HOW
FOREIGN
WAS MY
SERVICE

HOW FOREIGN WAS MY SERVICE

WITH THE U.S. DEPARTMENT OF STATE

BEVERLY LaVIGNE LEDBETTER

Desert Wind Press

The events and conversations in this book have been set down to the best of the author's ability, although some names and details have been changed to protect the privacy of individuals.

Cover and Book Design by Robert Brent Gardner
Illustrations by Jean-Dwight "Dewey" Ledbetter.

Independently published by Desert Wind Press
ISBN 978-1-7356957-9-2 (print softcover)

Dedicated to the memory of my brilliant, erudite husband,
Edwin Dwight Ledbetter,
with whom I spent 43 wondrous years!

To the
Other Ben —
miss you and the
sazarac days!
Ben

Acknowledgements

In deep gratitude to Robert Brent Gardner for the production of this memoire, including the format for text and photos, photography, design of cover, scanning etc. Brent did a yeoman job, was my mentor and all-around hero. (Also thanks to Becky Gardner's assistance in scanning of pictures and varied tasks.)

I am wowed by the talents of artist Jean-Dwight (Dewey) Ledbetter, who provided the sketches herein. I'm proud to be cast in the role of his Nana!

I also appreciate the input and steady encouragement from my Placitas writers group: Norma Libman, Gwenellen Janov, Daisy Kates, and latest member Denise Raven.

Also thanks to eagle-eye friend Barbara Rockwell, who proofed the entire memoire.

Table of Contents

My Life

My Beginning

Okay, if anyone needs to tell about my life, I guess it has to be me! In a way, my life did not begin until I fulfilled my dream of travel. Yes, I know, I hear, I was conceived in Montana, born in Wisconsin, and was carried to the home state of Illinois at 3 months. But I need to put that aside for now to tell you about my epiphany at age 13. I was in the 8th grade and had just finished a test. When I turned it in my teacher said I was early, why not just look through those books on the table over there? I picked up one and out jumped a poem. I recall the author was anonymous, but it leapt out at me, as follows:

> *"To think I once saw grocery shops with but a casual eye*
> *And fingered figs and apricots as one who came to buy*
> *To think I never dreamed of how bananas sway in rain*
> *And often looked at oranges, yet never thought of Spain*
> *And in those wasted days I saw no sails above the tea*
> *For grocery shops were grocery shops, not hemispheres to me!"*

Eureka! I thought. I knew that I was meant to travel, I did not care how I did it! That stayed with me the rest of my days.

I guess I should give more family background. My mother ended up marrying three times. My father was a French Canadian and had been the distiller for Hiram Walkers of Walkerville, Ontario, Canada. After prohibition Hiram Walker opened a distillery in

Peoria, Illinois and my father was one of the original three sent from Canada to do so. He perfected the formula for Canadian Club. Eventually Hiram Walker accumulated small distilleries throughout the U.S. One of them was in Red Lodge, Montana. My father was sent there as a troubleshooter and there met my mother who was a divorcee with three young boys. They fell in love. Hiram Walker back in Peoria kept trying to get my father to return to his position there, but as you can surmise, his love life had become more complicated. They married, my older sister Patricia was born in Red Lodge. He was eventually assigned the task of visiting yet another distillery in Laona, Wisconsin before returning finally to Peoria. The father of the three sons, with no consideration as to the welfare of the children or their mother, decreed the eldest Wallace would remain in Montana with him. The youngest Robert could go with my mother. I never understood the status of the middle child Gary for he would visit us through the years but often lived with his grandmother in Red Lodge. As I said, I was conceived in Montana but ended up being born in Laona, Wisconsin, the first child born in a lumberjack hospital. I don't remember much of my time as a Wisconsinian since I moved on to Illinois at three months.

One of the vivid memories I have of age four is that I managed to break my nose twice. My mother said I had a perfect nose before that, but the pug nose I now have was my own creation. The first time was when my parents' bedroom was being wallpapered and the bureau was placed next to the bed. So sister Pat and I would climb up on the bureau and do swan dives onto the bed. Finally I went too far and smashed into the headboard. Second time I used a doll's bunkbed ladder to try to climb onto a rocking chair. Clever! The prongs on top of the ladder jammed into my nose. The doctor had to remove a lot of cartilage; I can still recall the feel of the metal instruments he used. His final admonition: " Beverly, stop using your nose as a rubber ball!"

Skip through a not-so-happy childhood as a tomboy, always being the pitcher in softball games, becoming a lst class girl scout, riding bikes and adventuring with my best friend Mary. Death seemed to haunt us every few years. My mother's father died of a heart attack at age 62. Two years later we learned that Gary at 17 had drowned in Montana the night of his junior/senior prom. All five drowned when the car driven by a friend's father veered off a rugged dirt road into a muddy creek. Toward the end of my 8th grade, my father died at the age of 48 on April 28, 1951. He had been ill and passed out coming down the stairs, landing in a pool of blood at the bottom. My mother and I raced back and forth with wet towels to soak the blood from his body. My older sister screamed as she and younger sister Judy watched from above. He was able to dress himself awaiting the ambulance he did not want to take to the hospital. He died a day or so later of a cerebral hemorrhage. We took his body to Canada to his mother and family on several trains, an expensive proposition, since a solid copper lining had to be inserted into the coffin in order to cross the international border. With death haunting us every few years, I became aware of how precious and transitory was our time on earth. I vowed to account for my days in a diary, and began one at 13 and continue to this day!

A big event at age 13 other than my father's death, was this: The ride on the Peoria Rocket train to Chicago with my mother to attend a Chicago Cub/Brooklyn Dodger game at Wrigley Field. I was thrilled! I had for several years been an avid Brooklyn Dodger fan. When there arose a controversy of hiring the first black in major league baseball, Jackie Robinson, I wrote Branch Rickey to defend him. At Wrigley Field I stood in line to get an autograph from Jackie Robinson, but he stopped signing a few people before me, and walked away. If I had been less timid, I would have shouted out: "I wrote Branch Rickey for you!" Somehow I don't even recall who won that game.

We left behind the saddened house where I had lived 8 grades and bought one only several blocks away from my new high school, Woodruff.

My widowed mother, my two sisters and I then had the happiest three years in utter freedom in a male-free environment. (Robert had spent two years in Korea with the Illinois National Guard and later worked in Mississippi or Alabama before coming back to attend Bradley University.) We sang and danced around the house, with our dog Snooks even standing on her hind legs to dance with us. Then gradually came suitors for my mother, eventually easing their way into our time with her. She was a lovely, graceful beauty, born and raised in Montana, "God's Country" she always claimed. She had been a contestant in the Miss America contest in the 1920's. My memory was that she was second to Miss Yellowstone, who had always won the title of Miss Montana. Sister Judy claims she was Miss Yellowstone and politics played in her not making THE title role. But back to the story. My widowed mother married again and soon thereafter we were to move to a small town in Iowa, where my new stepfather had property. I had finished three years of high school, where I was a good student, active as a French horn player in the band and orchestra, basically quiet and reserved at school, but a riot with my close friends. Now I need to insert that Dan Fogelberg was one of the three sons of the band director Lawrence Fogelberg, about whom he'd written "Leader of the Band" in later years and acquired some fame.

Facing a senior year as a new kid on the block in another state, I had a decision to make. To my mother's everlasting credit, I had a choice to stay in that small town, go from a high school of some 250 students in my class to one of only 30 students, or return to Peoria to finish my last year at Woodruff High School, living at the home of my best friend. We arrived in the summer before school, having opened a restaurant in the small town of Columbus Junction, named because it was situated between two rivers and two railroads. Its population was 1200. Peoria was ten times that amount. My two sisters and I worked at the Busy Bee Cafe. The motto on the stationery added "where you don't get stung!" My older sister Pat, more gregarious, loved meeting and chatting with the townspeople. I presented a more reticent approach. But it wasn't long before we were being auditioned by the town boys, being asked out for dates on our time off. Wow, such good looking boys came forth and both of us had a retinue to choose from. Younger sister Judy was only 11 and not in the running.

By the time school was to begin, I had pretty well decided that I would stay my senior year. From a shy, retiring soul I had more confidence and began to like being a big fish in a small pond. I had made some girlfriends as well, was dating interesting fellows, and looked forward to the new experience.

One day three newcomers came to town to work on faulty telephone poles/lines in the area. They were in town a few weeks and came often to our restaurant. A particularly friendly one I had begun to know asked me about my girlfriends. Would I and two others like to join them on an outing? I agreed, as did they. So one evening six of us were in one car and headed for a movie out of town. Suddenly, we were run off the road by a car filled with town boys. They jumped out with raised fists and started a rumble, right out of James Dean. "What makes you think you can take out our town girls?" they shouted, and started to fight. To the telephone boys' credit, they did not encourage an all-out struggle. They mostly fended off blows. The town boys finally left, with a few bruises and blackened eyes on both sides.

We three girls were angry at the local boys' actions, not at all flattered (well maybe just a touch!) but the beginning of school began in a deep freeze. The boys were football players, automatic members of the Pep Club who decided the candidates for homecoming queen. All three of us were blatantly dismissed from that agenda and consequently, for the first time in school history, a sophomore was chosen Homecoming Queen. Herein lies a confession. When I was musing over whether or not to return to Peoria to finish high school, the captain of the football team came into the Busy Bee and said "No, stay here, we'll make you homecoming queen!" Okay I admit it was a factor in making my decision to stay, but by then I had some friends I enjoyed and really did appreciate coming out of a very tiring self-conscious shell that had enclosed me my entire life up to then. The plot thickens. Before school began and I was chatting with the manager of the hotel next door, he came right out and asked: "Beverly, are you going to be homecoming queen?" (Why I had it in the bag!)   Modestly, I answered: " Well, maybe just a princess." So when the telephone boy situation occurred and school began and homecoming came around and everyone knew the final result, the hotel manager, each time he entered the door of the restaurant, greeted me with: "Hi Queenie!" To this day, it goes down as my most embarrassing moment.

The local Columbus Gazette had a high school page in the back and I became the main writer for it. That cinched a seat on Quill and Scroll club. I was secretary to the Student Council. At graduation we chose the class motto: "Don't just itch for success, scratch for it." We chose colors pink and black. Both were rejected by the small town school superintendent who chose for us: "Not finished, just begun." And blue and white for the colors. We fought over where to go for our Senior Trip, so it was cancelled entirely. So much for our rebellious nature! But the year had its successes. I sang a solo in the Boys Minstrel Show, singing "I'm just Wild About Harry." Harry was the name of my stepfather and I wasn't wild about him. I played a southern girl in the Senior Class Play and kept losing my accent. I wrote an entire pep show program and wrote the lyrics for our school graduation song. I had spread my wings and felt liberated. I was in love for the first time, writing devoted letters to Ted in air force training in Texas. Others waited in the wings. The second half of the year a new attractive girl came to town and we became friends. She years later became the Governor of Nebraska. By my Senior picture in the yearbook was the quote: "She's witty, she's wise, she's a terror for her size."

During this very poignant year in my development, my sister had become a freshman at the University of Iowa. She also met her husband to be, introduced by new friends. I joined her at school the next year. I spent one semester at the freshman dorm rooming with my friend Margy, recently crowned valedictorian from our high school class, and joined my sister in off campus housing the second semester. One day I found my sister with a pile of books and ice skates in the middle of the room to be hocked so she could get money for a trip to Dallas. She had decided to audition to become a Braniff Airways stewardess. She did not pass the requirements, but that planted a seed into my cranium. That would be one way to travel and see the world!

So after a year or so at the university, I set out to Dallas with a friend and we became Braniff reservationists. After a fun month of training, meeting girls/women from other states, we were then assigned to a large room with headsets and a blackboard in front of the room listing Braniff's 52 flights. A supervisor stood with chalk and eraser updating the seats sold by us reservationists connected by phone to potential passengers. It was a wild scene, we were in trouble if we oversold a flight. Impulsive me, just as we earned free flights after three months of torture, I quit. I did not seek another job at Braniff where I could have been more suited, I looked elsewhere for yet another adventure. My dear friend Joyce stuck it out and ended up marrying a handsome Braniff pilot we both had our eyes on. I was maid of honor and happy for them, knowing I yet had a lot of living to do before settling down.

I then entered a phase of my life shuffling back and forth to Peoria to work awhile, returned to school for another semester, back to Dallas to work temporary jobs for an attorney, or serve as secretary to the manager of the Dallas Country Club, etc. I enjoyed flitting around with my new found freedom from family.

In the late 50's in Dallas I encountered drinking fountains labelled "Colored Only" and "White Only." I found it ridiculous and in defiance often drank from the "Colored." I also often went to sit in the back of the bus, rebellious lil Northern girl that I was. At one point I worked at Peoria City Hall for the Traffic Engineer, Public Works Director, and City Manager and fell in love with my first real beau. We were both aware of the fact we weren't good for each other, so several New Year's Eves we'd go out for a nice prime rib dinner, end up at his family home while his folks celebrated at the country club, and sadly toasted our goodbyes. That usually lasted about two weeks before one of us would give in.

My family lasted three years at the restaurant in Iowa before returning to Peoria to our house there. That small town of 1200 people could not sustain three restaurants, though my mother's reputation as a great cook had gained recognition throughout the area. I worked haphazardly at adding up semesters toward an eventual college degree. My mother's health began to fail. First a hysterectomy due to uterine cancer, where she learned she had an enlarged heart, then several years of heart trouble. I had been planning a European trip for myself, then felt guilty for my selfishness and cancelled the trip. I drove my mother, along with my younger sister and friend, to Montana for her to visit her mother and brother. She died in the second week of her visit, after the rest of us had returned home to school and work. She was 58 years old. My stepfather had died six months earlier in his sleep on the sofa, found by younger sister Judy.

Once I lost my mother, an orphan at age 27 (she died 4 days after my birthday), I figured nothing would now hold me back from my world travel adventures. I completed an application for Foreign Service of the U.S. Department of State, took appropriate civil service exams for secretarial skills, had a six-month security check and was informed I was in, as a secretary for the Foreign Service. I was 27 years old. The personnel person presented me with three choices for a first assignment: Saigon, Vietnam; LaPaz, Bolivia; and Tunis, Tunisia. I had no idea where Tunisia was! I ran to the library to look up the choices. There tiny Tunisia was, tucked between two large countries, Algeria and Libya. I reasoned, why its parked right across the Mediterranean Sea from Europe! I quickly gave my answer.

Friends gave me a farewell party, along with a gold charm bracelet with a pendant which said: "Your Peoria Friends 1965". It came with the stipulation that I add a charm for every country I visited in the future. I've done my best to fill it, along with another bracelet as well.

Off to Washington, D.C. for training; our group of about 12 young women were housed in an all-woman's hotel, which we soon named Menopause Manor since the rest of the inhabitants were well over 50. How depressing it was that first night as I lay on a single bed in a single room, with a dresser, chair and one bare light bulb hanging from the ceiling over the bed. I called my sisters to bemoan my fate. But in youth hope springs eternal and our little gang attentively attended classes and ate out cheaply on our per diem, a term with which we'd soon become acquainted. And I became particularly acquainted with Kathy Mathiot from New York City.

After our training she was to head for Karachi, Pakistan and I to Tunis, Tunisia. I had made plans to take a ship onto Naples, Italy and then on down. Kathy convinced me to change plans and fly together to Paris and Rome and then split to go off to our assignments. Having dated an Italian boy in NYC, and after I faked a knowledge of French, she said we'd survive with our language facilities. Well, we ended up with a lot of jambon sandwiches in Paris with my command of the language, discovered our first bidet in our hotel room, wandered and became, as do so many others, enamored with the magic of Paris and Rome. Boys followed us down the streets in Rome. Kathy had been pinched, which at that time seemed like a badge of honor. We met three Italian boys, all speaking English, at Trevi Fountain. I learned later that it was the ultimate pick-up spot in Rome. They offered us a tour of the Seven Hills and in our innocence we felt there was safety in numbers. Mind you, this was 1965. We had that tour, and all was fine, stopped for coffee afterward and exchanged addresses. It turned out they never even knew the third boy! And what's more, we kept in touch, Kathy with Daniel and I with Luigi. Luigi was going to school and also serving as a flight attendant on Alitalia Airlines. He visited me once in Tunis and in later years in Chicago, and I visited Rome a few more times to see him there. After a few days in Rome, Kathy and I parted ways and went on to our assignments.

My lovely mother Irene Ingrid Marsyla .

Daddy's brother Uncle Victor, Etienne A. Lavigne, and Aunt Irene.
Aylmer Quebec, Canada.

My mother Irene Ingrid Marsyla .

My father Etienne (Stephen in English) Lavigne as a young man.

Dad and Mom courting in Montana.

Cousins JoAnn, Pat, Joyce, Bev in Montana.

Pat, Mom and Bev on Montana visit.

Bev (always shy and demure) and natural curly red haired Pat,
pretending to be shy!

Bev around age 4.

Yours truly, somewhere in grade school.

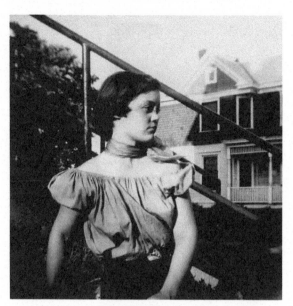
A pensive, high school kid in Peoria, Illinois, 1954.

Sister Pat's high school graduation, 1954

Half-Brother Robert high school graduation photo.

High school graduation photo, 1955

Sister Judy's high school graduation photo.

Ted Allen, my first real boyfriend, airman cadet. A charming,
thoughtful person. 1955

Half brother Robert Stetson, Illinois National Guard, about to be sent to Korea, 1952.

Columbus High School Junior/Senior Banquet, 1955.   Margy Vannice, Bev, Kay Stark (later became Governor of Nebraska!)

My bosom buddy Joyce Shellabarger in Muscatine, Iowa. 1955.

The highschool graduate Beverly Ann Lavigne. 1955

Tunisia

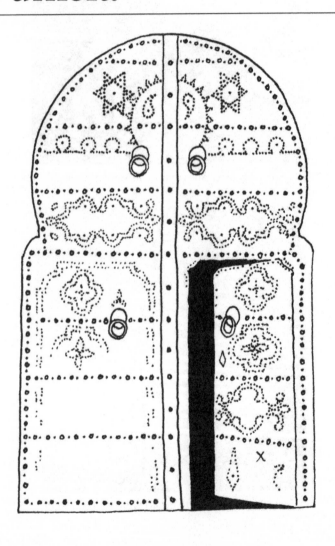

Tunisia

The Arab world opened up for me in Tunisia. All seemed exotic with robed people, men in black robes and red fezes atop their heads, and women in white safsaries. Unlike a stricter Muslin world, they did not have to cover their entire face, some even wore lipstick. Donkeys and taxis shared the crowded streets. My room at the Tunisia Palace Hotel opened up to a patio of fragrant jasmine and unknown flowers. It was a bit frightening, "what had I got myself into?" were my first thoughts. I was assigned to the political section of the Embassy with three political officers, and was soon immersed into taking dictation and typing up cables of government exchanges. The Embassy was comprised of the Ambassador, the Deputy Chief of Mission, and political, economic, administrative and consular sections. There was also a mystery area known as Pol 2. They had separate communications and their officers were allegedly assigned to separate sections, but they soon became known for what they were: the CIA.

After about a week at the Tunisia Palace, Norma, the secretary to the DCM, invited me to share her two bedroom apartment near the Embassy while I looked for an apartment of my own. She greeted me each morning with a friendly cup of coffee and I was most grateful. She was tall and big boned and I sank even further into my 5'1 frame. As all agreed, she was a warm, friendly presence. I found a two bedroom apartment on a street over from the Embassy and happily adapted to the routine. I liked my political officers very much. I was fascinated in dictation by the head boss Stephen McClintic, becoming aware of his extensive knowledge of Tunisia's role in the Maghreb states. I developed a slight crush; intelligence has always turned me on! Art Lowrie was the Arabic speaker in the section.

I bought a darling Triumph Herald white convertible, red interior, walnut dash, inherited a fluffy white puppy, which I eventually turned over to a family with children, since I had neglected Scruffy with all my activities with new friends.

I quickly became connected with Gary and Roslie Shann, a lively couple with one young son. I had dreaded my first Christmas away from home and family, but we had a congenial group gathered at the Shanns which dispensed that fear quite readily. Later on when she was with child, she prepared to go to Wheelus Air Force Base next door in Libya for delivery at the AFB hospital. It was November, the time of the annual Marine Corps Ball. Not only did she offer her husband as an escort for me, she loaned me a lovely blue long dress! Such a friend! Speaking of Libya, we would also drive over or fly to take advantage of the commissary for food and household needs. Once I flew and an air force person offered me a ride to the base on his motorcycle. I accepted. I had a straw handbag which rested on the manifold and suddenly caught into flames with my passport inside of course! It was badly singed and I feared being rejected by the Libyan immigration people as I returned to Tunisia . Thankfully the surly guard accepted my explanation.

Hedi Benamor was a Tunisian national who briefed the political officers each morning from the news in the Arab press. We quickly became friends. He lived with a lovely Belgian woman and soon included me for dinners and parties. I dated a certain Marine Guard. Despite that, a Consular officer took a shine to me and would often leap up the stairs to the third floor with a bouquet of flowers in an attempt to woo me. This happened so often that I finally suggested he include a vase, which he did, gleefully. I would have to turn to my diaries of those years to count how many flowers I received from Ralph, with no happy ending on his part.

I believe it was less than a month at post when I noted stirrings in the Political section as my boss rushed out to meet the Ambassador, and looked askance at me upon his return. My suspicion was soon answered when an FBI agent from Rome was introduced and requested that I show him the air freight trunk I had received from the States. I took him to the apartment where I was staying and showed it to him. He checked the numbers on it and referred to those he was carrying. I took him back to the Embassy. Later on that afternoon my boss, now more cheery, announced I was in the clear. Well, I knew that! It seems that a trunk loaded with drugs showed up in Madagasgar and seemed to have travelled on my bill of lading from Chicago. Interesting, if true, I thought. After work I ran into the FBI agent at a downtown shop. May I say that he was tall, dark and handsome and invited me to dinner? I took him out in my little Triump Herald convertible to one of our charming places on the Mediterranean. We wined, dined and danced. He told me that his orders had been to simply check the numbers, arrest me and take me back to the states. At that time I was just sizing up Tunisia and said I was willing to return home. A very pleasant ending to a crisis in other people's eyes. Back in Peoria, my sister Judy was also approached by the FBI and she thought I was in real danger. It was weeks before she received assurance that all was well.

Tunisia had lovely fish and Thibar wine which the Canadian White Fathers produced in an area outside Tunis. We had the ruins of Carthage in our back yard and visited other Roman ruins such as El Djem. There were lovely seaside communities for weekends away : Hammamet, Sousse, Sfax, Monastir. We had the mountainous cooler area of Ain Draham which boar hunters frequented, stayed at a French-owned hotel which served tiny wrens for appetizers. They were soon pushed aside. Having been raised in the midwest in the 50s and 60s, fish had come in the form of frozen fishsticks and swordfish, so I wasn't too enlightened to the wonders of the seafood world. Invited out to an officer's home early in my tour, I was astounded to have a fish eyeball staring at me on its appetizer plate. I quickly covered it up with a lemon slice and picked, I hope delicately, at its body, watching for clues from the others at the table. But soon enough as I entered into this strange French/Arabic world, I often requested sole meuniere and could delicately (finally!) dissect it properly. It became one of my favorite meals, along with calamari (calamar doree). Oh yes, the first New Year's eve was at Hedi Benamor's where he forced me to slither down a raw oyster so as to begin the year with good fortune. It took me many years afterward to appreciate raw oysters.

When I first arrived in Tunis, I was aghast at the black spots which frequently appeared in rolls served at meals. Spying a bug baked in the batter, I would indignantly send them back to the kitchen, but that would have been a daily occurrence. It wasn't long before I merely picked out the spot to put aside the plate without interruption in conversation.

I took French lessons religiously between the office activity initiated by three officers. One day Hedi came to look for my boss. "Ou est Mssr. McClintic?" I responded "Il est manger." Hedi cried out: "Mon Dieu! Que triste!" and put on a doleful face of sympathy, teasing me. I had tried to say he was at lunch, but said he was eaten. He never let me forget that one. While we're on the subject, the wife of one of the political officers (Art's wife Nancy) and I were in the same French class. Several times at various receptions we would pretend to be speaking good French and whisper to each other: "Unit 2!" Then we would go through the dialogue of that lesson. "Ya til un bon restaurant predici? Oui, je quois qu'il y on a au coin de la rue!" We'd have some laughs over our antics.

We were always hungry for novels written in English. I recall on a trip with a few friends, I was reading James Michener's "Caravans." I remarked on how well written it was, describing Afghanistan. Suddenly the others were ravenous to read it. So, it being a paperback, I'd read a chapter, tear it off, and pass it onto another, and so down the line. The Marines usually had a collection of their own, but sports and military action were not always to our taste.

I was invited to a party of a USIS (U.S. Information Service) official. The guests of honor were the Ink Spots, a popular singing group in the 60s. Their name carried on through at least six different groups of singers. We danced and had a good old time. Ray Beatty 1/4 inkspot, invited me for dinner at the Tunis Hilton the next evening and a ringside seat at their performance. My new friend D.J. and I both adored Harry Belafonte, who was visiting

President Bourguiba's son about the same time. He was not performing, it was a social visit. D.J. knew the FAA airport official so we could go on the tarmac to the plane. His plane pulled up, and we meekly waved to him as he exited the plane. He gave us a huge smile, we fortified our resolve and met him in the VIP lounge to ask for his autograph. He graciously asked us to sit down and we had a nice visit with him. I still have his autograph on the back page of my 1965 diary.

As you might have surmised, my Tunisian tour was to experience a land of happy people. The Tunisians I met and worked with were welcoming, had joi de vivre. They felt free under the protection of Habib Bourguiba. He as Prime Minister dominated Tunisia for 31 years. He was seen by some as a benevolent dictator. He established rights for women unmatched by any other Arab nation. He combined tradition and innovation, Islam with a liberal bent.

I served two years 1965-67 and left the post just days before the 6 day war when agitators stormed our Embassy compound, setting fire to cars. In fact, the American Ambassador to Libya was on the same ship as I returning to the States and gave a lecture on the current happenings in the Arab Maghreb. The time of innocence seemed to be over, but it wasn't until the Al Qaeda attacked the US Embassy in 2012 to make that certain. Tragic times were foretold with 2 lost in the Embassy attack; 2015 was a horrid year of terrorism with the March Bardo Museum attack, killing 22 tourists; the June attack at a Sousse beach with 38 tourists (mostly British) killed by a madman; and the Nov. suicide bomber attack where 12 Presidential guardsmen were killed. I thankfully escaped all latter events of this paragraph.

I took the ship back from Tunis, first a smaller ship I called a tugboat, from Tunis to Naples. I had a sweet champagne and flower sendoff from my dear officers and their families, all crammed into my tiny cabin. I had the day in Naples and met a naval lieutenant at the base who told me the Blue Angels were to fly over that day. He took me to the spot to watch them and was also sweet to see me off at the dock.

I boarded the SS Independence, an ocean liner, a sane precursor to the massive cruise ships of today which can hold 5000 passengers. It held 395 passengers, quite civilized! Government personnel were allowed to travel first class but that often meant an inside cabin with no windows or portholes! Being young and spending most of the time in activities aboard ship: bars, movie theatres, dining rooms, dance floors, we formed a small gang of navy, coast guard, and foreign service people filled with enough action we barely made it to our beds to sleep. It was a fun filled week from Naples to New York. We had an all-day stop in Lisbon, Portugal. Four of us (navy and coast guard men and another foreign service girl and myself) had a marvelous day of laughter as we wended up the narrow streets of the Al Fama region (the oldest section of Lisbon) to St. George's Castle, and hopped about the grounds. That day set the stage for my all consuming love of Portugal, and I was to return many times. We all parted ways in New York with no plan of any further contact. Then for me, several weeks of home leave and a check into the State Department before heading to yet another adventure.

U. S. Embassy chancery, Tunis, Tunisia - 1965

Scruffy and my wonderful Triumph Herald convertible. Felt guilty
for always deserting Scruffy so soon gave it to a family with children.
Tunis 1965

I was accused of causing damage at Carthage, just outside of Tunis - 1965

Sidi Bou Said outside Tunis, a favorite spot for ordering Tunisian bird cages and drinking mint tea. 1965-67

El Djem ruins, Tunisia. Rosalie and Gary horsing a bit. 1965

Marine Corps ball - Tunis 1964. I dated the Marine on the left, Carl J

Friend Ed Casey, the Greenes, and buddies Rosalie and Gary Shann.

Ed Casey and I found a suitable Christmas tree, Tunis 1966

D. J. Washinger, my closest friend in Tunis We also ended up in
Saigon together. 1966

Bev and Carl, Halloween, Tunis, 1966

Bev, Charles and Kathy aboard SS Independence. Left Tunis on what I called a tugboat and picked up larger ship at Naples, Italy. - 1967

The Big Four - Friends since kindergarten in Peoria, Illinois. Mary Johnson, Bev Lavigne, Joyce Green and Phyllis Shadid (maiden names). We had a get together each time I breezed through between postings. I'm guessing this was 1967.

Vietnam

Saigon

While Tunisia was for me a nonthreatening time, coming away with a positive view of the Arab world, I found action in my next tour to Saigon, Vietnam, an assignment for which I had no choice. I landed at Tan Son Nhut airport in August 1967 and was met by a political officer in an Embassy car, whisked through customs, and dropped unceremoniously at a bleak downtown hotel, the Excelsior. My assigned room had one window which faced a concrete wall. I became immediately depressed to land in such a dump, my new home.

The streets of Saigon were dirty and crowded with military vehicles, army jeeps and trucks emitting hazy fumes. Wending through this presence were cyclos or pedicabs, and families perched on Honda scooters, zig zagging with amazing dexterity through the traffic. One soon learned to dodge and make one's way along with the rest of the pedestrians. Within two months I was able to transfer to another hotel, the Park, and this time had windows, all windows on two sides. The room was perched on the roof, the 9th floor, along with just three similar rooms. I had no complaint. I called it my penthouse apartment, though it was just a regular room with small bath. It was amazing to awake with sunlight. We were next door to the Presidential Independence Palace, and at least one time, I watched a VC mortar fly over our rooftop onto the palace grounds. After a jittery two months of reacting to battle sounds, I gradually became acclimated and somewhat relaxed, with not quite a devil-may-care attitude.

Work at the Political Section was lively and interesting. Two secretaries handled the work of five officers. I landed before the active anti-war demonstrations began in full force back in the states. When I first arrived, we occupied the old Embassy building, unsafe by any measure in downtown traffic. A Viet Cong car bomb had exploded there in 1965; three Americans and 19 Vietnamese had been killed. Within two months of my arrival we were transferred to the new Embassy building with more land space and added security. We all felt we were there for a purpose, to free the South Vietnamese from the northern invaders. I would often see General Westmoreland at the elevators, after his briefing Ambassador Bunker on "pacification" of the provinces, which meant gradually turning the governing of those provinces over to the South Vietnamese.

A mortar also hit the palace grounds when VP Hubert Humphrey visited in October and was inside, but no one was injured. My friend Kathy and I saw his helicopter land earlier at the Embassy, and the Vice President gave us a two fingered wave. Later at a gathering on the back steps of the Embassy, high officials had gathered: General Westmoreland, former Ambassador Henry Cabot Lodge, Ambassador Ellsworth Bunker and others. Vice President Humphrey had made a stirring speech to lift our spirits, and I was able to shake his hand. We had many codels (congressional delegations) during my time there where the war seemed to pause as they were ushered around allegedly safe battle fields.

In all modesty, I was a whiz at shorthand and sometimes found myself upstairs taking dictation from visiting Assistant Secretaries and various senators, so the work always presented new challenges for me. Once I was called to the Ambassador's residence to take dictation from a senator from Pennsylvania, I believe Joseph Clark.

I very much counted on letters from family and friends, which refortified me. I made it to church most Sundays, a needed reassurance for my sanity. Even as bombs exploded outside and rattled the windows of the church, I was more or less complacent that it would all work out well.

We managed a few parties. One evening meal out with several officers, six of us went to a restaurant on the outskirts of Saigon proper on the river. We sat outside and were presented with lovely food such as shrimp grilled onto sugar cane, rice cakes, marvelous soft shelled crab. We were served tender beef which we cooked on our own charcoal pots, then wrapped with rice paper and dipped in the Vietnamese ever present sauce nuoc mam. One hundred yards away was rifle fire, flares surrounding the area for nighttime fighting. It was all quite dramatic and remains one of the most enchanting memories I have of Vietnam.

When we didn't have curfew at 7 pm (depending on war activity), we'd occasionally go to the International House for drinks, dinner and dancing. There were always available men who wanted to entertain us "round eyes." But it didn't happen often, as we had late working hours at the Embassy. There were also remnants of French restaurants for very lovely food. At least one specialized in souffles. My mouth waters as I recall the lovely spinach and cheese souffles. Always good fish, sauces, some baked alaska. But those places weren't available when we had curfew. Twice we were flown by military plane, once to swim at Conson Island in the south and once to nearby Long Binh for New Year's Eve to a base which shot up nine flares over the dance floor at the stroke of 12, several colored in red and green. I recall one fact of military expense. Each flare for nighttime fighting: $50. I used to add up a portion of the national debt from my rooftop. My dear friend and I would often sunbathe on the rooftop, and often boys in helicopters swooped down to look. Yes, we had on bathing suits!

The political compound consisted of 4 or 5 houses clustered on several acres of land. The occupants were mostly political officers, including Arch Calhoun, the Political Counselor, and several officers from USIS. Sundays were often set aside for a gathering of those serving in the political section, lunch for all of us and water polo for the men. A nice diversion.

One amusing time Jo Sloane had asked me and two men from USIS for an afternoon of bridge. She had forgotten she had scheduled a Vietnamese woman to do her feet that day. What to do? She and I received pedicures as we played bridge with the fellows! Such decadence!

Embassy personnel were allowed on R & R (rest and recuperation) military flights to the surrounding areas of Bangkok, Hong Kong, Sydney, Singapore, Manila, Taipei, even Australia. Kathy did an R&R to Sydney and loved it. I looked forward to the offerings from the Personnel officer. I signed up for an R&R to Bangkok in September, taking a military flight from Tan Son Nhut, just about 40 men and Bev on the plane. I was told to close my ears at the VD lecture. I had no trouble finding a seat companion, they were hovering over me. Three of us chatted and agreed to stay at the same hotel in Bangkok. The next day the three men and I visited Tim Land, which offered examples of Thai life: elephants, rice patties, pottery making, classical dance, cockfights, snakes and swordfights, the classical dance being the most charming. The PX was on my list, as I needed so many essentials like bathing suits, dresses, shoes, records, temple rubbings. Somehow we ended up at the Copacabana night club in the hotel for dancing. Gerry (was he the captain or lieutenant?) requested a polka and I was amazed I could follow him, as we hopped and swirled on the dance floor and were cheered from the sidelines. We returned to that spot three more times to dance. The floating market was fascinating, watching river peoples' daily lives and habits unfold before us: teeth brush, wash clothes, bathing. They seemed very conscious of hygiene in a rank, murky river. Boats floated along laden with exotic fruits and vegetables for sale. Made a quick trip to the Emerald Buddha.

Hong Kong became a favorite city, surpassing Paris on my list. It was in constant motion, from taking the Star Ferry from Hong Kong to Kowloon, to riding rickshaws or taxis, from large glamorous hotels to neon studded streets on the other side. Wonderful Asian food, reasonable prices for Asian souvenirs. On an R&R I stayed at the Hilton Hotel in Hong Kong and went down to the shore for a reported cruise, only to find the dock empty. A boat pulled ashore and a Chinese man offered me to join his private group: three Chinese men in the export-import business, one South African, a dress and beading manufacturer, and one Chinese girl (who resented my presence) and me. We spent four hours cruising the Aberdeen, Repulse Bay area and stopped to eat at Soc Khu Wan at a seaside spot where they pulled shrimp, garoupa, lobster and assorted fish out of roped-off sections of the sea at our request. We sat at a huge round table with our chopsticks, ate crudely, hungrily. I can still envision the girl chewing the meat off a fish head, a true delicacy. It was a delicious, intriguing experience with nice people I am relieved to say.

On my R&R to Taiwan, I had people to look up for others and had a nice offer to stay with another Beverly from the Embassy, who had a charming house with fireplace. Got fitted for some dresses by the "French Lady" and still remember them, though not their ultimate fate. In old Taipei I saw the impressive temple of Buddha and Tao, which was eery at nighttime. Sidewalk restaurants had steaming soups, octopus and jellyfish. My guide said, when he forgot something: "Ah, I almost remember!" At a Japanese bar the owner kept toasting me with warm saki and soon both of our cheeks became quite pink! I flew to Hualien for a trip to Taroko gorge to view spectacular mountains of pink and green marbling, a massive marvelous birthday cake of granite. A man at a party in Taipei read my hand and said I was a mixture of great passion and a cool cynic, and would overcome the lifeline break in my hand. (So far it's true!)

President Johnson had provided Ambassador Bunker with a plane at his disposal so he could visit his wife Carole Laise, who was Ambassador to Nepal. I was offered a seat on the plane, but had just returned from a R&R and did not want to take advantage. I also won a ticket for the Bob Hope Christmas show, but my hair was a mess and I gave away the ticket. After a late day working for the Political Counselor, same hair mess, so I gave up on the annual Marine Corps Ball. Talk about regrets! Do you recall the old adage: "Come up to my apartment to see my etchings!" Well a charming officer once asked me: "Come up to my apartment to see my AK-47!" I did.

Late Embassy arrivals to Saigon had to stay in hotel rooms for an indeterminate amount of time. Those who came before enjoyed apartments and maids. I spent over nine months in my penthouse before being told I could move into an apartment if I roomed with someone. So friend Kathy and I jumped at the chance and were moved into a two bedroom apartment near the Saigon river. The war action heated up considerably with that move. Nightly rockets were launched across the river to land near our street. Vendors were killed, everyone was on edge.

Tet occurred in February 1968. It was a holiday replete with strings of firecrackers trickling down 3 and 4 story buildings. Light the bottom and up they go, popping all the way. Pistols shooting, fireworks flashing, a perfect time for the invasion of Viet Cong into Saigon. I was awakened by such noises at 3 a.m. in an apartment borrowed from a friend who was on R&R to Tokyo. I heard on the Armed Forces Radio that the Embassy and the Independence Palace had been attacked.

I realized I was to work for the Political Counselor that day and things would be lively. So I jumped into the car and drove to the Embassy on deserted streets. I saw cars with open doors and legs hanging out. All was silent. At the back gate of the Embassy Vietnamese guards with guns drawn told me: "No go in there, VC in there!" I went to the nearby house of the Chief of the Political Section and with him went to the Political Counselor's compound where gathered were those who lived on the compound. The Political Counselor was on the phone to Washington.

Soon some were heading to the Embassy. I went in a jeep with a political officer. The Viet Cong had entered the Embassy compound, but not the Chancery itself. Fighting between the Marine Guards, Embassy security men, military police and Viet Cong had just ended an hour or so before. The 101st Airborne had provided reinforcements. The bodies of 19 Viet Cong lay awaiting removal near the concrete flower circles in the Embassy's front yard. A Marine guard had been killed and four wounded, four MP's killed. The teak door at the entrance was riveted with bullet holes and could almost be folded back onto itself. In the Ambassador's office I was given a phone to take down from a military person all the hits, KIAs, etc. throughout the country during the night. I tediously took down the data, had the officer spell out the name of all the areas hit, spending hours on the phone, and then transcribed the notes in cable form. Those of us in the almost deserted building were provided with C-rations, a jeep sat in our lobby for a few days, a tank parked outside. We soon learned which ration had fruit and peanut butter, a favorite. I wrote up my Tet experience and it was published in the Foreign Service Journal in April 1968. I became a "published writer" as they paid $35 for the article.

When LBJ announced in March that he would not run again, I called it the April Fool Speech. When it was March 31 in Washington, it was April 1 in Vietnam.

In June 1968 Kathy and I managed a trip together to Singapore. We went for a Singapore Sling at the Raffles; Malacca where we stayed at a British guest house with mosquito netting round our beds; Kuala Lumpur where we partied with a group of Aussies; and Penang, staying at the Eastern and Oriental Hotel, which had often been frequented by Somerset Maugham. There we met a young GI named Wally Beckman assigned to the very dangerous DMZ in Vietnam. When he joined his outfit, only 5 of the original 32 had been left alive. But now on R&R he basked by the pool "in the loveliness of chatting with a round eye." When we went down for breakfast one morn, the headlines screamed "Bobby Kennedy is Shot!" Later in the day we were in the countryside looking for batiks. I saw a television set on in a house and asked a little boy about Bobby Kennedy. With a doleful face he told me: "He no live! He is passing away!"

After Tet

Saigon was indeed more tense, the Viet Cong having made known their presence in the city. There were background sounds of renewed skirmishes, more stringent curfews. We were escorted to work either by Embassy drivers or political officers. In some ways we felt protected, but at the same time felt strangled by not being permitted free movement. The workload was constant, even more energized. We even had a curfew party at the political compound, an all nighter with mixed results. After 9 months in a hotel we enjoyed being spoiled by our Vietnamese maid Xuan, who gave us lovely breakfasts and tasty meals. For a party we had, she and several friends squatted on the kitchen floor making egg rolls. Xuan was young and pleasant, a very good cook. She even made American dishes for us, following our recipes. If it weren't for the outside activity, we would have felt satisfied. But moving close to the river meant more mortars flung across that river. A woman a block away was decapitated after a mortar round, a street barber killed. There was a crater on the grounds of the Cathedral, just missing the church itself.

About this time John Tunney, a congressman from California, showed up in the Political Section and we chatted. He had accompanied his friend Ted Kennedy on a visit back in Tunis and I had mentioned it. He was accompanying a political officer to see some military head at Tan Son Nhut. I invited him to a party we were having that night and he accepted enthusiastically. He didn't show. I learned later that the colonel or whomever insisted they play tennis after their meeting.

We had a mini-Tet in May, the war came closer. Kathy became increasingly stressed by the barrage of loud noises outside our apartment door. She had also experienced a disappointed ending to a relationship from which she expected more. All of us had frayed nerves. One day she was writhing in pain and I called the Embassy doctor, who sent over his nurse. Her pain was exacerbated by day's end and we were told to go to the field hospital on the outskirts of Saigon. We took an Embassy car with a Vietnamese driver and waited a long time to get attention as they dealt with more bloody, urgent cases. The Embassy driver fretted as curfew time drew near, afraid to be on the streets. I released him to take a taxi and leave the car for us. We got more of a runaround and finally Kathy was looked at and given pain relief for her migraine headache. We were sent home when I had wanted her to be held overnight. So, long after curfew, I drove the Embassy car on silent streets. We were stopped at several MP checkpoints and reluctantly sent along to our apartment. The next day arrangements began for Kathy to have a direct transfer to Washington. She made plans to visit her last post Switzerland along the way. She departed within a week, the last of June.

Having felt this added pressure--worry for my friend-- along with the general discomfort from the war out there, it suddenly became too close and personal. I was prompted to turn my 18 month tour into one year. I had arrived in Saigon August 3, 1967 and departed August 8, 1968.

Saigon, Vietnam 1967

Saigon, Vietnam 1967

Saigon, Vietnam 1967 - Girls in the ao dai traditional dress they
wore 1967-68. So lovely and graceful!

Tour guides in Taiwan . When one forgot something he said: "Ah, I
almost remember!"

On R&R to Taiwan 1968

One of many Sunday gatherings at the compound of Arch Calhoun.
Philip Habib from D.C. liked the girls and we liked him. Kathy, Bev,
D.J., Eva Kim, Mary Frey, Marj surround him. Saigon 1968

Same Sunday session, Saigon. (Is that alliteration?) Dave
Lambertson, Bev, Lars Hydle, and Don Ferguson on right. 1968

Kathy Cardin and her boss Roger Kirk. Saigon 1968.

Mary Frey and I and a few others awaiting a flight to Long Binh for
New Year's Eve - Vietnam 1967

On way home from Vietnam, stopped in Yumato, Japan. 1968

After Vietnam

There was thought of returning to the States via the European route, but Bob had told me to stop by in Hawaii where he was now posted, and Jim sent a letter from Minnesota telling me I must come for a week! And here I was in the far east and had not yet seen Tokyo! My first stop out of Vietnam was my favorite city Hong Kong, where I spent 3 nights. The USS America aircraft carrier was in port and I was invited to a lavish reception at the Hilton Hotel. There were elaborate ice sculptures, plenty of food and drink. Women I admit were in short supply so I became the belle of the ball. I wore my white lace cotton dress with orange shoes and matching earrings and was greeted by many of the 400 officers of the aircraft carrier. I partook excitedly in my own magical Cinderella ball where a group of 8 or 10 would line up and cut in to dance with me! Chalk that one down as one of the highlights of my life!

I flew to Tokyo a couple days later, and what a shock that was! Everything a big whirl. Tall flashy buildings, crowded streets. The airport bus driver drove recklessly and in his jerking motion almost toppled an elderly Japanese lady down the aisle. Taxi drivers angrily flipped the back door shut if you couldn't say in their language where you were headed. So when I finally landed at the military BOQ or whatever they called it, I was ready to head out of Tokyo. The next day I told myself I would go to the train station and whatever train was there, head out of Tokyo for one hour. I was pushed into the train by the crowd and, standing packed like sardines, waited one hour and got off the train. I had landed in Yumoto, a small town near Mount Fuji, which they promised one could see on a clear day. It was not a clear day. I stood on the platform and shouted "ryokan, ryokan" (Japanese inn). A man guided me to one nearby which was fully occupied, and then another, where they granted me asylum.

All smiles, I was gestured to take off my shoes and into slippers. They guided me to my room, a large window displayed a lovely pine forest. I was given a kimono. An elderly man went to draw my bath (I wondered what else he was to do). But he withdrew and I was alone to figure out the routine. I believed I was to soap myself on the little stool and plunge into the hot relaxing water. Another window with pine trees soothed me, helping to erase Tokyo from my thoughts. I stayed in that room the rest of the day and night. A woman, bowing, came to take a futon out of a closet and stretch it out on the floor. A small TV was at the head, a John Wayne western with John Wayne speaking Japanese! Food was delivered, all with gestures since none of us spoke the needed language. I bowed often and said "Ohio." I was enthralled. Except I discovered the fish was raw. I ate shrimp, nibbled round fishy edges, and ate all of what I called seaweed and rice. All was silent. I slept quite comfortably on the futon on the floor. Breakfast was delivered and this time the fish was cooked. More rice and greens and hot tea.

When I braved the outdoors I found in a shop four lovely little pictures: a boy on a water buffalo playing a flute; a man perched with a torch over water; a woman in kimono with umbrella in the rain; the moon with pine trees, for my souvenirs of Yumoto. I keep them on my walls to this day. I looked around the ryokan and elected not to join the community bath. Meals were always delivered to me, too much raw fish, plenty of rice. After two nights there, I bowed goodbye and called out my destination at the railroad station. "Tokyo!" "Tokyo!" I realized later they had tried to get me to say a specific station but I finally made it onto a train and back to the military quarters. That night, my last night in that godforsaken place, I went to the Kabuki theatre. Again, with a strange ticket with symbols in my hand, I held it out and gestured where's my seat? I was eventually seated and became entranced with the show. Men played the female roles, all done so graciously, well worth the experience. I left the next day for Honolulu.

Bob greeted me with an orchid lei and for the next four days I received royal treatment from an intelligent, considerate fellow. He showed me Pearl Harbor and the SS Arizona, to the Polynesian village where dance and crafts of Fiji and Tahiti were depicted, ending with a spectacular show of folk dances from the Island, with a surrounding moat, waterfall background and a fountain spray as a curtain. We also flew one day to the island of Hawaii to view the Halemaumau volcano which was then only mad enough to give off hissing sprays of sulfur. We viewed a shoreline with craggy chunks of black lava which contrasted dramatically with the white ocean spray, long needled pines, needles shed to cover the lava flows in a soft carpet interspersed with small pine cones. Everywhere, signs of damaged land and gorgeous contrasts. Mesmerized, I did not want to leave the Big Island. My co-worker from Saigon was in Honolulu with her boyfriend on R&R and we dined with them one night and with her the next day. When we dropped her off, she stuffed two $5 bills in my purse when Bob refused to take them. I insisted later on giving them to Bob, saying "make Lois happy." Tired of fighting over the money, Bob rolled down the car window and tossed them out, saying: "That way we can make two people happy!" I left Hawaii having been wined and dined and very much pampered, and thinking I could get used to such treatment! (After all, I had been Cinderella in Hong Kong!)

Next stop was Montana, visiting 1st and 2nd and once-removed cousins in Billings, Red Lodge and Roberts. A sad trip to the cemetery to see my mother's grave, where her remains were placed just four years before. Visited with her two brothers and families. It felt at the same time strange but wonderful to be surrounded by relatives. We had always been the black sheep (or odd man out) living in Illinois, with my father's family in Quebec and my mother's in Montana.

What? I haven't mentioned Jim before? Jim O'Donnell. I landed for my week's visit to Minneapolis and he was at the airport to greet me. I had met him in 1965 in New York City, practically out the door for my new foreign service adventure to Tunisia. It was Easter and I arranged to see my friend I had known in Illinois in his Yorkville apartment in the City. I met his wife Mary for the first time, and she had a friend there with whom she had worked at Montana's Glacier Park during summers between college semesters. He was Jim O'Donnell. Mary had hidden easter eggs in their railroad apartment and we had a hilarious time searching for them. So much so that she sent us out to a nearby bar as she hid them again. I returned to NYC one more time before leaving for the great white yonder. I had never laughed with anyone as much as I had with this new fellow. Great! I thought, I meet the man of my dreams just as I'm headed for the unknown! We went to the World Fair, the Russian Tearoom, whatever we did vied for yet another best experience! He had graduated with a law degree from Univ. of Minnesota only to realize he did not want to be a lawyer, but wanted to travel! A kindred soul! So he became a tour guide for American Express. Aha! we could arrange to see each another in various places, all was not lost. I went onto Tunisia. But he had now returned to his home state, working independently as a travel agent.

Back to 1968, the next day I received a travel agent's tour of Minneapolis and St. Paul, with prissy Jim pointing out every bloody building and its date of birth. I even met his mother, 74 years of age but looking 60. He had mother issues and we didn't stay long. At one time he made a suggestion. We would become engaged when he turned 80, and I 75! That seemed fair enough! After only three nights there I was both ready to leave, yet a bit sorry. I spent about a week in the Peoria area visiting my sister and her family, and my 3 dear friends. We had known one another from kindergarten and called ourselves the "Big Four." My sister's mental condition was a bit flaky, but they were trying to work it out. It was many years later we learned she was bipolar. In those days it was called manic/depressive. In the meantime I learned from the Department that I was to work in the Office of THE Secretary of State and that would mean even more travel! I was excited to be considered. But at the same time my younger sister was going through her own crisis and I had requested a month's annual leave to help her out. I joined her in New Jersey Sept. 2 and we were back to Illinois Oct. 5. In the meantime, the Secretariat had called saying they could not hold the job for me any longer. I was then assigned to the Laos, Cambodia desk when I returned to the State Dept. Oct. 21. I was miserable that I had lost the Secretariat job.

A civil service secretary had worked forever in that office and figured she was the manager. The officers were okay. There were certain files in a certain safe we could not mention. I realized later that I could have been the Daniel Ellsburg of the State Department disclosing the secret background on the Cambodia bombings. I was very unhappy in that office. Luckily I had a two-week reprieve at USUN in New York, working for the press section and renewing my love for NYC. I stayed at the apartment of my college roommate Jane and also visited with friends Mary and Ed who had introduced me to Jim three years before.

When I returned to Washington, I heard that another section AF/N would welcome me, and attempted to transfer to that section. I learned it was easier to get transferred to other countries than it was an interdepartmental transfer. Frustrated, I gave them my resignation, but was even more disturbed when the man in Personnel said he wouldn't accept it. I returned to family and friends in Peoria over Christmas, went to New York with my visiting aunt from Chicago, and acted in accordance with my earlier action, having tendered my resignation. My Jewish aunt had been advised to visit the Catskills. We tried it one day and were besieged by pushy, aggressive men. So on New Year's eve we made our escape via a bus to New York City. The time in NYC with Aunt Bev was magical. We stayed at the St. Moritz Hotel and had a lovely view of the skating rink in Central Park. Had a tour of Lincoln Center, went to several shows: "Jimmy Shine" with Dustin Hoffman, "Plaza Suite" with Maureen Stapleton and E.G. Marshall, loving both. I even managed to look up a Lebanese concert pianist Anis Fuleheim whom I had met in Tunisia and we enjoyed a kibee reunion at a Beirut restaurant. Before our departure we met Mary and Ed at the Algonquin Hotel for Irish Coffee. Upon my return to D.C., I learned that an Ambassador had made a call on my behalf and the transfer to AF/N had been accepted and acted upon.

I reported to work Jan. 13, 1969 to AF/N (North Africa) bureau. My new boss was Hume Horan, in charge of Libya. Others headed Morocco, Algeria, and Tunisia. I felt instantly more at home with this crew. Hume Horan was to become one of my favorite bosses in the Foreign Service. He was later to become THE department spokesman for dealings with an increasingly terroristic Arab world, was a superb Arabist, speaking both Arabic and French fluently, along with other languages. (Later on he was often on national TV explaining the current uprising.)   I was delighted to meet a charming, self-effacing, obviously brilliant man. I was also pleased to become reacquainted with foreign service people from my other two postings, and had a very friendly social network with my former Tunisian and Vietnam co-workers. I walked to early morning French classes and took a writing course in the evening. I liked the apartment I had thrown together in Rosslyn, Virginia near the Iwo Jima statue, had illegal wiener roasts with Fred under the Key Bridge, and all was well with my world.

My article in the Foreign Service Journal regarding my experience in Vietnam had appeared earlier. One day I overheard Hume bragging about it to another officer, how well written it was, etc. I was pleased as punch! Also during that assignment, Tim Babcock, governor of Montana, came to visit Hume re oil in Libya. I mentioned to him that we were sort of shirt-tail relations since my aunt had been married to his brother Bill Babcock. That is another long story for another time. He suggested that I visit him at his office. I never did.

I visited Jim in Minneapolis and again in Bermuda where we faked being married for his tour group, which caused a lot of angst afterward. I had been reading Tolstoi's Ivan Ilyitch and questioned "what's it all about Alfie?" and decided to trap Jim, but at any rate leave the Foreign Service. I loved working for Hume Horan, but he was going off to do a stint as a Congressional Fellow, so I felt I wouldn't be deserting him. (But I learned so much later that the last month he had in that office all hell broke loose when Libya had a coup. He had needed my help.) But I gave my notice and was to be independent on the 4th of July! Impetuous soul that I was, I was always on the brink of poverty! Somewhere in there I had earlier interviewed at the Washington Post to be Ben Bradlee's secretary. He questioned my claim to leaving the Foreign Service, said if they offered me Paris I would go without hesitation. I denied it, saying I was ready to leave the Service. When we parted, there seemed to be a casual assurance between us that I would become his new secretary. Just when I had given notice to the State Department, the Post called to offer me a job working for the President, Kay Graham! A woman in her office would work for Ben Bradlee. Remember, impetuous? I handily refused. A major road not taken, just short of two years and Watergate!

So there I was jobless, this time for real, with little money in the bank as a cushion.

I went to New Hampshire to a friend's lakehouse; was on Cape Cod the night of Ted Kennedy's Chappaquiddick. Saw the moon landing on TV at Kathy's uncle's place in Mass. To Midland, Texas to visit Loretta and John where they had opened a new museum. Had my first trip to Mexico as the three of us took burros across the Rio Grande. Visited Dallas, Peoria, Springfield, Chicago family and friends, and the trip to see Jim again, allegedly for the Big Decision! It didn't happen. We cared very much for each other, but he had to come to terms with his own sexuality, and we parted with nothing decided but further frustration. So there it was! I could think only of escape. I returned to D.C. to sublet my apartment, loan my car, and off I went to sponge off friends in London, Paris, Bern, Florence and Tunis for a glorious three months. I was seen off at Dulles Airport with $33 in my pocket! Oh, I guess the timing had something to do with Jim. He had a tour group in London at that time. We met for two days, I told him we had cut the cord forever. I didn't know how we did it but we had done it. He hadn't yet admitted it, sadly for both of us. But we never did lose personal contact, just in a boy-girl sort of way.

My friend Jo in London informed me that Personnel had heard I was there and would I be able to work a couple weeks for a conference? Manna from heaven! I received a temporary clearance to work an IMCO (International Maritime something Organization) convention. Let's face it, I had been wondering where the next meal would come from! So I had a lazy two weeks tending to the office, resisting a few advances. At a reception I met Nasser Majd, an Iranian I had known in Tunis, and we were happy to become reacquainted. An earlier weekend Jo and her cousin and I took the hydrofoil to France and spent a night at Audreselles at a French home and delightedly drank cafe au lait in a big cereal bowl for breakfast. In London I went to some plays and ate a lot of East Indian food. Then a train to Paris.

I stayed with Barbara whom I'd known in D.C. in a charming French apartment with fireplaces and balcony. People from other worlds were there, Hal from Saigon and Ed from Tunis. Turned down an invitation to the Marine Ball, always a highlight in Embassy life. Then I was on a train to Bern, Switzerland, Kathy's favorite post.

A man in the compartment tended to me, lowered the shade, etc. When he got up to leave I said bon voyage. He then kissed my hand. While I was dealing with that gesture he asked in his most stilted English, "Can I kiss you?" I replied in my most definite French, "Non, merci!" So I checked in to Hotel Silvahof, of which the Embassy was attached (a unique arrangement) and checked in on Kathy's friend Coke, the owner's son. Had a nice conversation with him and he invited me the next day to an Embassy party of dance and frolic. Did a lot of wandering through the lovely town with moss covered trees and cliffs overlooking the peaceful Aare river. I decided to rent a car and drive to Florence. I was enchanted by the Swiss countryside even on a rainy, dreary day. I was in highest of spirits, soaring along with the Alps, besieged by friendly calls of road workers, high points, narrow roads, no guardrails, crosses to remember those who'd gone over. But by the time I got to Italy in constant rain, I was longing for it to pass.

Kathleen, with whom I had visited Paris and Rome enroute to our first assignments, was assigned to the Florence consulate. She had become engaged to Franco. In the course of several days I met and dined with her Italian friends Franco, Sergio, Angelino, Guido, such light and happy names for happy, carefree people. Franco's mother Mrs. Bensi had us for a lovely Italian dinner with pasta, chicken, salad, fruit and cheeses. " Mangi, mangi !" she would exclaim, as she offered more food. Franco, Kathleen and I drove to Rome with the diplomatic pouch, and we were all reunited with Luigi for a solemn lunch. Kathleen and I had met him 4 years before at Trevi Fountain. They returned to Florence and Luigi and I went on to see the Roman Forum in the moonlight. In later days we visited the Vatican and the lovely Pieta, tombs of popes, Sistine Chapel. Then he put me on a plane to Tunis on Alitalia, $39.80 one way, the final stop on my itinerary.

Larbi the Embassy driver and friend D.J. were awaiting me. Larbi breezed me through customs and D.J. and I jumped into her blue MGB for the drive to her apartment. How great it was to be back! She was so thankful I had arranged for her to work for Arch Calhoun again, now Ambassador to Tunisia. I was invited to Thanksgiving at the Residence. A fun and lovely American thanksgiving meal. Grateful Peace Corps volunteers heaped the food onto their plates. At the Embassy it was great to see old friends from just two years ago. Hedi Benamour arranged for me to take tennis lessons at the tennis club. Everyone complimented my sense of freedom, no job, no plan, just liberation! The American military USLOT had a contingent in Bizerte in conjunction with the Tunisian military, so we were encouraged to visit the Americans at any time. D.J. was to become the wife of one of them, and later on Ambassador Calhoun walked her down the aisle. But not just now! When I visited the facility with her, I became more interested in the Tunisians, and two cousins Habib and M'Hammad adopted me.

Habib had been a foreign airman at Chanute Air Force base near my home at Peoria, Illinois and was named THE Foreign Student at Chanute during his time there. M'Hammad was the Chief of Agriculture in Bizerte. We became known as the cousins. Their house was nearby on Cap Blanc, the furthest point north on the African continent. They had a lovely home on the Mediterranean sea, an Arabian horse, a dog, cat, fireplace, colorful Tunisian furniture and enormous flower and vegetable gardens.

When I met the head of the Smithsonian Marine Sorting Center outside Tunis, Dr. Higgins, he offered me a temporary job at 600 millienes per hour, or $1.10. So I became the new local! He gave me a draft on some strange sea creature and his dentures. And I wrote Christmas cards, painfully copying Seasons Greeting in Arabic! He was also glad to teach me complicated scientific names of creatures whose translation in English were somewhat obscene.

About that time the Admin Officer's secretary's mother died in the states and she was going home. I inquired and was hired to be her temporary replacement. More needed money just in time! I worked for the Admin Officer, put together the Tunis Bulletin, and filled in for the DCM when his secretary was ill. I loved the feeling of being useful and appreciated. Partied with a lot of Tunisian nationals from the Embassy and loved it. Saw my cousins and Hedi, visited the Souks and thoroughly enjoyed Tunis, my first post in the Foreign Service. Suddenly it was December. D.J. went home to the states for Christmas, I visited "my cousins" and had a marvelous Christmas dinner with the Americans at USLOT in Bizerte. Sadly on December 30, 1969 I left Tunisia for the States to meet my sister for New Year's Eve in D.C.; thereafter a blank slate.

Jo Sloane and cousin, London trip and onto Audreselles, France, 1969

Kathleen Mathiot and fiance Franco, Firenze, Italy 1969

My two Arabian "cousins" on revisit to Tunisia 1969 - M'Hammad and Habib.

Big Four: Joyce, Mary, Bev, Phyllis, sometime between posting.

I helped arrange D.J.'s return to Tunis as Ambassador's secretary for her boss from Vietnam Arch Calhoun. She met Paul Miller in 1969 when he was with USLOT contingent in Bizerte, married him in 1970 with the Ambassador walking her down the aisle. Tunis

Chicago

Chicago Tour

A surprise to myself. I had forgotten exactly when was to become my Chicago tour and it began in January 1970. My older sister was crumbling in her mental state and marriage, the mother of five children. My inner self knew I could not return to Peoria, too close to the action. So I chose Chicago where my main support was my aunt Beverley and was close enough to Peoria, 2-1/2 hours, within striking distance. She graciously allowed me a bed while I job hunted. I eased into town a roundabout way, visiting friends Gary and Rosalie in Michigan from my Tunis tour. Once in Chicago I searched the newspapers, several employment agencies, and ended taking a chance on the city's largest law firm in the highest building, Prudential on the edge of Grant Park. I was assigned to a managing partner, a corporate attorney. And there began a constant to-ing and fro-ing between our personalities. I liked him one day and hated him another. Work was always overflowing and I had a tendency to race through a project without having the leisure time to proof, thereby overlooking errors. At times I was superb and at times lacking. He had his own problems with an ex-wife, ex-secretary, ex-girlfriend. Work life was certainly not boring, there were many overtime hours into the night. One secretary devoted herself to the time and a half overtime, which she added up to pay for a studio apartment in the new John Hancock Building NOW (the latter part of 1970) the tallest building in Chicago.

My aunt was a very impressive, talented actress who had

graduated years before at Goodman's Theatre School. We met her first in Peoria when her husband's brother became my mother's husband. When she lived in Peoria, she played the starring role in many productions: Glass Menagerie, Shakespeare, Suddenly Last Summer, Bell, Book and Candle. Once in Chicago I encouraged her to a tryout. Once the director heard from her, he was saddened to report he had already chosen a lead. She and I often went to productions in the Chicago area. Highlights, all quite superb, were: "Dylan, Bus Stop, Who's Afraid of Virginia Woolf, A Play by Aleksandr Solzhenitsyn, Come Blow Your Horn, Hair, American Ballet of Swan Lake, Carlos Montoya, The Effect of Gammas Rays on Man in the Moon Marigolds, Man of La Mancha, Lady Audley's Secret, Status Quo Vadis." The very worst was "Outcry" written by Tennessee Williams in his waning years. It was so boring people fell asleep, but we were trapped and could not leave, as he was in the audience. (When it premiered in NYC in 1973, it lasted just 9 days.)

Meanwhile I was my free and flippant 33 yr. old self, looking for love and affection. I met possible future beaus in the Grog Shop bar in the Prudential Building. Laura and I were sometime vixens. We'd go to lovely dinners with visiting businessmen and dash off quickly when they wanted compensation. Once I ran into an acquaintance from my Univ. of Iowa days, who had become an attorney in Chicago. I signed up for what I believe to be the first computer dating service, was given eleven names for possible interest. I checked on a few. One I recall was the son of THE Werner von Braun, the maker of "wee-1 and wee-2's" as he pronounced them. He also said it was a "doggy doggy" world! We had dinner a couple times. One owned a greeting card factory and kept sending me kooky cards to woo me. Another was a Persian named Jim. I found him very straight forward, analytical and comforting.

I found a reasonable pleasant 8th floor apartment on Marine Drive, the extension to Lake Shore Drive. I often rode my bike down the lakeshore on days off, sometimes getting all the way to Chicago's loop. When Minneapolis Jim came to visit we rented a bicycle built for two. Luigi, flying for Alitalia, came for a two day visit and begged me to come to Rome and work there. I had occasional visits from other manfriends, Steve and Bill. Ralph Nader made our law firm a project during my Chicago tour, attempting to undermine the power structure of our firm. Notices went out: do not talk to Ralph Nader! I don't know the ending to that story.

I returned to Washington several times. In February 1970 I returned to be the maid of honor at my dear friend Kathy's wedding as she married a Foreign Service Officer and went on to their posting in Beirut. I hit it off very well with her father. At one point he said: "I'm going to have to talk to my daughter and tell her that you're going to be her new stepmother!" How we all laughed over that! I flew again to D.C. to be with old friends at Thanksgiving. Those were the days before TSA security checks and I often managed to dash to the plane within ten minutes of takeoff.

In July 1970 my younger sister Judy, who had lived with Pat's family for several months, broke away to begin her own life in California. She flew into Chicago to visit me at Christmas time 1970 and we drove down to be with Pat and her children and onto Springfield to visit our brother's family. She also came the next year in the summer, again a trip to Peoria. She enjoyed her liberation in

California.

Once settled in my job I took a French course, night school at Northwestern, a yoga class at the YMCA. I joined the Art Institute to save my fevered soul from the maddening, hectic days of dictation from an irascible, unpredictable boss, a Leo the lion. I would go for lectures on Art during rare spare time, and was always soothed by sitting in a roomful of buddhas, or viewing lovely, restful Japanese and Chinese paintings, always in nature. I laughed when my name was included in their bulletin as a "Donor Under $1000." (way under!)

Laura and I would head for Rush Street on the weekends for serious drinking and enjoying the "big band sound" at a popular bar. One time we picked up two baseball players from the Philadelphia Phillies in town to play the Chicago Cubs. She became friendly with a publisher/fancy bible salesman from North Carolina who came often to the Windy City. I met some of his co-workers along the way. She and I were free to choose the restaurants, so we chose the most elegant or trendiest: Chez Paul, Ambassador East, Cape Cod room. One time I had the staff on their knees hunting for what they thought was my contact lens. But I had panicked over my lost eyelash which had cost me $15. They immediately gave up the search.

After my sister's mental health diminished she was hospitalized several times. After swallowing pills in April 1971 she ended up in Bartonville, the Peoria State Hospital. Her husband eventually checked her out of the facility assuring her that all was fine between them, and then asked for a divorce the next day. He married another soon after the divorce was final, thereby dumping fragile Pat with five children. The oldest was 13. We learned later that his attorney had done exactly the same thing to his own wife, including the mental health scenario. When this occurred, I often made weekend trips to Peoria to shop, support and be with the very sweet, confused children. At the same time I did my best to bolster my sister's confidence and attempt to stoke her up for needed courage.

After the April incident I made almost weekly drives to Peoria, leaving on Friday night or Saturday, returning on Sunday nights. We had to move her out of her family home when one day he upped and took away the children, even though she was technically the custodial parent. When that happened she was placed in a halfway house. We stored her furniture in the basement of her friend Laurie from church. One holiday weekend I dashed to Peoria to pick up Pat and three allotted kids and we headed north again. We stopped at my apartment on Marine Drive so they could see it and headed north toward Wisconsin. Our college friend Ike lived in horse country near Libertyville. Her husband was a horse trainer. The kids were thrilled to ride them and have a wholesome childhood experience. On my other visits I would rent a hotel room with swimming pool so we and the permitted children could pretend we were on vacation and having fun. I drove an unreliable car, a Datsun, which would sometimes stall in the middle of a highway. When it rained it would not start. I put rugs and plastic into the hood to ward off moisture and sometimes forgot to remove them! I was always returning to a gas station or garage to fix the radiator or another serious part. I was always broke, but celebrated with great lunches with my new friends. The charge card was new and much too tempting. Overtime was a must!

Meanwhile, the ex would have moods and offer my sister 3 of the 5 children; then later change his mind and say they were all off limits. Whatever whim he and the new wife (who had two children of her own) would proclaim, they kept her from seeing the youngest child. The oldest at 13, 14, 15 (during my Chicago tour) was withdrawn and acted as though he were finished with both his mother and father. He proved it by later graduating from high school in three years and immediately going off to college on his own. The youngest had no memory of her own birth mother, as she had been whisked away at age two or three. The middle three had one another to lean on for whatever happened, and stuck together. Eventually the newly formed family was upended and moved to Florida, no forwarding address. There was a span of 30 years before they and I were reunited. I and their mother had lost their childhoods forever.

I was dating Chuck who worked for Bank of America and had a great apartment on Lake Shore Drive. I helped him decorate and stayed there when he was called out of town back to California. I met several people who lived in the complex and we would often go out to feast in Chicago's finest. I recall one day walking to work from his apartment on a bitterly cold day. Frost collected on my eyelashes and lasted to the Prudential building, up the elevators and to my office area so I could boast to my co-workers before they melted. I was so proud!

In Dec. 1970 I met Keith, who was an architect in Who's Who in the West and Midwest. He lived in the same apartment complex as Chuck. We had a mutual attraction which would move into 1971. The more I knew him, the more intimidated I became at this famous architect, head of his architectural firm. I guess I felt I didn't deserve him, we grew apart. My mental state between a workday of chaos and the chaos of my family, was not in good order. My dear aunt had her own problems during 1971, losing her elderly millionaire father, and then later her dear daughter in an automobile accident. Her father had made his millions with stainless steel. He owned the factory which made all the coin boxes for the Chicago Transit Authority buses. He had been a self-effacing White Russian, a kindly man. I still have a memento, a small tray he had made by hand. Her daughter Michelle had just become a nurse, was a talented potter and artist and had been a bubbly, effervescent person.

Toward the end of summer 1971 I met another Jim, also an attorney, one of the apartment complex gang. Just after meeting him someone had stolen his car and wrecked it. He soon left town for a new job in San Diego. Guess what? Noble Beverly kept track of the auto repairs, arranged for financing those repairs, when she had barely a dime for herself, and what's more offered to drive it to California once it had been repaired! When I picked it up and took off for California, the fan belt kept flipping off and the generator light lit up, first in Illinois, then Oklahoma, then New Mexico. I did have a magical moment visiting an old college friend who lived in an adobe house north of Santa Fe, at the edge of San Juan Pueblo. She and hubby had baked their own adobe bricks and remodeled several buildings, making their own kiva fireplaces, skylights, bancos, and painting the interior all in white. Red chilis, squash, corn hung from a kitchen rafter, with snowcapped mountains in the distance, a black mesa out their front doorstep. The day after my arrival I climbed up on the mesa with Lanny to gaze at primitive pictographs on the rocks, and wandered through an old railway depot. I was enchanted with my first look at the land of enchantment, did not want to leave. (I returned to this haven the next Thanksgiving.) But off I went and three fan belts later from the trip's beginning, I pulled into San Diego for the delivery. I had a two-fold purpose as my sister also lived there, and I was happy to deliver the car to Jim, who was grateful. I was later to endure the hassle of his repaying the debt for repairs.

In 1972 I continued the see-sawing with my boss. I did not take his outbursts lying down, gave back as was given. He would become enraged if I was not on the other end of his buzzer. One frustrating time I answered an ad for an ideal job in a travel agency, always with a view to travel and see the world. I was in the top 3 but did not get it. No change of plan. My boss's clients were always more generous than he. One bet on a horse for me at the track, it won and I received a $50 bill. One took me to a very gentlemanly dinner, all were generous in their compliments. And I began secretly investigating a return to the Foreign Service, applying anew, fingerprints, medicals, security investigations, all done gradually like putting a little money at a time into a bank account.

A hairdresser was a vital person during my Chicago tour (let's face it, all my tours!) I played with wigs and hair pieces, going to extremes. There were always at least weekly trips for resuscitation of hair follicles. The highlights for plays in 1972 were Death of a Salesman, Butley, How the Other Half Loves, Company, Godspell (Musical), Old Times, and the opera Cosi Fan Toote. I was to see my favorite movie Cabaret, the first of many times throughout my life. TMT (too much trouble) to put them all in quotes!

So in January 1972 Jim returned from San Diego, that job not working out, and I took him in, ready or not. He was a great cook, kind of a non touchy-feely fellow, but I worked hard at working it out. There certainly arose a tension when two months turned into three and onward. When my friends returned from Beirut and visited, he stayed with a friend but prepared some lovely meals for us. Boef Bourguignonne was a specialty but he was a master at many dishes. One weekend he and I and another couple took a car trip to northern Wisconsin, where I had been born. We stayed in small cabins in magnificent woods, I saw the lumberjack hospital where I was born, the first baby! now a doctor's office in Laona, Wisconsin.

Friend Laura and I spent a week in the Miami area in May, mostly baking in the sun, her favorite pastime. We met dental students attending a convention. They took us to a hotel with a floor show and made a grand scheme of running out on the check. Talk about feeling violated! I took French Prose at Northwestern. I joined a ski club. In Chicago it meant driving north to Algonquin, Ill. for some rolling hills, sometimes with a chill factor of 28 below. On one occasion others were in the warming house and I charged down the hill, wondering where the brakes were. I and my skis got tangled in the lift ropes going up. Often trips were cancelled for lack of snow. The ski club was an excuse for partying and we eventually skipped the skis.

My aunt and I took a trip to Europe in August. She had not been before, so we hit London, Paris and Rome, seeing all the obvious sites. Saw Butley in London and Robert Morley in How the Other Half Lives, clever and funny. In Paris, the obvious sites, and enjoyed a lovely dinner on the Place de Vosges with Dave who had been a

Saigon boss and Amb. Calhoun then retiring from Tunisia. Saw Luigi again in Rome and my aunt, approving of him, offered to "make" a wedding for us. When we were bumped up to first class on TWA back to Chicago and they rolled the prime rib cart down the aisle, serving us champagne and caviar, she remarked "This is the highlight of my trip!"

Upon our return the apartment was a mess, Jim was not there. Fed up with him, I packed his things and began our "divorce." The next day I learned that my car had been stolen; of course I had no theft insurance. What a welcome home! But I felt so relieved that I had kicked Jim out and weeks later the car was retrieved with minor damage. That car's history was full of minor damages! The police had been thrilled to arrest the suspect as he had his own history with them. I went to court to see him convicted.

Sister Pat visited a couple times that year, as well as Minneapolis Jim, archaeologist Joe Ben Wheat and wife Pat from Tunisia days, dear friends Joyce and Larry.

In October I met Julius, a handsome lovable Jewish fellow, divorced with 2 children, ten years older than myself. He was everything Jim was not, liked to touch and snuggle, was considerate, kind and thoughtful.

And on November 17 I was fired. At noon Leo the Lion came storming down the hall because I wasn't at my desk when he had buzzed. We commenced to exchange loud words. I said "The next time you scream at me will be the last time!" He said "Okay, this is your last day!" "That's great with me," I shouted and that was it. The entire area heard him and I found out later that all were on my side. I was of course humiliated and cried. A higher ranked partner wanted to talk with me. I was too upset. He passed the word I could come stay with the firm and work for someone else. I wanted to be away from it all and applied at an agency and worked a few days for another law firm. Unhappy there, I returned to Kirkland and Ellis to be a temporary secretary. After my famed firing, I worked for about a dozen attorneys when their secretaries were not available and found genuinely nice, considerate people. By then I had been accepted again by the State Department and was to go to Recife, Brazil. Soon the assignment was changed to the Embassy in Panama to my favorite section, political. Nineteen people attended a farewell luncheon for me at a popular Italian restaurant, arranged by friend Laura. I made a farewell trip to Peoria to say adieu to my dear sister and friends. My sister supported me in my new move, knowing that I was born under a wandering star and now needed to return to the Foreign Service. She appreciated the three years I had devoted to her.

Chicago ski club meeting with Marylou, 1972.

Buddy Laura Czukla at Kirkland & Ellis Christmas party, 1972

Aunt Beverley Enslin on 1972 tour of Europe - Chicago tour

Return visit to Roma and Luigi from Chicago, 1972.

Visited college roommate Loretta Vincent in northern New Mexico,
my Chicago tour - 1972. A talented artist.

Childhood friend Joyce and husband Larry Spurgeon on Chicago
visit, 1972. (Jim O'Donnell in background)

Eternal friend James O'Donnell, cherry blossom time in D.C. 1969.

Julius Hankin (a tender fellow) and me - Chicago 1973

Chicago buddies Laura Czukla and Clara Douglas.

My Chicago cousins: Scott, Ann and Brad

Bev, Scott, Aunt Bev in Chicago

Niece Renee - 1972

Nephew Steven - 1972

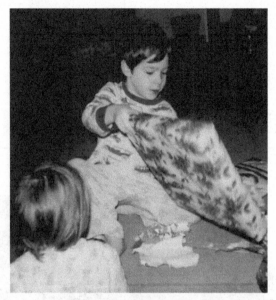

Nephew Mark - 1972

Niece Leslie, Christmas – 1972
Doug, 13, didn't want to be photographed.

Panama

Entering Panama

On January 13 I left Chicago, sadly saying goodbye to Julius. I was to see him in D.C. before my departure to Panama, as he was heading out for a new job in Philadelphia. I stopped in Dayton for a couple days to see Jim. In D.C. I ran into Steve Whilden, who invited me to see the very lovely civil war house he was renovating in Maryland near Harper's Ferry.

I entered a class of 13 secretaries, having already received our assignments. Three happened to be legal secretaries from Chicago, small world. We four coalesced immediately. We were subjected to various lectures and workshops for several weeks before our departures to new adventures. I renewed my acquaintance with my Spanish hairdresser and friend Petra, who always made me look good. Got my shots for Panama: yellow fever, small pox, a polio check.

January 20 was Richard Nixon's inauguration day, no celebration for me. Then Lyndon Johnson died two days later, only 64 years old, a defeated man after Vietnam.

Mary Frey from Saigon days and I took a bus to New York City to see "Last of Mrs. Lincoln" with Julie Harris, which was spectacular. Mary Phillips had arranged for us to stay with another Mary, her cousin, on Long Island. How Merry! We went to Rockefeller center to watch the skaters, always enchanting: an old man, an older couple, and young sprites gliding and enjoying themselves. Also went to see "Don Juan in Hell" with Ricardo

Montalbán, Agnes Morehead, and Paul Henreid, all outstanding. Back to D.C. on the Metroliner, a 3 hr. trip. I went to dinner the next day at cousin Joanne's. She looked so much like Aunt Ione and had the same sweetness. We discovered we had a lot in common. I had seen her just a few times on trips to Montana while growing up. Her husband worked for the Forest Service. I went again to give her and her daughter some winter clothes; all looked good on them. I was heading for the tropics!

Julius drove into town a few days later. Took me to his brother's home one eve and to his parents the next. His mother told me instantly how she liked me and hated Julius' ex. His father was sweet and gentle. The same eve he took me to his sister's home, who also approved of me. Was I being auditioned just as I was to leave town? All wanted me to not leave for Panama. Julius said he would come to visit this summer.

On February 5 I headed for a brief visit to Guatemala to see friend Ed Casey from Tunis days. In Miami there was 2 hr. wait as they investigated an engine malfunction, which necessitated a switch to another plane. Landing in Guatemala, they had lost one bag, and there was no Ed to greet me. I checked into a hotel. The next day Ed reported that he had just received my letter of arrival. His mother was visiting, he had luncheon plans, so she and I took a tour to Antigua with two other people. Antigua had a volcano which destroyed much of it in 1500 and then an earthquake demolishing even more in 1773. Had an enjoyable tour, my missing bag had materialized, and Ed and I went out for a fine dinner. The next day I had lunch with new friend Sally from the tour, along with her husband. All were old friends by the afternoon and I departed for

Panama. The ride was only 1 hr. 45 min, landing for my new assignment on February 7. I was met by Ken Bleakley and his wife, who assured me that morale was fine, the weather great, and delivered me to the Executive Hotel. My room was on the 11th floor with a marvelous view of the city and lights on the bay. I was surprised to find Panama City to be somewhat attractive.

Panama

How joyous it was to be back in the fold! I was one of two secretaries working for three officers in the Political Section. People were friendly and included me in their plans. I was home! I could not wipe the smile off my face. I rolled with the punches and came out victorious, happily playing my role at the Embassy. In preparation for future negotiations with Panama and the U.S. concerning the Panama Canal, there was a Security Council meeting in Panama with the USUN. A month or so after my arrival four American Ambassadors (including our own) kept us quite busy for almost two weeks. I worked long hours for Ambassadors Scali, Bennett, Schaufele, and Sayre. I signed up for daily Spanish classes. My new friend Joyce worked for Security and had been active with a local orphanage of 23 children, ages 6-20, mostly girls. I became her co-pilot in April, and we had taken them on picnics, to the circus, and to swim several times at the Marine House. At one picnic we played both softball and volleyball, a real hit. The children were lovable and so appreciative. When Joyce left later I was to become Chief Orphan. She also knew the person who headed the crafts program for the Army: Sam, and introduced me to the potters wheel. What a thrilling sensation to release tension with a lump of clay!

Dating was a bit sparse in comparison to Chicago, but there was a lot to explore. In March and April I dated a couple USAID fellows I had met at a fun party. Four had formed a singing quartet called the Marshmallows. About that time I found a classical guitarist Ronald Radford's performance enthralling. Then there were the visitors from the American Geodetic Survey who came to Panama for a conference, end of April and into May. Joyce and I flew with two Phd doctors to Contadora island for a Sunday outing and had our pictures taken by a photographer for the local paper. We had a few fun filled days with them. I got the better one Joyce had been trying to seduce. We were sorry to see them leave.

A new courier to Panama informed me that Hal from Saigon days had left both the Foreign Service and his Paris-met wife. I've wondered if he thought I had "turned him in." I never did. Some of you will know that story.

The end of May a group of eight of us flew over to Bogota for the weekend. We enjoyed our nice hotel and the cool air at 8600 feet. Dined at the Russian Balalaika restaurant where we all got hilarious and cozy with the vodka and high altitude. It was a gay, beautiful group and we seemed to click instantly. Even sang hymns on the way back home. The next day some of us visited the gold museum and an interesting salt cathedral which had been built underground. A very successful weekend jaunt.

My first boss Harry left several months after my arrival, having landed a posh job for the State Dept. He later became the Ambassador to Nicaragua. I became good friends with his wife Iris as she managed to stay almost two months in their home. I'd deliver her mail and enjoyed lovely lunches by the pool. She was an attractive, vivacious woman from Honduras and our friendship remained unbroken long after Panama. She had been a huge hit in London when she had been married to a Honduran diplomat and attended the wedding for Queen Elizabeth and Prince Philip. She showed me pictures of herself in London society papers, lots of them! What she recalled most about the wedding was they had to arrive hours earlier to be seated and then endure what it seemed more hours for the ceremony, not being able to get to a bathroom!

Having access to the PX in the Canal Zone with all the comforts of home, did spoil us. I would mutter that it robbed us of the foreign feeling of finding our way to discover the joys of life overseas. But who was I to argue? We had access to military PXs and Officers Clubs at Ft. Clayton (Army) and Fort Amador (Army); Rodman was the Naval Station; Air Force (Albrook) and Howard Air Base we flew in and out of. The Army ran Gorgas Hospital, all based in the Canal Zone. But Embassy people lived on the Panamanian side, and I was grateful.

Once some of the Embassy was invited to transit the Canal aboard a US Navy Guided Missile Frigate (I am not swearing!) so of course I had to tag along. We had a strange notion that we would be entertained royally with a large buffet on deck. As it turned out we had baloney sandwiches and weepy jello in the ward room. The trip did not take the promised eight hours, but twelve. The Canal pilots had chosen that day to begin a slowdown. An electronic/computer lad latched onto me and gave me a fascinating trip into his Startrek world (showed me how a computer could land an airplane!) Afterward I tried to shake him, with no luck. Worse yet, he had invited me to the Admiral's cocktail party the next night, so I couldn't dump him overboard! The Admiral's affair was just all right. The odds were 40 to 1 and could have been delightful, but the more I tried to escape, the more he clung and would not permit others even to talk to me!

A favorite hideaway was Contadora Island, 20 minutes from Panama City via small plane. It had white sparkling beaches with clear snorkeling water unpolluted but for sharks. It later on became the spot to begin Panama Canal negotiations on which country was to finally run its operation. Occasionally birds clogged the engines and the plane went down, but it was worth the risk. The flight scheduling was erratic. Often we were told we'd depart a certain time and then would see Panamanians take off on our scheduled flight. Once Joyce and two male companions and I hopped in on the return to Panama City and refused to disembark when they said it was not our plane. Once back to Panama City we were accused of hijacking the plane. If they were going to arrest me, I said, I'd better let the duty officer at the Embassy know about it. They backed down. Other than this incident I managed to stay out of trouble.

I worked for the Political Chief John Blacken and we got along very well. There were two secretaries in a section of only three political officers and the aide to the Ambassador, so work was not that demanding. It was a piece of cake after Leo the Lion in Chicago.

Dini the Administrative Secretary became a special friend. We'd wolf down voluminous lunches one day and made bets for diet loss campaigns on another. Embassy parties were plentiful, with lots of dancing. Irene the personnel officer was a good cook . We went on a siege of eating escargot at her house (yes, in the tropics!) and would try to out eat one another. I recall the time we had fresh lobsters and can still hear their tortured claws scraping the pan in their attempt to escape the pot! I took tennis lessons and kept up a regular stream of classes at Florida State in the Canal Zone. By the time I added up credits from various universities as I left Panama, I had the senior year to go before a B.A.

Three of us took a train to duty-free Colon one day off to check out bargains. We didn't find it too exciting for being duty-free and bought little. On the way to the Hotel Washington for lunch, a man with a gun shot after a running boy (fortunately up in the air). When walking back we went through a seedy section of town, and were stopped by two men of the national guard. They said 15 men were about to mug us, they had been following us. We got into their official car and were escorted to a safer section of town, whereupon the police there reaffirmed our potential danger. On the train back we breathed our sighs of relief and decided Colon left nothing to desire.

One time in April, Ardith, Lorraine and I went to see "Camelot." It was good, frothy, but too long. The message: "All of us are but drops in the vast sea, but some of us sparkle." I unabashedly took that message for myself.

In October a very nice thing happened to me, the arrival of a new officer, Harvard Law School, an older (49) wiser, witty, good looking, bright, salt and pepper haired man, divorced, a precious and gentle person. His title was Special Assistant to the Ambassador for Narcotic Affairs. His name was Edwin Dwight Ledbetter. We became an instant ITEM. I was never as happy as I was with him, felt comforted and protected. Others wanted to feel the same way. The personnel officer tried to claim him, as did Joyce. When Joyce left for her next assignment she announced to the personnel officer, "I guess I'll have to leave you and Bev to fight over Ed." I won.

When first a passenger in my car he said: "I like the way you drive, like a fighter pilot!" He had been the captain of a B-17 bomber during WWII, shot down over France and was a POW for almost six months before being rescued by Patton's 3rd army.

Ed rented a tux for the annual Marine Corps Ball in November. When we went to the military base, we were disappointed that it took place in their gym. Several parachutes covered basketball hoops and other paraphernalia in the ceiling. Our table was placed near the smelly food laden steam table. The venue looked like a high school dance! But we adjusted and it was fun to dance with Ed, my boss John, and others and we made the best of it. Ed made the decision that it was his last Marine Corps Ball.

He and I continued in a warm, very warm relationship. Let's put it this way, my face had a virtual glow! We could not hide the intensity of our feelings. But all was not perfect in paradise. His "other" in D.C. poured out letters of longing to him, would not let go. He was indeed torn and confused. When she threatened to come down to Panama, he mentioned it to me. I said "I will then consider you have decided between us." She did not come down. They had even talked of marriage before he had presented himself to this new assignment. After several months he went to the states to see his family and then her. Each day he was gone I endured an agony of wondering, but he returned with no commitment made and was again amorous for me.

It was great fun to shop for Christmas gifts for my kids, the orphans at Bella Vista. I decided rather than have the gifts from me, they could draw names and give to one another! Aside from our party together, I managed to farm them out two at a time for a day with an Embassy family during Christmas week. All of us were better for that event. In over two years there I was always buying turkeys and hams and school supplies at the commissary for Bella Vista needs, and we were often picking them up for picnics or swims at the Marine House. One Christmas they came to the Embassy to sing carols for us, ushered into the Ambassador's office. It was a thrill for everyone and they received special treats.

Ed and I went to the San Blas Islands over New Year's Eve. Housing was an iron bed on white sand in a thatched hut, ate lobster every meal, bought molas from the Cuna Indians, all stretched out on a clothesline (the molas, not the Indians!) Ships would pause in Cuna territory. We ran into some Greek officers and when he heard them speak, Ed greeted them in Greek. The delighted captain invited us back to the ship and off we went with a Cuna Indian rowing us in a dugout canoe! We had a few lovely hours with the officers in their board room and returned to our island haven. Awaiting the plane the next day, I managed to pass out, crumbling onto the soft sand. A doctor happened to be in the crowd and came to attend me. Worried Ed held me as we staggered to the plane. Lobster turned out to be overpoweringly rich for every meal!

His children all came down, one after another. Daughter Suzanne, aged 23, came first. We took her to Coronado Beach for the weekend. She was elegant and slim in a provocative white laced bikini and am certain she was an eye popper for the VP's house next door to us on the beach. (Make that Vice President of Panama!) She stayed a few days, was very sweet, seemed to accept her father's relationship with me. John a bit of a con artist at 19 came next, always seemed to have his hand out for a "loan" from Pop. He stayed longer, several weeks. Cathy, next year had turned 23 and she was easy to talk to, also very accepting. An artist, she spent a weekend with the Cuna Indians and was fascinated, acquiring their molas.

Astrologically speaking, Ed was a Pisces and I a Virgo. He cut out one description that summed us up: "Virgo will give shape to Pisces' rather muddled reactions; Pisces will warm and relax Virgo. While Virgo works, Pisces will dream." That has always seemed on the mark.

Secretary of State Kissinger breezed through for a day or so in February 1974 just long enough to upset normal operations. Chicago friends came, first Laura and a week later Clara and Patti. The AID fellows were thrilled to entertain such attractive women. In March I made a whirlwind trip to visit my younger sister and "significant other" on his sailboat in Hawaii for a lovely few days. They lived on his 32 foot boat in the LaMoana harbor in Honolulu. Much of Judy and Van's closeness reminded me of Ed and myself. I stopped first to see Dallas friends, and returned via Chicago and Peoria. I saw again Chicago friends who had visited me, along with Julius, who happened to be there on a visit from Philadelphia. We each confessed we had found replacements in our new locales. It was great to have a luncheon reunion of 11 of us at LaTour in Chicago. My older sister seemed to be doing better mentally downstate.

Later visitors to Panama were college friend Ike, and Iris returned as well. Ambassador Sayre left and William Jorden replaced him. He had been born in Montana just sixteen miles from Red Lodge, my mother's home town.

After several months in a transient apartment with another woman, I had been assigned to a two bedroom apartment in new

Embassy housing just across the street from work. Small, but had a great view of the water (the Gulf of Panama). The next year when Magdelena Kalodimos came as the second secretary in our section, I turned my apartment over to her and found one away from the Embassy family. I liked my new hideaway, but missed the view.

Ed and I took a trip to San Andreas island off Columbia. Clear skies, smooth flight. When a lovely breakfast was served to us on the plane, the tray shot up and the plane dropped about 35 feet. We had run into a tropical storm. All were frightened; there was not one word from the cockpit. We were no longer hungry, the plane landed safely after a long hour of bumpy sky, and we were quite relieved to land. We enjoyed the clear water and gorgeous reefs of the San Andreas area. Took long walks during the full moon. Later we went to Mexico City together when he had a Narcotics Conference. The first night we landed we enjoyed a superb performance by the Bolshoi Ballet. We drove one day to nearby Taxco, gave a man a lift. I had carelessly left my bag in back and when he hurriedly left the car, he had stolen $55. His conscience made him leave $200 plus a 500 peso note.

Another trip was made to Costa Rica where we walked up a mountain to a volcano, saw a mystical pine forest, the grass a fluffy feather bed of soft pine needles. Costa Rica was clean and sparkling with lots of flowers, in contrast to Panama where you had to search for special pristine spots.

Student demonstrators from Instituto Nacional began a peaceful banana war protest in August of 1974, burned a U.S. flag and an effigy made of banana peels. A banner said: "Hoy bananas, manana el Canal." They threw rock and bricks, eventually breaking 83 windows of the Embassy building. The Guard Nacional watched and made no attempt to stop them. I had to dodge flying glass as I entered the elevator. My boss wrote a protest note in strong language on behalf of the United State government to the Panamanian foreign office. The students began another protest a week or so later, but this time the Guard Nacional fended them off several blocks away.

The next day we received the news that on that same night in Arlington, Virginia, outside the Orleans restaurant a few blocks from where I used to live, our Security officer Jack Herse, who had recently left Panama, was shot and killed. Three blacks attacked as he and his wife were headed back to their hotel after dinner. Dini had felt particularly close to him; we were all desolated. The crime remains unsolved. It was a time of violence. Less than a week later the Ambassador in Nicosia was shot and killed at the Embassy during another demonstration. Ed had served in Cyprus in the early 60's.

When Honduras was struck with Hurricane Fifi in September 1974 with at least 5000 lives lost, we collected from Embassy personnel, bought and sent several shipments of food and supplies.

Ed wasn't in town for the Marine Ball in November, so I went with Sam our gay friend from the Canal Zone. We had a rip roaring dancing time. The next day Col. Austin's wife said to him: "Beverly has a new boyfriend." He replied: "I'm not jealous. Everyone is Beverly's boyfriend!" It makes me laugh each time I read it, saucy person that I was!

Ed's job was a tenuous one. The U.S. vacillated on its treatment of drug pin Manuel Noriega and the drug scene. He was in an on and off relationship with the CIA, and currently it was "hands off" Noriega. Ed set about justifying the abolishment of his position there. In the meantime they used him to write up talking points for future Panama Canal negotiations. When the negotiators came to Panama I was sent to Contadora island for dictation and they came often to our office. Later they brought their own support staff. I would occasionally be called to the phone to take dictation from Ambassador Bunker in Contadora to Kissinger, Secy of State. An efficiency report for Ed was nebulous, written by an insecure man acting as Charge d'Affaires and it was cause for concern. He also fretted over his next assignment, once his current position was abolished. His term there was fraught with tragedy. He lost both his father and his brother, the latter succumbing to the rampant flu epidemic in February 1975. I was learning to take on my love's "bag of rocks."

Lovely moments were our star gazing times, either from the roof of my apartment building or on beaches as we spent weekends out of Panama City. He taught me constellations. Orion and the Southern Cross shared the sky on a rare occasion in February. I had bought him a book by H. A. Rey which showed constellations as stick figures, making them easier to spot. It became our bible.

I extended my tour by three months, hoping that Ed and I would come to some sort of conclusion. I was granted a European tour, to Geneva. Would he accompany me, or would I follow him to his next assignment, which would most likely be Washington. Back and forth we went, with no answer. Just two days before my departure I had dinner with John Morrison from the Chicago law firm who was in Panama on business. We had a very nice dinner at the

Continental and never stopped talking for three hours.

Ed and I managed to depart post together May 21, 1975, taking a freighter to New York, the SS Santa Barbara. The orphans came to see us off. I wanted to take them aboard, but sadly kissed each of them goodbye.

At a lock in Panama Canal, aboard US Navy Guided Missile Frigate. They promised 8 hours to transit canal, but took 12 hours due to canal pilot slowdown!

Joyce Ford, the vamp, in the middle. Panama 1973

My best buddy Bernadine Chenevert, and Irene Bauer, Personnel Officer, Panama. 1973

A weekend trip to Bogota from Panama. Sammy Williams and Joyce Ford on the right. 1973

Visit to Honolulu to visit sister Judy Lavigne, 1973.

Sister Judy and Significant Other Van Elkins in Honolulu - 1973
Panama Tour

My sweet Panamanian orphans. We took them on picnics,
swimming at the Marine House, carloads of fun. 1973-75

Panamanian orphans, mostly girls, all fun and sweet.

Sammy Williams, Panama - Picnic with the orphans - 1974

A Cuna Indian woman and child, San Blas Islands, Panama 1974.

Cathy Ledbetter, appreciating her mola purchases after San Blas visit, Panama 1974.

Iris del Valle Bergold - Met in Panama 1973 and remained friends into infinity.

Ed and Greek ship captain - San Blas Islands, Panama. Ed greeted them in Greek and the captain insisted we come to visit the ship. A Cuna Indian in a dugout canoe delivered us for a fun afternoon - 1974

Magdalena Kalodimos, fellow secretary in Political Section, a lovely person, a dancer - 1975

Ed and Bev in Panama at Marine Corps Ball, 1973.

At Ambassador's Christmas party, 1974.

Freighter "Santa Barbara" we took leaving Panama 1975, trickling through the Bermuda triangle during an eclipse of the moon!

Washington D.C.

Wash. D.C. '75

Ed and I had two adjoining cabins on the SS Santa Barbara with huge windows. One cabin got little use. There were twelve passengers on the ship. All the rest on the manifest were returning from a six week cruise around Cape Horn and were looking for new bait and diversions. Some Embassy people had seen us off, but the big disappointment was the purser. I made the mistake of asking if the orphans could come aboard and he said they were loading the ship and it would be too dangerous. I should not have asked. I endured two days of seasickness and Ed tended to me. We had decent meals, but I could never get accustomed to the 5 p.m. call to dinner. We had the same dining hours as the crew. I was reading a book on the Bermuda Triangle as we passed through that area of mystery. I called out portions of the narrative, talk of planes and ships disappearing, leaving no trace. And not only did we have a full moon, but a downright lunar eclipse! Ed whispered I should stop the announcements or superstitious sailors would have me walking the plank.

We had three lovely days in NYC, staying at the Hotel Moritz on the Park. We were met at the dock by college friend Jane, now sporting three small boys. First night there we went to see Voltaire's "Candide" highly enjoyable. Next day "Absurd Person Singular" a waste of the talent of Geraldine Page and Sandy Denis. Next: "Goodtime Charley" with Joel Grey, clever dialogue. After the theatre I conned a handsom cab driver to take our picture in the cab.

We thought the ride itself was too expensive, but tipped him. We dined at sumptuous French, Italian and Hungarian restaurants during our stay and drove south down the Jersey Turnpike.

When we landed in D.C. May 30 after our NYC landing from the freighter, I was still scheduled to go onto Geneva for my next assignment. Ed went off to the State Department to determine his next assignment and was fretful. I spent time renewing old acquaintances, we stayed with Tunis and Saigon friend D.J. and her new husband until Ed's temporary apartment arrangement was finalized. On my home leave I pranced off to Chicago and Peoria for nine days. My sister's mental state was in flux and was a concern, but I enjoyed the renewed company of my old buddies. I returned a week later for home leave in Dallas and Santa Fe.

Having missed me on these occasions, D.C. - assigned Ed wrote letters from the heart, pleading me not to actually go to Geneva, but stay with him. Absence makes the heart grow fonder! For both of us. When I returned to Washington, and spoke with Personnel, I broke the assignment to Geneva. The reason I cited was my older sister's health and that she needed my support and attention. No word of hot romance! So eventually I was assigned to the office of ILO /CMD (International Organizations) which deal with USUN, and I reported for duty on June 30. I began nagging Personnel to change my orders to D.C. since my Household Effects had been sitting in Geneva for five weeks.

Soon thereafter we went to the Kennedy Center to enjoy the National Symphony with Rostopovich directing. In that performance his wife sang arias from La Boheme and Madame Butterfly and it was a brilliant and moving experience. Later saw

"Ramonda," Russian Ballet. We bought season tickets to Arena Stage, always providing quality productions. "Enemy of the People" was the first for us in November. The message was: "The Strongest Man in the world is the man who stands alone."

There were five men in my section to tend to. I was the Foreign Service Secretary and we had two younger civil service secretaries. One had her desk next to the door and entertained the fellows who were constantly stopping by. She was young and flippant. The other was more reasonable and would accept assignments, but let's face it: I was the slave of the section. It usually worked well enough, since I was filled with the ethic of production. If a task was there, someone had to do it and it was usually myself. The head of the Section had almost daily dealings with the 7th floor, the Secretary of State's quarters. Male officers at meetings were note takers, and they passed those notes onto secretaries for completion. The finished product had to be perfect. The people upstairs had typewriters that corrected themselves; I had a more humble model and often had to begin again to seek perfection.

Ed and I began a fling with Transcendental Meditation. I was assigned a mantra I could not bear, always gave me a headache. Instead of switching my mantra, they told me to relax and take it easy. I had a lot of headaches, but admit that just 15 minutes of meditation is quite soothing. That project didn't last long for either of us. The Cafeteria was a meeting and greeting place, often running into people we had known at other postings, so it was a lively spot to renew old acquaintances, have a fast lunch.

In July Ed had awakened with a breathing incident, rasping throat, choking, gasping for air. It panicked me and it seemed to be several minutes before he could get his breath, relieving the grey tinge to his face. After speaking with a nurse in George Washington's emergency, she speculated that he had had an anxiety reaction and hyperventilated. Later in the week we learned that he had acute bronchitis plus an allergic reaction to something or other.

His son John came for a visit the day after that scare and stayed three weeks. John had had his own traumatic situation. He had been with a friend in Puerto Rico surfing and working for the summer. They had been painting in a warehouse and the friend had been electrocuted before his very eyes. In the semi-professional emergency vehicle which took them to the hospital, John had to hold his dead friend's body in his arms. I appreciated John more this time. He was affable and a very good cook, making us delicious vegetarian meals. He had worked for a famous Chart House in California and had become disgusted by red meat, so he stuck to fish, eggs and vegetables.

As Hurricane Eloise graced us with three days of downpours, I learned that marriages of my friends were failing. Mary and Ted in Montana were divorcing after 18 years; he had beaten her a few times when she was finally beginning to "assert" herself. She and daughter Julie would return to Peoria. Closer to home Iris at Watergate announced that Harry was seeking a separation after 14 years. He had someone waiting in the wings.

About this time Ed and I decided on an apartment in a building between Watergate and the State Department, which was a bit tricky in 1975. We were supposed to be married, not " living in sin." Since it was a Cooperative Apartment, we had to seek approval from the Board. So we told them we were engaged but had not set a wedding date, all of which turned out to be the truth! So in our interview for acceptance, two lil ole ladies decided to be big and grant us acceptance! I believe they giggled a bit as they said it. The added problem was that we had no furniture, heaven knows where that was! In the latter part of August we had signed the papers and moved in, straggling with a few suitcases; someone had loaned us sleeping bags. After a few days we graduated to a rented rollaway bed, borrowed some dishes and utensils from Iris, and began to make a nest, awaiting my household effects which did not appear until Oct. 16, almost five months after landing back in D.C.

Washington, D.C. crime was always a worry at that time (haven't compared it to now). Ed would go off to meetings in the evening and I fretted when he came home later than usual. A taxi driver was slain just outside of our apartment during the early morning hours. We would walk to Kennedy Center and back in the evening, just three or so blocks away, and returned home gratefully that we encountered no problem on the street. Saw "Sweet Bird of Youth" with Irene Worth and she was tremendous. Later, "Long Days Journey into Night" superbly done.

In September we visited friends in Ocean City, New Jersey whom we had met in Panama, and enjoyed tossing bread to the gulls and sleeping to a lovely ocean breeze. We visited them again several times before the next separation. We also spent a day on Iris' friend's speedboat on Chesapeake Bay, five of us on a boat that seated eight. Some waterskied. After mooring the boat, we had cherrystone clams with hot sauce, a new culinary delight, along with Sangria. A lovely day.

In November I took an Icelandic flight to Luxembourg,

Heidelburg, Frankfurt and Munich, visiting Irene in Frankfurt and Dini in Munich. She and I went to the Opera "Die Fledermaus", checking our humble woolen coats midst mountains of what was that soft white fur? oh yes, ermine! At intermission German lovelies would promenade up and down the corridor, showing off their lovely gowns, gems and furs. After Germany I visited a few days with Barbara in Geneva, enjoying the very attractive place I had given up for Ed, and onto Luxembourg to see Louise from Tunis days. I had a lovely reunion with Ed in D.C. and we stayed put through the end of the year. We had several always great meals with Iris, keeping her company in her newly saddened state at her Watergate apartment. We went to the National Theatre in December to see Katherine Hepburn in an enjoyable "A Matter of Gravity." We spent Christmas day visiting three venues. New Year's Eve was quiet in the rain and also feeling "under the weather."

We began 1976 with a trip to the theatre. Saw Moss Hart's "Once Upon a Lifetime" and enjoyed it thoroughly. I signed up for two classes at George Washington University: "U.S. Diplomatic History" and "American Drama." I was offered assignments overseas every so often in February: how about DCM Secretary to Copenhagen, then an offer as Amb. secretary to a small African post; then South Africa, no, no, no. Finally, with no hesitation, I accepted in March an assignment to Lisbon, Portugal for June 1976. It was perfect timing to finish my courses at GW!

We drove to Arkansas in March to visit Ed's family for me, the first time. His fragile mother was small and sweet and I knew we'd get along fine. For one thing, we were both born in Wisconsin! (even though my stay was only 3 months). Met his lovely sister and brother and nieces and nephews. Seems the Arkys stick together, all lived in the same town, and all were very kind and accepting of me. When I left his mother said, "Thank you for taking care of my son!" I left him with them and went onto St. Louis, Chicago and Peoria to check on family and friends, fretting as usual over my older sister Pat. In May we had a three-sister reunion in Florida on younger sister Judy's houseboat. She and her "significant other" Van had moved from Hawaii. The dog and cat sparked Pat's allergies, but we managed to have a rare songfest and a very healthy, reassuring reunion. Pat was not at a loss for songs to sing. (I can still remember her voice in "Side by Side.")

With Ardith I saw the Royal Danish Ballet and it was simply gorgeous. Ed and I loved "Our Town" at the Arena Stage. Earlier we had seen "Rex" at Kennedy Center, Shaw's "Heartbreak House", witty but dragged on, and "Dandelion Wine", marvelous and nostalgic.

Contented with my lovemate, I tried matching friends with old boyfriends, Barbara with Julius, Celeste with Steve. Have no idea how that turned out!

At the end of May Ed went to Arkansas, I to Chicago and Peoria for my farewells. My sister Pat was super mentally and told me she did not mind my venturing off again overseas. Back in D.C. my major boss, with whom I'd gotten along very well, did not stand in my way for breaking the assignment. Farewell parties, packing, and off I flew alone to Lisbon, Portugal. Ed was to follow.

Office gang 1975 in D.C. Wendell Woodbury, Gloria, Richard Poole, Birney Stokes.

Joan Stokes and Bev, a picnic on the mall at lunchtime. 1975

Bev, Scott, Aunt Beverley in Wash D.C.

Sisters Pat and Judy on her Florida houseboat - 1975

Portugal

Portugal 1976

I landed in Lisbon on June 2. The Embassy was housed in an old pink building, a former villa, on a side street off the Marquez do Pombal. I was assigned to be secretary to the Economic Counselor. The country was reeling from its African nations having declared their sovereignty and thousands of expats from Mozambique and Angola were converging upon their homeland. The country had endured six months of communist rule in 1974 which had been defeated in a bloodless coup. Graffiti on the monuments and buildings still screamed out in shame, but gradually the cleanup became noticeable. During this time of upheaval, we blissfully attacked the countryside in our yellow Volkswagen Bug on weekends, luxuriating in castles for $25 per night. On our Lisbon weekends, we took the commuter train on the Marginal from Alges to Cascais, where the Tagus river insinuated itself into the Atlantic. The Cascais area entertained the tourists and disenfranchised royalty from smaller European nations. But for all of us awaited the lovely and humble seaside eateries with the freshest seafood, sparkling Portuguese wines, caldo verde (cabbage or kale soup) with local cheeses and chewy peasant breads. All at very reasonable prices.

On my assignment there, one drove on winding two lane country roads, appreciating the bare bark cork trees in the south and vineyards in the north, stopping by monasteries and castles. Ed called the Alcobaça monastery the temple of gluttony. Along with its enormous ovens, a stream with varied fish meandered through the spacious kitchen. The monks planted luscious gardens. The Portuguese countryside beckoned with tidy small houses, often with an ajuelos (tile) planted on a front wall, in stark contrast to the lavish more exotic display of ajuelos on Lisbon walls and buildings.

Ed had taken a military flight to our air force base in Madrid and made his way to Vigo, Spain to meet some people. Therefore, less than a week after arriving at my new posting, I was on a milk run train to Vigo, Spain, which was allegedly to be a six hour trip. I was tense that somehow I was on the wrong train, it ended up two hours late, but miraculously Ed was at the other end! How happy I was to see him! After a couple days exploring lovely Vigo, we took a 1st class train back to Lisbon and were there in a matter of hours. Much of our discussion dwelled on how we were going to explain him to the Embassy crowd, what story to tell on where he lived, etc. We were not in a typical Embassy relationship. Back in Lisbon, we had been invited to tea with an older British couple, Reg and Barbara, where I wolfed down her lovely tea and scones. At one point she remarked, "Would you like some more, gutty?" With that insult I roared and knew we'd be friends.

I was able to rent a charming penthouse apartment in a suburb of Lisbon called Alges, nestled next to a small park and with a view of the Tagus River beyond the trees. It was partially furnished and the furniture provided blended easily with what I had. We soon had a crisis, I had barely got my pictures onto the walls.

Ed's friend Paul was to take a freighter which meandered around Europe, with a stop in Lisbon. He sent his son via air for us to pick up and join his father when the boat landed. Well, the son came, a noncommunicative teenager, but his father did not. The freighter went on by! What to do with Paulo? Thank heavens he slept a lot, but we dragged him off to restaurants and finally to the Marine House for movies. He enjoyed their company and often spent evenings playing basketball with them, or swimming or whatever. It was over three weeks before father and son were reunited! And I was thinking in my mind (an old expression) that I was happy I escaped motherhood. An overlap occurred when Ed's daughter Cathy and her friend Annette descended upon us, with the view of living and working in Portugal. They were generally easy to have around. I told them early on that I was a neatness freak. They could mess their room to their heart's delight but the other rooms had to remain tidy, dishes washed to avoid roaches, etc. They concurred.

After we had the dubious pleasure of Paulo's company for several weeks, Ed, Paulo and I made a trip to London to meet his father and have a theatrical experience. Somehow I saw "Equus" on my own. It was a poignant, penetrating, perfect play. All of us saw "Chorus Line" and all appreciated it, Ed even more so. "No Sex Please, We're British" only Paulo loved it. During that trip Paul and Paulo left early for Lisbon. Ed and I met his niece Judy and Roby and family in Oxford where her orthopedic surgeon husband was assigned to a U.S. base. Had a tour to Woodstock, Churchill's home. Eleven yr. old Roby Dan guided me in the art of brass rubbing in cathedrals. We later saw what was touted as play of the year: "Otherwise Engaged." We were not.

Returning home to Lisbon, our full house, now Cathy, Annette, Paul and Paulo, were there to greet us. We had a fun evening meal at a local restaurant. The next day we had to take Paul to the hospital with stabbing back pains and he remained there a couple days. The hospital seemed dirty, the doctors sported pipes and cigarettes. I vowed to stay healthy for my tour. Then we had the good news that Paulo was going back home, and he left! We had father Paul for another week. After taking him to the airport, I thought to myself, 2 down, 2 to go!

When we returned from a Labor Day weekend to Evora and Estremoz I discovered an utter mess in the kitchen, days of dishes, garbage all over. I was on fire, had a knot in my stomach and wrote a furious note about cleaning up. I cared not for the consequences and if Ed took it personally, I would accept that as well. As it turned out, Cathy and Annette had felt guilty upon leaving the mess, but it had been a full day, they had talked with a potential landlord and it was the first day of trial at the language school. They came home submissive, did the dishes and cleaned their room. We chatted and all was well again. So one month and 2 days after arriving they moved into their own apartment. The place was totally ours.

Did I mention work? It always seemed to be busy in the Economic Section. My boss James Ferrer and Ambassador Frank Carlucci worked closely on arranging to provide a loan to alleviate Portugal's economic miseries. Added to their problems was the onslaught of returnees from Africa as Mozambique and Angola declared their independence from Portugal. There was also another economic officer to tend to, a rotating officer and the Commercial Officer for any classified work. Two Portuguese national women worked in the Commercial Section and I was to become very fond of both, Carmen Neves and Graciete Oliveira. So I became happily ensconced in my new work world.

The World Bank was involved in the loan to Portugal so several of them became familiar faces at the Embassy. One of them asked me if I thought the U.S. should lend money to Portugal and I answered, well they certainly need it but I'm a Virgo and practical. I would want to know what they would use the money for. "Spoken like a true banker," he responded.

One weekend in October I had the entire ECON section (Americans and Portuguese) over for brunch, making my tried and true l'oef escoffier dish (egg, mushroom, onion, bechamel). It was a hit. A junior officer brought over the game twister and we had a good time with that one, a real ice breaker. And Ed blew our cover, walked out to the balcony with my boss and commented "great day, he hadn't been out yet," so subtle!

Early on as duty secretary I went to the Ambassador's residence one Saturday and he showed up casually in swim trunks. I was at ease in dictation but found the typewriter there to be an antique and insisted on another to replace it. Several hours later I handed him the finished draft. Later on, as the Ambassador and my boss the Economic Counselor worked on a cable regarding the U.S. loan, it was dictated into the typewriter as they say. When the Ambassador commented on how good I was, my boss bragged he had the best secretary in the Embassy. (I heard that remark!)

In the fall more visitors popped in. D.J. from Tunis and Saigon days came with new husband (another Paul) and their tiny poodle named Titan. After a couple days with us, we drove them to Madrid. When we arrived at the Hotel Capital, a baggage man raced out and screamed "no pero, no pero!" Paul and D.J. quickly moved to the higher class Ritz at four times the cost, but Titan was welcome. We four checked out Hemingway haunts for restaurants, visited the Prado museum and had a good time before they returned to Monrovia.

As in Panama, I also became active with another group of orphans, mostly little girls, shy and always smiling. We bought food for them at the commissary and various markets. At one point Ed and I looked into adoption, but it was very complicated with Catholic restrictions and rulings. They loved visiting our penthouse and stretching out on the large balcony, and we often took them to the beach.

In October I flew to Great Britain to meet Kathy and Dick in South Hampton as they returned from South Africa, enroute to Washington. Ed was entertaining his good friend Hal in Lisbon. From Southhampton we took a ferry to the Isle of Wight. They took me to Winterbourne, which Charles Dickens had bought in 1849 and where he wrote his favorite "David Copperfield." My friends were banned because they had their young daughter with them and no children were allowed overnight. We had a wondrous dinner there and Kathy spent the first night with me, talking to the wee hours. A pot of tea was quietly placed outside the door by 7 a.m. Watching a gorgeous sunrise at the end of the grand expanse of lawn, listening to the ocean's roar, I thought how Ed would love this place. I walked the grounds, feeling very much a part of the 19th century. I spent three wonderful nights there and vowed to return.

One of highlights of the year for me was the visit December 1 of Elliot Richardson, then Undersecretary of Commerce. There was an elegant luncheon for 14 at Tivoli Palacio do Seteais, an elegant villa in Sintra. We had a big round table for 14 and on either side of him were the Ambassador's wife and moi Beverly. I mentioned to him that my friend (make that Ed!) had worked for his firm (Ropes and Gray) while in law school. He remembered him and asked an update on what he was up to. (Ed was spending three long weeks in the states, visiting children in California and family in Arkansas.) I can't recall all that I said but we went onto other subjects, such as his fascination for bullfights. He appreciated the immediacy of it--not what the matador had done before had counted but what he did at that very moment. Mrs. Richardson was quite lively at the table, said they had gone to a Spanish bullfight on their honeymoon. He also mentioned that when they left the UK (where he had served as Ambassador to the Court of St. James) they had breakfast served by their 14 servants, and by the evening in the States Anne had made dinner herself and washed the dishes. I could sense that they were very fond of one another.

Cathy and Annette had their own adventures at their apartment. They had been hired to teach English as a second language, and the facility was across the street from the Embassy. We met often to have dinners with them and going to our favorite place, Sintra. But in December they announced they were through with Portugal and were off to have a go at Italy, where Annette had relatives. Unhappy to see them go, off they went on a train to Italy Dec. 23rd. I packed a lunch.

Ed and I went off to spend Christmas in Spain. Went to Sevilla, Rota (military base), Aljeciras with grand views of Gibraltar, to Tangiers on the hydrofoil. Our tour of Tangier was: our Arab guide naming street names, mint tea, Moroccan musicians, couscous, and a fat belly dancer horsing around, decorating a German, most memorable the downpour of rain, and the silver necklace w/phony turquoise I bought for $20. We then went back on the hydrofoil to Marbella, Torrelimos, Granada to the Parador San Francisco where they miraculously had a room for one night. Back to Rota, Cordoba, where another Parador had one suite left and we took it. To Mesquita with the impressive mosque where Christians had plunked a church right in the middle of a mosque, which seemed sacrilegious somehow. Cordoba was known for its courtyards green and lush in the midst of narrow city streets. Everything would have been nicer with sun, however. On New Year's Eve we returned at 11:30 pm with revelry at midnight downstairs, and ended 1976 with a kiss.

Portugal 1977

When we returned from Spain, we heard that the $300 million loan had been given to Portugal before New Year's Eve. When it had been announced on television, a crowd gathered at the Ambassador's residence and they warmly applauded him. Such appreciative people!

A few days after our return home Annette called from Italy and Cathy was in the hospital with hepatitis, in solitary confinement. She had left the train with a high fever. Ed made plans to visit, but she discouraged him, as visitation was limited to ten minutes per day.

Sometime in 1977 Vice President Mondale made a trip to Spain and Portugal. I recall shaking his hand but not much else, except for the thought that I could've been his secretary. Yes, to the VP of the U.S.! Back in Washington when I interviewed Ben Bradlee of the Post I also went to Congress and there was an opening in Senator Mondale's office. Another road not taken! "But," sez Ed, "you wouldn't have met me!"

During February's cold weather Ed and I had taken a trip to Madeira. It was an absolute delight since we left Lisbon in heavy rain and were greeted on the island by the sun and blooming flowers. We stayed for five days near the famed Reids hotel, a favorite of the Brits. We would go over for tea. Winston Churchill had stayed there often, painting Madeira's captivating scenery. We had been aware that Madeira sported a very dangerous, short runway. In fact there were two fatal crashes there later in the year, within a month or so, at nighttime, in bad weather. Our Consular people had the sad task of flying over to attend to American bodies.

We spent a week in Paris, staying in three different hotels to experience their particular flavor. I was particularly fond of the small bedrooms with proverbial flowered wallpaper (usually quite faded) and mismatched curtains. A bed, an armoire, a bidet. I could not appreciate glossy modern hotels. A favorite was Hotel Navarin de l'Angletaire, where Benjamin Franklin had signed a friendship treaty between France and U.S. We loved our morning cafe au lait and croissants. I was proud to be using my French and having Ed rely on me for a change in the language department. When we went to see Monet's water lilies at Palme d'or, I thought how lovely it would be to skate silently across the area soaking it all in. Walking in Paris, our eyes feasted on seeing the eternal displays of offerings in shop windows. Even the vegetables were seductive! We went to what Frommer dubbed the cheapest restaurant in Paris housed in an old dusty building. We were greeted by a smiling crone with just two remaining front teeth. A four course meal was offered for the franc equivalent of $2. We had a choice of beet or bean, couscous, dried hunk of cheese or orange, but all the wine you could drink! We also found great food in small bistros, soupe d'oignon, formidable! And how nice to be in Paris with the man you loved!

I was to lose 4 months and 13 days of my recorded life in 1977. Ed's daughter Suzy was visiting us from San Francisco. After exploring fascinating Oporto, we ran into gorgeous country along the river Douro. Heading home, we stopped for lunch in Nazare, a fishing village north of Lisbon. We locked the car on the same street of the restaurant. While we ate thieves broke the window and helped themselves to an overnight bag. Suzy lost a $200 camera, and $50. I lost my favorite navy Cardin shirt, my diplomatic passport, my diary! Ed lost his dirty underwear.

Sometime during my lost life I bought a guitar and began taking classical guitar lessons. The man didn't speak English, so often he first got out the clippers to trim my nails before proceeding with the lesson. And just when they began to grow for the first time in memory! The first moment I was to wrangle a decent sound out of it I thought "With a guitar one never had to be lonely!" And Ed was soothed by the sound of it, mistakes and all.

The Algarve on Portugal's mainland became a popular weekend diversion, with lovely beaches and a relaxed atmosphere. At that time it was in sharp contrast to Spain's southern shore of wall to wall skyscrapers. Hotels in Portugal were more spread out, closer to the ground. We would drive through the Alentejo, with miles and miles of cork trees. We'd point out the red patches on their bottoms where the cork had been harvested. Portugal had been a main supplier of cork to stop up millions of wine bottles throughout the world. While Suzy was with us, we went to stay in the Algarve with a British couple, Michael and Rosemary. I noted he was quite smitten with Suzy, didn't know how his wife felt about it. Later, in a talk with Suzy, she told me that their family growing up showed little affection for one another. She confided that her father acted as though I was his first love to date. That thrilled me, of course. She won the title of our best houseguest. About that time in the Embassy it was EER time, which happened once per year. They were the Employee Evaluation Reports, so we were kept busy with reports and review statements. My boss and the DCM were kind to me.

In the office it was a time for departures. Lee would leave, as would Bob about the same time. I had written a poem about Lee and the role he played during the 6 month revolution. He liked it so much he had it framed. Ray and Jack came into the fold, a period of transition. All occurred when my main boss was on home leave for almost two months. It was a fairly quiet summer. Ed and I spent four days in Barcelona, a lovely city of lovely ladies, lovely food. I was later to blame Barcelona for a major mishap in my life.

After glutonizing in Barcelona, Ed and I went on a four day fast. On the third day I felt very strange and weak. We had gone downtown, parked the car and walked for a morning coffee. I could not make the walk back, he went for the car to pick me up. During the four days I had lost 8 lbs., was weak but very happy. I gradually got weaker, with a pit in my stomach, yet managed to crawl through each day. The boss man returned from home leave, the Ambassador had us over for a pool party, I enjoyed my time in his sauna. The day before, Ed and I had a tiff and I threw a glass to the tiled floor, smashing it, feeling some relief. On a Monday at work I had a hamburger patty, carrots, salad, and 3/4 glass of wine. It still makes me sick to think about it. It did not settle well. Later I was not in the mood for either wine or booze. The next day I had no appetite, got a partial ride home with the intention of taking a train, but could not do it. I called Ed and sat on the steps until I was rescued. The next day at work people told me I had yellow eyeballs, so I went to the doctor and he believed I might have the beginning of hepatitis. I had a blood test.

The next day friend Dini landed from Munich. I went to the

HOW FOREIGN WAS MY SERVICE

hair dresser in Alges, and while under the dryer Ed came to put a phone number on my lap. I knew something was dreadfully wrong and was hit with the realization it had to do with me! Called Dr. Andrade and he said I had a very bad case of hepatitis, what was I doing at a beauty shop? I dashed out, rollers still in my hair, and went to bed, a contamination to both my friend and lover. I sent them off to get gamma globulin shots and felt desolate. I slept fitfully, with Ed on the couch and I forbade them use of my bathroom. I awoke with a great loneliness at the tragedy of it all and cried crocodile tears. Ed held me, figured he'd been exposed as much as he could be. Dini looked at our feet wrapped around one another and smiled: "They lasted 24 hours!" Dini kept Ed and therefore me in good spirits. She made plans to leave, after a three night visit. I felt that Ed would lose patience fast if he had to wait on me for very long. Dr. Andrade said the two of them would know in two weeks whether or not they had my disease. I was turned over to the British Hospital on Monday. I guess it was past contamination time, as I was permitted to have visitors. Cathy in Italy had endured much worse.

The British Hospital was situated next to the British cemetery. When dusk arrived, there was a recording of TAPS being played. Henry Fielding was buried there along with an American diplomat who died in a duel in the 1700s. When a minister showed up at the foot of the bed the next morning, I asked if he was trying to tell me something. He laughed, ministers and priests visited hospital patients as a matter of course. This was my first ever experience in a hospital, hooked up to a gluclose drip. And I felt surprisingly good compared with the malaise of the last couple weeks. I was spoiled by visitors and flowers to match my complexion, as well as the attention from my love. After he was declared hepatitis-free I encouraged him to go home to mother. My sentence here was for a minimal two weeks. I didn't want him to fret over me. He took my advice. I passed into another decade, turned 40 during those two weeks. I admit I felt well enough to enjoy the attention. People brought me books, more flowers. The Ambassador called to console me, as he had the same history as I. I had my Adelle Davis bible, "Let's Get Well" and she encouraged me to wolf down Vitamin C's. I had smuggled a bottle into my night stand drawer and followed her advice. As my numbers on the liver Richter scale kept going down, Dr. Andrade happily took credit, but I knew better!

And so, two weeks went by, no one I knew contracted the disease, and I went to Liz and Jack's for a few days of pampering, then home, edging my way gradually back to work. When thinking about how I got it, I thought of the hotel in Barcelona, which had water problems while we were there. I recalled taking morning vitamins with water out of the faucet. I had rather blame Spain than my beloved Portugal. My favorite meal in Lisbon, however, was amejois espanol (clams in tomato/onion sauce), a more likely candidate.

Ed returned after three weeks and we had a lovely reunion. I had been in the hospital two weeks and spent another two weeks in recovery before permission to return to work. That period was complicated by more visitors, Jimmy Young from Scotland, Laura from my Chicago law firm and the vamp Joyce from Panama days. Annoyed by Joyce coming on to Ed, I sent her and Laura to the Algarve so we could have a respite. We joined them there a few days later to take them back to Lisbon. Once Joyce headed back to the states, Laura, Jimmy, Ed and I took the car on the train to Oporto to see our British friends Norm and Patricia in their gorgeous, newly renovated 300 year farmhouse, a definite candidate for Architectural Digest. We also had a stayover at the wonderful Bucaco, a former hunting lodge for Portuguese royalty. All of us were mightily impressed. Also, for good Catholic Jimmy, we made a visit to Fatima. Ed and I had not been impressed by the enormous paved area to accommodate the crowds of the faithful.

Ed's son John came around Halloween. "Gabriela" was the telenovella that Portugal stopped what it was doing to watch in the evening. It was created in Brazil and all were mesmerized. John was enchanted by the lovely Brazilian girl and her loves. Years later he named his only daughter Gabriela. He was also enchanted by the surf. A California boy, he brought his surfboard, and he and Ed would often be out on surf checks. He stayed a few weeks and we missed him when he left. I liked him much better this round.

My assignment toward recovery according to Dr. Andrade was to avoid fatty foods, and worst of all, not drink for six months! When a visiting American doctor saw me, he suggested avoiding it totally. So I decided to abide with the former. I continued to make good progress. At three and one-half months Dr. permitted one glass of wine every two weeks, but two beers per week! How I savored them!

Then occurred the accident in November on the dreaded, fast moving Marginal, the main highway from Lisbon to Cascais. I had received a lift halfway and Ed met me in his VW yellow bug. When he turned left he was at fault, attempting to enter the traffic heading west, which was our normal routine. A mini bore down on us, hitting our left fender, which turned the mini around, backing into oncoming traffic, smashing into a Peugot. If he hadn't been turned around he would have been killed, because his mini crumbled like an accordion. He had minor injury. What a mess! We stalled the traffic for hours on that busy road, and later limped our car on home. All parties to the disaster were later called in and were asked if we wanted to sue the perpetrator (Ed). Insurance covered damages for those involved, and all of us, the involved, did not wish to sue. Did I not say I loved Portugal?

This year Ed did not have a choice, we went to the annual Marine Corps Ball, which I had missed last year. With no drink I was not lively, or even close to being the belle of the ball. He was more lively than I. But a day or so later an Embassy driver said I was "la flor do embassade." So that perked me up.

So boss man Jim Ferrer began to gather a choral group together for the Christmas holidays and I joined eagerly. We'd go to his residence for rehearsals and as a consequence I got to know Marcia, the Ambassador's new wife much better. We had a lot of laughter, fun together, along with Liz, Jack's wife, and the boss's daughter Annette. Our carol presentations in a small sweet church were welcomed by the community, wanting more. I had become annoyed with him earlier, because at one point we were to have a small group (six?) sing a carol, but he changed his mind along the way and dropped us. I was also tired of xeroxing sheet music by the pound.

I had no time to pout because I was designated to fly to Warsaw, Poland to be part of the support staff for President Carter's trip to Poland just after Christmas. Thrilled, we first went to spend Christmas with Dini in Munich on the way. After all, we I should say I, had ruined her trip to Portugal in September! Irene, also from Panama days, came down from Frankfurt to join us and we had a lovely Christmas dinner, decorating the tree German style with live candles! Two days later we three took a train to Vienna, stopping at the Polish Embassy for visas. Requirements were a real pain since you had to get a money order for the visa fee plus an exchange control for required money in Poland. I had to dash to the tourist agency for that and back to the Embassy before the noon closure! For some reason I flew via LOT an ancient Russian jet from Vienna to Warsaw, with Dini and Ed taking the train. I went the next day to the Embassy and made reservations for them at the Grand Hotel. I stayed at the Polish guesthouse called the Parkowa Hotel. We had dinner in the Grand Hotel's restaurant. Waiters sat down when not serving, we almost had to make an appointment. The waiter kept trying to find the correct English words for us and Dini fell in love. I had greasy onion soup I could not finish and a greasy pork cutlet. Ice cream was a healer, they asked if we were going to tip. I took a taxi to Parkowa Hotel; the room was austere but warm.

I was not to go on duty until 10 p.m. to the control room after President Carter landed the next day. So I made my way to the Grand Hotel and Ed and I made love right there in his trundle bed, room 659. We joined Dini at breakfast. We went to Old Town to view lovely churches and buildings, to the ghetto and Jewish crematorium and prison, too overwhelming thinking of what they had endured, make that not endured! Went to Embassy for lunch, bought some gifts. Dini charmed people with her easy manner and ran into people she had known elsewhere. I bought an amber necklace for $10 and to this day wonder if it's truly amber. Don't want to light a match to find out. Got hair set and I always feel renewed when that occurs. I had dinner at my lodging, sat with Carter's translator, had a lovely veal cutlet, lovely service. They had a small glass of vodka at table, refilling when empty. Obedient Bev had one beer.

I went on duty, the Carter entourage landed and the group showed in the control room at 11:30 p.m. It was very calm and organized before the S/S (Secy. of State) people on Air Force One landed and a woman named Nancy came in. Ron said she was the type who created a crisis so she could solve it. How true! Things were so quiet that night they let me leave at 5 a.m. instead of 8 a.m. I bummed a ride to the Grand. Ed, Dini and I wandered through a department store and saw a line of 30 women waiting to buy a simple cotton nightgown. We had a desperate urge to buy something, but everything began to look alike, so we were frustrated. We tried to settle on a restaurant. The 1st looked dismal, 2nd we couldn't communicate, 3rd too crowded and 4th was a snack bar with marvelous goulash and beer. My shift was 6 p.m. to 2 a.m. I went to eat good turkey beforehand. On duty I typed a four page memo from Secretary Vance to President Carter on the mid-east. But not much else.

On New Year's Eve at 2 a.m. it had been a very slow night and I could hardly keep my eyes open. I went to bed at 2, read a minute and conked out. When I awoke at 8:45 Ed called me. Lovely snow was falling and had accumulated. The herd had departed on schedule. Dini and I later had beef stroganoff in the dining room of the Grand Hotel, now filled with butterflies for New Year's Eve. The Embassy car picked us up and took us to the Parkowa to pick up my bags. The man at the desk kissed my hand, which overwhelmed me. It was the first sign of cordiality from the Polish Guest House. Then the Embassy driver did the same! We had no way to dispose of our zlotys at the airport. If I had known, I would have given them to the driver! It was freezing on the LOT plane to Vienna. When Ed asked the stewardess for a blanket, she pointed and said: "That man over there has it!" We took an airport bus to the Hilton air terminal. It was very cold and began snowing. We sat near our luggage and listened to Strauss music sneaking in from the ballroom next door. Ed and I had one dance and he said "You can't say I didn't take you dancing on New Year's Eve!"

Thoughts on Portugal:

What strikes and warms me most of all is the sense of community among the Portuguese. "A queue" (or line) is not something to be endured, but a chance to chat with your neighbors or even strangers about the price of milk or the political situation; perhaps to pass on the current joke about a particular politician. Voting day October 5 demanded long waits, but the chestnut stand was outside and the crowd chatted amicably. Men in their villages play horseshoes, sip in the local adega; holidays are a community affair with parades, folk dancing in their native costume. There is not the "bubble" spacing of the USA on a bus or train. They sit near one another, and when a family member dies, he does not wander to his grave in his own separate hearse. The family is on either side of the casket, still a cohesive group, before that final separation.

Portugal Ending 1978

The boss man and I began the new year in a cool period, sort of sizing each other up. He said I was more subdued, at peace with myself since I returned from Poland and Germany. In the meantime, one of my favorite Portuguese left for the Azores, due to her husband's assignment there. I worked on a 2000 piece jigsaw puzzle, becoming madly compulsive to finish it, only to find one piece missing!

Our highly regarded Ambassador Frank Carlucci was lined up to become the Deputy Director of the CIA. At last, I muttered to him at a party, there will be some semblance of honesty there! I remained active with the orphans. Whenever I hit the big PX in Madrid, I had lists of their various school supply needs, and whenever I kissed them goodbye after visits, I had to endure gladly 31 hugs and kisses at one sitting. I continued to practice my classical guitar with an occasional lesson from Tony of the Consular Section, with the goal of eventually learning to play Anonymous, my favorite piece for guitar.

In March my sister's companion Van died of a heart attack and I urged her to come to Portugal for a visit. I felt guilty that I was the only one of the three sisters with a loving relationship. She came for several weeks and during that time got introduced to the orphans, which delighted her. We also we made a trip to London, Edinburgh, Glasgow, Dublin. Signs on roadsides puzzled us: "loose clippings" "acute bend" "road up" "lay-by." Ed asked for heat at a hotel and the owner blew his top on how he was "cheesed off with the yanks." Ed's friend Paul Dwyer accompanied us and was proud of his heritage after we viewed "You never can Tell" by George Bernard Shaw. It was a grand production, everyone top of the line. It was an interchange between boy and girl pretending to deal with love intellectually. We were all charmed and it made Dublin memorable.

We discovered Cullentra, a 200 yr. old farmhouse with fireplaces roaring, cows in the front yard, stone fences, greenest grass, lovely dinner of cod, baked chicken with banana, soup, salad. Hot water bottles for our bed, beamed ceilings. Onto Kilkenney, with a tooth causing me pain. I was forced to head for a Dublin dentist with dirty fingernails. He diagnosed an abscess below a root and gave me penicillin, suggesting I soon see my dentist in Lisbon. I was relieved he'd not do more. Meanwhile Paul coughed up blood and was frightened, so he headed back to the states via London. My sister left at the Shannon airport to return home. I realized I felt so much closer to her this time, even more than when she came to Tunis. Our plane to Lisbon could not land because of fog and we were made to wait an hour in the Algarve before the half hour flight back home. They were happy to have me back in the office after two weeks away. The dentist concentrated on the next step to repair the damage.

At a May reception on USS Nimitz, I met a Dave who had been POW in Hanoi for two years. He said in order to keep themselves sane, they would retell movies they had seen in the States, tapping out word for word on their cell bars. He later gave me a long tour of the ship. When we visited a Canadian ship a week later called the

"Iroquois", it was so much homier than the streamlined American ones: it had curtains, exercise bikes, and a "wet bar" on board. The latter part of May we were off to Spain again. We always treasured our copy of Michener's "Iberia", reading the history of the area where we stayed. In Badajos Franco during the civil war had lined up thousands of citizens in the bullring and had them gunned down. But now in saner times, red poppies were profuse in the fields, strolling troubadours with guitars and velvet suits roamed the plaza.

In Madrid we'd continue to pick up Lladro statues for friend Laura in Chicago, shipping them to her from the PX. In Segovia we got caught in the rain and dashed into a cafe where they played "American in Paris" with Doris Day, dubbed in Spanish; people were glued to the TV set. The Alcazar castle was lovely with a grand view. Dinner was enjoyed at a homey place with flowers and grapes painted on the walls, old furniture. We felt we were the only foreigners in town and loved it. At our hotel a raucous herd of 12 yr. old boys dashed and screamed in the hallways. Ed went out in his red striped nightshirt, a mistake, which caused giggles from the miscreants. I later went out to say "Bastante! Okay?" and finally got silence. The owner permitted us to eat breakfast before the herd and I muttered "nyeh, nyeh" as we walked out. We took a picture of the ancient aqueduct which stretched across the field. Such a magical, poetic place, Segovia, it rolls off your tongue like a limerick! Onto Salamanca, the old university city, once the learning center of Europe, spending the night in Parador Ciudad Rodriguez, and home to Lisbon.

Back at the Embassy boss Jim prepared for his spring concert. I boycotted it, miffed at how he had handled the last one. I believed he was a much better boss than a choir director. He had passed the endless xeroxing of music sheets onto another. So I attended the performance. He had a mix of nationalities in this one. The Japanese soloist had a good voice but continually mispronounced all the words in "Summertime." And yours truly was called to the stage, winning the door prize, a Hoover pressure cooker; the director presented it to the upstart.

In June Lisbon had its second earth tremor in two months and everyone thought we were due for the big one. Lisbon had been virtually destroyed by one in 1755 with at least 75,000 killed. But now we were thankfully passed over. We continued to have events for the orphans, hot dog lunches, walks, swings in the park, or to the beach. There were never any traumas, they were eternally in good humor, so we enjoyed them even more.

In July we flew to Casablanca, a short flight over the Mediterranean sea. We took a bus to the capital, Rabat, where we stayed at a splendid hotel called the Splendid, and visited the medina. Moroccan people wore more colorful robes than the black and white of Tunisia. A train to Fez. The Palais dur Batha gardens at the Palais Jamai hotel had lovely Arabic fountains and trysting places. We took a normal non tourist bus to Marrakesh, had been told it was a 7 hr. trip but it turned into 12. At first we felt virtuous going so native. We noted women with henna designs painted on their fingers, demure solemn children with enormous dark eyes, listened to tinkling in a can as robes hid their toilette. We clung to our bottles of water, afraid to drink lest we had to use the two- holer in dirty pit stops. At a particular pit stop, we noted scores of children dashing to the tourist bus as they completely ignored our native one.

We gave ourselves points for that. As the day progressed, hot and sweaty natives that we were, we began to look longingly at the tourist buses with Air Conditioning painted on the sides. Then eventually we were unloaded and weary in the medina of all medinas the place Djemaael Fna. Snake charmers, cobras lured by musicians rising out of their straw baskets. Story tellers. Goods for sale. A young boy told Ed: "I can get you anything!" I was so involved in taking pictures, I almost backed into one cobra as I clicked the camera at another.

Weary from our journey, we saw a sign Hotel de Paris and headed there to check in. It was a dismal place, no air conditioning, but no other hotels were in the plaza. Later, after a fitful rest, we ventured out, found a taxi, and hunted for a cool place. We ended up at a former Holiday Inn and sat in the lobby with a drink, listening to classical music in air conditioned splendor. It was the highlight of our trip! French women in long gowns went out to celebrate Bastille Day. At dinner there was a conglomerate of Italian, German, French and Americans at the tables, plus one token cat. Camels were parked outside the hotel for rides. The taxi driver was afraid to go into the medina at night and told us to have our money ready and hop out. He would not take potential passengers who converged in a mob onto us as we leaped out. It was miserably hot sleeping at the Hotel de France, reminiscent of childhood summers in Peoria. We managed to get out of our cell in the early morn to take a train. Ed wondered if we were on the right train. I responded "anything out of Marikesh is the right train!" We spoiled ourselves in Casablanca, settled on George V Hotel. It had hot water so we considered it the Ritz! Bought an 18k gold hand of fatima.

Ate at Maxims on Mohammed V and the food was simply divine, bread with anise seeds, stroganoff, veal, mushrooms with garlic. The next day we flew home to Lisbon.

In the Saturday morning market in Alges, we loved to mingle with the people, stand in line at the bakery for pao integral, faz favor! the only gringos in sight. We had a favorite flower lady, always smiling and generous with her blossoms, as well as fruit and vegetable ladies, no nonsense but always polite.

July 28 was the collapse of the Portuguese government. President Eanes asked Soares to step down as Prime Minister. My boss played tennis the next day with General Haig.

In September Dave, the Commercial officer, brought in a 3 wk. kitten, weak and listless. I held him as he purred, tried to cry but had no squeal left in him. Saved his last breath for Dave when he returned in the afternoon. Sadly we took him to Dave's place and buried him in the garden. Dave had become attached to him during his three weeks on earth, and I for just a day.

Barb and I went to visit the Italian ship Amerigo Vespucci, a 3 mast sailing ship, lovely wood throughout. We were served good chianti, sausage and sweets by attentive Italian boys. A Frenchman asked me to dance and invited me for dinner with the officers tomorrow nite. I did not go, had my own man at home.

I continued to take correspondence courses for the Univ. of Iowa, working toward my B.A. degree.

In October we took a train to San Sabastian, Spain where the church bells rang wildly to announce the new pope was chosen. We were in the second class section with a Spaniard, Israeli and German. Ed found himself speaking three languages and I was proud of him. In Bordeaux a waitress at Restaurant Caveau lamented over "papa communista!" since he was from Poland, and warned us that the Algerian and Moroccans stole purses along the waterfront.

Onto Paris where we saw gorgeous chateux along the way. We thought 100 francs for a hotel on the left bank was an obscene price at $25 per nite. We had dinner on the Ile St Louis, Le Menestral, a congenial spot, very good steak au poivre. Yet Paris (my 6th time there) seemed to be different. Oct 20 I recall a very poignant scene in our hotel room, sobbing because I was getting old (then 41) and withered. Paris hadn't changed, I had. Men didn't look so much anymore, no admiring second glances. I had the sad realization that I was aging and couldn't do a thing about it! It was thrust upon me in that 100 franc rumpled wallpaper room in the latin quarter and I will never think of Paris again without remembering that scene I had that very morn. What an ingrate! I had a marvelous man there in that room, who was there, in person! to comfort me.

We visited Musee Cluny, a great collection of medieval art, tapestries, Lady and the Unicorn. Stopped at Jeu de Palme, Van Gogh still my favorite, Room in Arles, etc. Flew to Nice settled for Hotel Flots d 'Azur on the water for 89 francs with a lovely view of the Mediterranean Sea, cozy and luxurious. Later, a walk along the bord de la mer for our most expensive meal at 35 francs each, dining among French, American, German couples. The next day we tried Antibbes to visit the Picasso museum, closed. Onto Cannes for a fast picture. We thought St. Tropez should have been more exotic, perhaps only for the wealthy ones tucked into the hillside. We took the autoroute to Aix-en-Provence, Cezanne territory. Tried an almond tarte at a patisserie which was heaven sent! To Marseilles, Hotel Richelieu, nice room on the Med, later to bed, the Med lapping at our feet.

Then a flight to Madrid to stay at Hotel Lope de Vega for the third time. I called my favorite hairdresser from D.C., Petra, now home in Madrid. She looked better than ever, now 31. Petra brought her curlers and paraphernalia to our hotel room to cut my hair ala mode, made me feel much more the sophisticate, and younger! She also trimmed Ed's hair. We three went tapa hopping to the Plaza Mayor: shrimp and squid and fish and clams and olives and who knows? She was the liveliest of the group as it neared 11 p.m. She had given us a souvenir of Don Quixote and Pancho Villa. I gave her a Parisian scarf I had intended for myself. We put her into a taxi, missing her already! A day later, we went back home to Lisbon.

Barb and I had been fascinated by the circus tent in Alges late October, so we went after dinner. The greatest part of all was watching the three elephants outside before the show, swaying to the music like the Andrew sisters. When they did the show inside the younger one refused to jump on the back of her sister; she knew the rules but ignored the trainer. He screamed and tried 3 or 4 times. We thought it terrific and voted for the elephant.

The Halloween party was at the same perfect mansion in Sintra as last year, but this time we dressed! The dramatic house welcomed us with lit torches to either side of the massive door. We had rented costumes where the Lisboa Opera obtained vintage wear. Ed was Julius Caesar and played him to the hilt. I was the Marquesa do Pombal, in a splendid velvet, wine colored dress. John D. from the

Embassy was a London Beefeater and fun dancer. I made up for the drinks I couldn't have last year, post hepatitis. We lasted until 2 a.m., a lovely frolicky night.

In November Iris and daughter Celeste from Panama days came to visit. We went to Sintra to tour the fascinating Pena Palace. While they were there we had our farewell streetcar ride. One could rent it for a few hours, bring your own snacks and drinks. It was decorated in old Victorian style with red velvet seats, lampshades, fringed blinds, etc. with a friendly streetcar driver in front. I dashed around playing stewardess, pouring spumante, serving chip and dip to 18 chosen passengers, all in great holiday moods. At that time it was a unique thing. I'm certain that it later became a tradition for others. We were all dropped off at our apartment and had a potluck lunch at our penthouse which consisted of veal, gnocchi, salad and dessert. It was a happy family sort of day and diehards pitched in to clear up and do the dishes.

Our British friends Barbara and Reg had a lovely farewell feijoada buffet for a group, with great food and charades. Nov. 23 was Ed's farewell, off to see London friends and then home to the States. We would have a 10 day separation. I "packed out" as the term goes. The movers spent an entire day packing up dishes, books, and loading furniture I had purchased in Portugal. I then moved to the Ritz Hotel. Nov. 25 was my farewell to the orphans. I puzzled them when I began to cry and could not stop. I gave money for Christmas gifts; they sang Auld Lang Syne in Portuguese as I left them. I departed my beloved Portugal via TWA on December 1, 1978.

Among Portugal's treasures, 1977

Fishing village of Nazare, north of Lisbon, Portugal, 1977

Receiving a Meritorious Award from Ambassador Frank Carlucci in
Lisbon, 1977

Bob (Commercial Attache) and Fran Pastorino, James (Economic Counselor) and Dolores Ferrer my first week in Portugal at St. George's Castle, an economic event. 1976

The famed Amalia Rodriguez, fado wonder of Portugal - 1976 at St. George's Castle.

Buildings resplendant with azuelos (tiles), always a pleasure to behold! Portugal 1976

My precious little orphans in Portugal. Always cheerful, always grateful, a real delight! 1976

With the orphans on a shopping tour - Lisbon 1977

Orphan cuties grabbing some rays on our balcony in Sunny Alges,
Lisbon suburb, 1977

Brad Morrison and buddy Barbara Lutz - Lisbon 1976

At the Isle of Wight with lasting friend Kathy Cardin Searing just back from Beirut assignment. I got to stay in the former home of Charles Dickens where he wrote Great Expectations. 1977

Our Christmas choir, mix of Embassy and business people in Lisbon community, 1977.

Road closed in Madeira 1977

Economic officers Jack Pavoni and Ray Marin, Commercial Attache
David Wilson, Lisbon 1978

My buddy Carmen and husband Marinho Neves, Rochal Cabo da
Roca, Portugal. Westernmost point of Europe. 1985

Friends Jack and Liz Pavoni, Lisbon 1978

British friends Patricia and Norman Wilson at pool of their
wondrous 300 year old house near Oporto, Portugal - 1977

Boss James Ferrer, Economic Counselor. He and Ambassador
Carlucci became heroes in 1977, working to provide Portugal with a
$300 million loan.

Dear Portuguese friends from Embassy. Helen, Carmen , Judite and
Graciete - 1980 - Visit from T&T.

Ed as Julius Caesar for Halloween party held in a Sintra mansion, Portugal 1978

Julius Caesar and the Marquesa do Pombal, Lisbon 1978

Dear British friends Barbara and Reginald Windsor on our farewell streetcar ride - Lisbon, Portugal 1978

Farewell streetcar ride - Lisbon 1978

Iowa

On Way to Ioway

When I landed in NYC, I called college friend Jane to rescue me at JFK, 45 min. from her home in Brooklyn Heights. As I reflect, it was not a nice thing to ask, but she did it. After an overnight with her, husband and 3 young sons, I visited Iris and Don at a Manhattan hotel. Then I flew to Dulles, Wash. D.C. to stay with Kathy and Dick for a few days. I visited other friends, had the medical exam at State, lunch with an old boss. Ed flew in, we bought an old 1973 Honda which we soon labelled the Junk Car, since it was continually breaking down. And this was the car to transport us to the Midwest, to the University of Iowa! I won't bore you with the times it wouldn't start and had to be pushed. I was returning to my original alma mater to finally finish off the credits for a B.A. In the middle of winter! First we make it to Wilmington, Delaware to see Emily and Paul and have a luscious brunch at a posh hotel. About that time we learned there wasn't even a spare tire in the trunk. Yet we plodded on in December's bitter temperatures, often 15 degrees below at dawn. In Illinois the car slid into a snow drift and it took 5 men to lift it out and place it back onto the pavement. Visits to friends and family in Chicago, Peoria, Winfield, Iowa, and finally landed in Iowa City to house hunt. The snow along the highway was 8 ft. high after being plowed, what had we done? Time out for Christmas. Ed went home to Mother in Conway, Arkansas. Sister Pat and I headed to spend the holiday with sister Judy in Littleton, Colorado. It was a lovely, comforting visit.

By now 1979 had arrived and we were in Iowa City territory. We rented a duplex in the country with a required fireplace. Two young girls lived in the basement below. They would be handy in the summer when tornadoes threatened. We admit to not being married but Ed called us a subdued couple! Being subdued is worse for my reputation than not being married! The snow settled itself into the deep driveway to the garage and we were snowbound a few days before the beginning of the semester. Iowa almost closed down in blizzard conditions, mailbox was blocked off when the snowplow came by. We made a welcome fire. Ed shoveled snow to keep ahead of the storm. A man on a snowplow said it wouldn't do much good to dig out because rural roads had been closed with 6 ft. drifts. Snowbound, 40 degrees below with the chill factor! Ed had adapted to America and to Iowa and to blizzards better than I had. My sister said the storm was the worst in Peoria's history. Somehow I make it to the scheduled first class. I've stuffed a lot of literature classes into my semester, faintly aware of writing papers and reading volumes. I was the oldest student in class, often older than the professor, but I was not deterred! We learned from Reg and Barbara in Portugal that their kidnapped banker son was still being held in El Salvador.

All I did was read, read, read and write, write, write. Our household effects arrived and I was torn between opening boxes and doing my school work. I plodded along from assignment to assignment. At spring break I dashed to Dallas to visit Joe and Helen and Bob Davis. In April I learned from Pat that her daughter Renee visited with her for 3 hours and brought her up to date on her children she had not seen for years! Ed and I went to see Superman. He wore his superman nightshirt and charged down the aisle with arms out in a V, like Superman, and got some laughs. On TV I watched the Boston Symphony perform in China. The Chinese concert master had not been allowed to play his violin for ten years until that time. It was one of television's finest and most touching moments.

I'd been reading so much you could have used my eyeballs as a road map to San Francisco, they were that bloodshot! The prof returned my Renoir paper saying "Beverly, that was the best one in the class!" A big fat A!

Paul Dwyer came to visit Ed and show off a new car to drive him to Arkansas. It was May and I set about my yearly lilac thievery. Ever since I left our gorgeous bush back on Phelps Street in Peoria, I had given myself license to steal them wherever and whenever. I loaded up the house with stolen blossoms. I needed solace for the end of semester finals. Then Ed and I drove off this time in a new Buick Skylark to Peoria, then Cincinnati to see Jim, Emily and Paul near Atlantic City, NYC to see the Blackens on the East River with a fantastic view of the Manhattan skyline. Onto D.C. to use Lee's bed and cat sit, with the cat watching our lovemaking, rather nonchalantly! Back to Kathy and Dick and Meg; saw Iris and Don. Upon return to Iowa for summer school, we stopped in Pennsylvania for an overnight visit and great dinner out with Ed's law school friend Jay and family. Then Chicago, Peoria, the usual suspects. And onto Iowa City. Ed told me that he'd received permission to audit my Shakespeare Class. I was not pleased! It turned out the instructor and Ed had a good time with their particular theories while I had to do the work and write papers! I went to C.J. for a high school reunion since I could not make the 25th the next year.

I saw a few people from my class; Margy and Rich came with us.

In January we were inundated with snow. In June were dodging tornadoes. Sixty-three tornadoes were sighted in Minnesota and Iowa during the week. Mid-June we went to the basement aprt. when a tornado was sighted in the next county. Lots of high wind and rain until the worst of the storm blew over. Hurricane David killed hundreds in the Dominican Republic; Frederick wrecks havoc in Mobile, Alabama; Mt. Etna erupts; Skylab, 3 Mile Island. We named the Junk car Skylab, but Skylab ended up in the Indian Ocean, and we still had the car. Sister Pat and friend Deni visited, then Deni and Ed took Skylab on the road to Arkansas with the hope of dispensing with it there.

Somehow in July there was talk of marriage, ours! I asked Ed "Do you think God loves us if we live in sin?" His response: "Will you marry me?" I responded that he didn't have to do anything he didn't want to do and he said: "I want to save your soul" then "I'm serious. I've been thinking about it for a long time but was afraid you'd reject me." And I said: "Darling, I love you!" Somehow we were agreeing and it seemed a splendid idea. So we made plans. We had already planned to go to Portugal during the summer. Why not have the ceremony in my favorite place? That proved complicated in a Catholic country, posting bans etc. But we could have the civil ceremony here in the States and the religious one in Portugal, doing his friend the favor. There was a Baptist minister in Alges with whom he'd have theological discussions. We'd give him a break and make us honorable. We got mixed responses as we told people. Mary in Dallas, now in her 80's, responded: "You know I never said anything but you have to die some day and God loves you, but not that much!" Ed's mother was happy and had been praying for it. Ray in Dallas said "That's fantastic Fifi (nickname)" My first year roommate at Iowa Margy called to say that Iowa was saying: "conform, conform! " Others said "what took you so long?"

Reg and Barbara would be in England, so offered us their apartment in their Lisbon suburb. So July 28 was the big day. We drove in our new Skylark to Chicago and prepared for the civil ceremony, license etc. finding a dress. Friend Laura, her mother and sister got me ready on the big day. When we got to the Chicago city hall, my aunt and Scott were already there, saving a place in line. Then Msgr. McDermott, whom Ed had met in Portugal, showed up with a cake and pulled us out of the line. He had run into a Judge friend who had asked his reason for being there. When he told him his friends were getting married, the Judge insisted we all come up to his chambers and he'd marry us himself! What an eclectic group we were: A Monsignor in the Catholic Church, my Jewish aunt and son, the Ukrainian mama and two daughters, and Ed and myself, he of British and Swedish ancestors and me with French and Finnish! It was a wonderful ceremony, I suddenly became serious with a new feeling of responsibility. My aunt treated us to a lovely brunch at the Drake Hotel, and in the later afternoon we flew off to Portugal.

We had a week to wait before the religious ceremony and I had the feeling of being half in and out, a blushing bride at one point and a half-filled person on the other. We renewed old but new acquaintances, had left just 7 months before. There was a special luncheon with my Portuguese buddies, a visit to our flower lady in Alges for the bouquet of white roses. Barbara Cake (I'll explain later) was in charge of a reception and keeping me in line. It was comforting to be back in such a peaceful, happy place. August 4 was the date for the second ceremony. A small group of British and American friends were in attendance, held at a Scottish Presbyterian Church, officiated by a Southern Baptist. Many Portuguese friends spend the month of August in the Algarve and were not available. (Just as the Parisians head for the south of France.) Ed and I had been raised Methodist. All went well according to the liturgy, but I had forgotten the Southern Baptist penchant for drawn out prayers. Rev. Shepherd said: "Dear Lord, we know you are with us today, for we have been praying about this for a long, long time!" I could have kicked him. We had a small ceremony with cake and champagne at Brad's apartment.

Later at home, we sent out wedding announcements, requesting no gifts, but they could donate to our Portuguese orphans. Barbara my buddy handled those donations. Okay I called her Barbara Cake because she had won the Pillsbury Bakeoff as a teenager in Pennsylvania and could whip up a sumptuous cake in a flash. Our other Barbara the Brit was Barbara Pie, since she always delivered an apple pie to our dinners.

When we returned to Chicago, we collected our car with the mission of seeing Ed's Uncle Art and Aunt Mable in Marinette, Wisconsin. We stopped for lunch at Whitefish Bay Inn in Milwaukee, introduced to me by Jim years before. In Marinette we stayed at a motel nearby and had dinner with Art, now 87 and younger wife Mable, 69. He stood ramrod straight and could still fit into his WWI uniform. He was proud of his atomic physicist son then working on SALT II, travelling with Mondale to explain the treaty. Heading south, we made a slight detour to Madison,

Wisconsin to see Claude LeRoy whom Ed had met in Brazil many years before. He was the head of the Portuguese department at Univ. of Wisconsin and had a room which housed six exotic birds from Africa, parrots from Brazil, and cockatoos from the South Pacific.

Back home we went to Iowa City and I learned I had received an A in Shakespeare and a B in Literature and Film during summer school.

A late August wedding dinner was held in Peoria at Hampton Court with Pat, Joyce & Larry, Phyllis and Rich, and Ed and me. Then onto St. Louis to see brother Robert and Sandy, onto Conway, Arkansas for Ed's family, Dallas with Judy and Roby, Helen and Joe, Joyce and Ray. Dashed back through K.C., Des Moines and home.

And now to face the second and final semester! This time Ed signed up for Shakespeare with Miriam Gilbert, a New Yorker, the creme de la creme Shakespearean expert. I signed up for Film and Sexes, French, Southern Women Writers, Ecology and Evolution, Spanish Civil War. Also a pottery course for stress relief. I kept making clunky pots that weighed a ton. The instructor kept refining her clay into thin elegant pieces. I found such pleasure just having my hands in the clay, trimmed off a few pounds eventually, but they always emerged quite rustic. Toward the end of the semester she announced to the class, "I'm starting to worry about myself. I'm beginning to like Beverly's pottery!" We all had a laugh.

Speaking of stress relief, a friend of Ed's took us several times to Davenport, Iowa's Coliseum, known as the COL, to dance. Couples in their 70s and 80s whirled around the huge dance floor as in a roller rink, making laps. I had never seen that before! But they certainly enjoyed themselves and we joined them. Dave's friend Ron, who worked for Ralph Nader, came to visit on business. We enjoyed our time with him, had a dance with him at the disco in his hotel in Cedar Rapids.

In September Hurricane David killed hundreds in the Dominican Republic; Frederick wrecks havoc in Mobile, Alabama; Mt. Etna erupts; Indonesia has the worst earthquake in some time; all occurred in a matter of days. Then we had Skylab, 3 Mile Island. In October the State Department called to say that in January I'm to be the Ambassador's Secretary in Trinidad. I was on Leave of Absence to finish my degree. Ed was excited to have a stimulating teacher for his Shakespeare course, but she was demanding, made him write papers, and was very critical. Ah, justice!

We went to see the Houston Ballet do Giselle and thoroughly enjoyed it. Campus life can be rewarding! Phyllis Diller had come to town during that year, but we found her too raunchy.

What a year this had been! Sixty people from our American Embassy in Iran were taken hostage on November 4. Thanksgiving found us in San Diego to see Ed's daughter Suzanne and her husband Howard. His son John and friend Katha joined us. We also had a stop to see Joyce of Panama days in San Juan Capistrano, and Ed's other daughter Cathy in Santa Monica.

The last weeks of December were quite neurotic, attending last classes, studying for finals, writing papers, not to mention packing household effects for the Trinidad assignment. Discovered that the Shah of Iran had fouled our dear island of Contadora in Panama. We sold the Honda to a neighbor, paid $10.50 for my cap and gown, paid Mayflower $1026.95 to deliver our household effects to

Washington. The State Department would pay onward to Trinidad. We left Iowa on December 21 for Peoria. I found my sister Pat in a panic as she learned her ex had sold his restaurant and had plans to leave town with her children, address unknown.

On a happy note, my graduation ceremony was held in Joyce and Larry's house with Joyce playing Pomp and Circumstance on the piano. I came down the stairs in my cap and gown. All of the Big Four were in attendance plus mates, plus sister Pat. Joyce, Mary and Phyllis and I had been good friends since kindergarten. A speech was given by Larry; we were a jovial group.

Onto St. Louis Dec. 23 to Robert and Sandy's. Judy came from Colorado and brought Wayne, her fiancé, to meet us for the first time. Ed, sporting a new beard, became known as the Family Philosopher. On Christmas Eve we attended their church to hear sister-in-law Sandy and Judy sing a stirring Holy Night, with the rest of us serving as church choir. We parted ways Dec. 26. Ed and I went onto Arkansas for a festive turkey feast at Clara and Bill's. Left Dec. 29 and Ed's mother said she was happy Ed had me to take care of him. We shed some tears when we left and wandered thru Memphis, Nashville, crossing over Looseahatchie and Buffalo rivers in Tennessee. Dec. 30 we meandered into the West Virginia hills, crawled up route 50 and down again. Ran into snow in higher places, finally ending up at Laura's place in Virginia by sundown. The next day I checked in at State and saw a bunch of old friends and acquaintances. New Year's Eve was in Bethesda at Iris and Don's, a party with Latinos, Arabs, gringoes. Ed met an old boss who was married to Iris' daughter Celeste's friend, small world! 1979 ended for us at 2:30 a.m.

The Big Four - Peoria, Illinois. Joyce Green Spurgeon, Bev Lavigne,
Phyllis Shadid Boland, and Mary Johnson Ball.

A blizzard and snowstorm to usher in the first semester February
1979, University of Iowa.

High school friend Margy Vannice Nelson, organist at a Lutheran church in Iowa. 1960-ish? She published a book on an esoteric musical technique.

Wedding day, Chicago City hall, July 28, 1979

Religious ceremony a week later in Lisbon, Portugal. Jorge Lagido
and Barbara Morrison as attendants.

Ed and I after religious ceremony in Lisbon, Portugal August 4,
1979. A lot happened on my Iowa tour.

Crudely made pottery collection at University of Iowa, done to temper the madness of eternal reading and writing of essays for bachelor of arts degree. 1979

The Graduate, 1979

Trinidad

1980 – Trinidad

I spent several weeks in the Department of State, attending the Terrorism Seminar, having lunches with old bosses, friends. On January 9 I spent a grueling all-day Foreign Service Assessment Program. It was an evaluation whether I would be officer material or remain a peasant secretary. I was later informed that I passed that lap of the race, and now await further developments. They said about 1/3 manage to survive the Assessment, so I'm happy to have jumped that hurdle.

We spent a few days in Miami on the way to Trinidad. Dini of Panama days met us there and we met Ed's friend Paul. Then onto St. Croix for a night, a lazy, luxurious little island with a bunch of yachts parked out in the harbor - good restaurants, D.C. prices. We enjoyed the taste of an island before being sentenced to a two-year tour on our own. We rented a car and practiced driving on the left-hand side of the road, as they do in Trinidad. Tricky, tricky!

We were, upon landing in Port-of-Spain, Trinidad introduced to our Grand Canyon Suite at the Trinidad Hilton, rather luxurious quarters with a view of the harbor. We soon found we could not turn down the air conditioning, even plastered folders to the vents to no avail. Ed and I could not bear the cold and soon transferred to the Queen's Park Hotel, on the Savannah (Trinidad's sexy name for a large plot of green). The hotel was a rundown relic leftover from the British rule. The elderly waiters must have served Queen Victoria. They would shuffle along, taking several minutes before acknowledging your presence. Once, when fearing I'd be late for work, I asked about my toast. "Whole wheat takes longer!" the waiter responded. We use that term in the family to this day! I had seen only one Trinidadian roach in our bathroom, so the quarters were considered to be clean. The Hilton had provided us with a lizard who stood guard duty on the dressing room wall to ward off any such invaders.

The day after we arrived we had luncheon with Ambassador and Mrs. Irving Cheslaw on the patio of the Ambassador's Residence, overlooking Port of Spain, some of us sipping rum and bitters, local products. Both the Ambassador and his wife were very sweet people, almost too good to be true. He had been very understanding about my taking time off for house hunting. I spent much of my time in the office keeping track of four appointment books: the Ambassador's; my calendar of his events; Mrs. Cheslaw's functions, and lastly, our own. Phone calls turned out to be a major feat - when they went through! One had to dial the same number at least 4 or 5 times before achieving success. Soon after our arrival we attended a reception for three visiting poets. It turned out one of them - Mark Strand - had taught at my alma mater and we knew some of the same people. Later I learned that Derek Walcott was an up and coming poet from St. Lucia and Joseph Brodsky, a well known Russian poet. Ed took it upon himself to learn a lot more about him later on.

A week or so later, I attended a reception for officers of US South Carolina. Ed had other plans. *I* began dancing and kept it up: with sailors, some short little kid, and the Ambassador. I was one of the first to arrive and the last to leave. Then a day later it was Panorama, with steel drum bands lining up in the streets, to compete for presence in the grandstand at Carnaval. The steel drums were created in the 1930s where discarded oil drums from the naval base were cut and shaped, and pounded into musical tones. Warming up to Carnival, one got invited to various Calypso houses to learn the lyrics of songs written just for Carnaval. (They spell it one way and I another!) It is a great way for you to become familiar with the songs early on. At one spot, I was kissed on the cheek by the Mighty Sparrow, a well known Calypso singer.

Mid February we went to Dimanche Gras, with a grand display of Queens and Kings costumes. They were elaborate and massive. The only rule was that they had to be self-propelled, so many were on rollers at the hemline. It was quite a lovely display, I got excited taking pictures, so beautifully done. On Jour Ouvert everyone hit the streets by 5 or 6 a.m. Bands gathered and a motley crowd follows them, dancing, many drunk from the night before. And on Carnaval Tuesday, Mardi Gras, comes the Parade of Bands. Enormous, colorful costumes on fantastic display, some bands with over 1000 members following in the same colors, musical back up trucks playing the theme of the season for that particular band. I spent 6-1/2 hrs. there, rather mesmerized. Trinidad's carnival wins 10 times over that of Rio's, as I was later to observe.

I received my diploma in the mail: Bachelor of Arts, 20 years after it could have been received, had I attended college straight through. But I was proud of my accomplishment. I attended 3 years total at Iowa, but supplemented it with night school courses at Northwestern in Chicago, Florida State classes in Panama, and two night school classes at Geo. Washington Univ. in D.C. Oh yes, a couple correspondence courses from Iowa. Now that is determination! And there was my first semester at Iowa this last time when I nearly made the Dean's list. I received 3 A's and 2 B's and one curmudgeon gave me a C+. I should have fought for a B-.

Back to Trinidad. What an eye opener it was to go to a poultry store! There are live chickens in a cage, pick the one you want. It is then stoked head first into a funnel and weighed, squawking away, wings folded, legs tied, and then tossed in thru a burlap flap in the door to the slaughter house beyond your vision. The patron returns to collect his dismembered, defeathered friend. I immediately asked "Do you have any frozen chicken?" and was relieved that they did. It had been a gagging moment and I never returned. There were always food shortages in Port of Spain: Butter, chicken, etc. Onions too, such a necessary one! When they were available, they were sold under the counter.

While wandering on weekends, we encountered the ex US naval base which was a ghost town. The buildings and houses were deteriorated from lack of use. The US navy was kicked out in 1971.

Most of the Americans at the Embassy had been either robbed or burglarized. Even the Ambassador's residence noted a shortage of silver spoons. John the GSO and his wife were robbed in daylight of several of her rings and his combat boots. Several days after, Ed and I were mugged by five fellows on the Savannah by our hotel at twilight. Two held his arms, while the others searched his pockets. When I began to defend him, I was hit on the forehead by the tallest one. "Take it! take it!" Ed shouted and they ended up with his watch and billfold with about 40 TT. ($1 US = 2.40 TT) I yelled after them "bastards!" One was a rastafarian.

So we entered the role of victims of Trinidad's hospitality. The next day John reported it to the police and we looked at mug shots. Several weeks before the German Ambassador's secretary, mother and aunt were robbed and at least one was stabbed when they tried to resist, so we were fortunate. The mother was still in the hospital recuperating. Several days later the shop-keeper at the Chinese bakery warned us to watch our money. I said we'd already been mugged. He pointed to the front page of the newspaper he was reading, and our story was on it!

How leery we were when we saw any dark men in a cluster, ominous to us now. We made our sojourn to the armpit of the city, bought 8 small loaves at the bakery, all whole wheat, made it back to the car and sped away and felt we had accomplished a major heist. Later Ed took me on a date to the Holiday Inn by the pool. The waiter was singing and I encouraged him. He offered a calypso number and we both sang "Brown Skin Girl" and it was such a moment of tenderness, it helped me forgive Trinidad. Weeks after the mugging I felt down and threatened. Ed had a mole on his chest I fretted over. It seemed I had transferred Trinidadian fears to that mole until I convinced myself there was something critical about it. It turned out okay.

Off for a picnic to Maracas beach, fairly deserted, we saw some sinister types along the road wanting a ride, which made us uptight. But as we soaked in nature's beauty, the rolling hills, it eased somewhat. We watched a fellow climb barefoot up coconut palms with a machete to hack coconuts down with great expertise. And we appreciated his skill.

We were treated to Senegalese dancers, box seats compliments of the Ambassador. Great costumes and effects. A bride on the shoulder of the man with a flowing gown over them, the constant beating of drums. Thoroughly enjoyable, my kind of rhythm.

Oh yes, househunting, We had looked at several places, some interesting, but the fact they were miles from the Embassy made them less desirable, because traffic during the morning hours was always horrific with school children and others needing to go to work. So we saw the house of Kathy, an officer who would be leaving in April, and decided to wait for it. Yes, we got here in January! The Admin officer offered his place for us to housesit and that was about a month out of the hotel. We loved the lush and luxurious hanging foliage on his front porch, the wide variety of colored butterflies, the varied birds chattering away every morn, and in the evening the keskidee. I often felt the urge to paint, green, green and green! At other times the sultry tropical clime made me languid, feeling hopeless about the world, myself and my role in it. Oh, remember the hummingbirds in the hibiscus!

After Nixon's trip to China, the Red Chinese Embassy invited us for dinner. Was that Chinese glasnost? They made an attempt to serve us forks with delicious Chinese food. I smiled and asked for chopsticks. We saw a film of the Premier visiting Tibet. The evening was enjoyable and the next day I had a Red Chinese hangover from their potent rice wine.

April 3 we moved into our own house after 3 months living out of suitcases. It was small and had two levels, but built with a lot of open space - Frank Lloyd Wright would have approved. Four small bedrooms, ceiling fans. The small yard in back was lovely with a giant Travelers Palm outside the sliding door, hibiscus trees/bushes, and at least three banana trees in joyful production. Just settling into our house, Jorge and Wanda came from Portugal for a visit. There was a complication because back in 1974 Portugal had been communist for six months and a visa was required for Trinidad. After 3 hours at the airport they were granted overnight permission to stay. The next day the plane was held up awaiting their arrival, with the DCM's wife on board. Back and forth talking among Trinidadian officials finally released the plane and Jorge and Wanda were permitted a week's visit with us! Virgoes Wanda and Bev got along fine. Jorge treated us to dinner at the Hilton. Since the Ambassador and Mrs. Cheslaw were away, we often sunned and swam in the pool at the Residence. When the Cheslaws returned from their Barbados visit they said that the Barbadans thought Trinidadians were wicked, voo doo-ers who drank blood and dealt with snakeskins.

We took Jorge and Wanda on a trip to Tobago. Have I not mentioned Tobago? It is Trinidad's sister island, lovely, calm and innocent, in contrast to Trinidad's suspect character. But we had no clue of calm when we went to the BWIA Tobago building at the airport. There was no semblance of order whatsoever. We encountered a mob waving tickets, pushing up against one another, struggling to get their baggage to the scales. We asked for politeness at first, a girl said it was the survival of the fittest, so then we joined in the push. We got our boarding passes, finally made it, and even then half the mob wandered to the wrong plane. Fifteen minutes on the BWIA jet and we were there. We had not told Ed and Jorge that we would be kicked out of the first hotel after one night. Finally, after a poor breakfast, we announced it, had a lousy lunch there and we took a taxi to our new home, the Robinson Crusoe.

It was Night of the Iguana decadence, the jungle was closing in to reclaim the land stolen earlier to build the hotel. The road in front was split in two levels, and the sea was encroaching to reclaim its own as well. Wanda laughed hysterically when she saw the rundown place. Ed and I had room #17, the hotel's best, and we loved it! Open windows with the ocean pounding the shore outside, flowered curtains, window seat, all quite cozy. Downstairs there was an enormous veranda with a baby grand piano, lots of sofas and chairs with faded chintz upholstery. We were all surprised at the fine dinner, chicken with a lot of vegetables. We could not resist the guava dessert.

The owner Kurt Nothnagel, 82, was dressed in a tuxedo no less. They "dressed" for dinner, had come from German and British heritage. He played us Gershwin tunes on the baby grand, expertly. It was altogether enchanting. I've never known such a heavenly night's sleep, I was back in the womb with the reassuring whoosh of the ocean in my ears. No mosquitos. The place was delightfully decadent! For breakfast, Ed got his pa pa (papaya to the unimaginative). The Robinson Crusoe was THE place in the 30's, 40's, into the 50's. Kurt's sister (also) Wanda showed us the newspaper clippings in their scrapbooks. They even had Queen Elizabeth's birthday gathering on the lawn! --see there's the photo to prove it! And movies were made here: "Heaven knows Mr. Allison" with Deborah Kerr and Robt. Mitchem; Walt Disney had done "Robinson Crusoe." Vivian Leigh was here once. She loved to party, had danced with Kurt, and wanted to take him home with her.

Jorge and Wanda decide to stay a few more days in Tobago. When they returned Wanda was as black as a native Trinidadian. They loved Pigeon Point and felt Tobago was the only saving grace for Trinidad (T&T). They left later on a plane to Puerto Rico. It was also the time of the aborted attempt by Pres. Carter to rescue the hostages in Iran.

Alba returned from over a month medical leave in the States and I was happy to turn her boss (the DCM) over to her. The Pittsburgh Jazz Ensemble was great. We went to a reception to meet them two days after the performance. Then it was our first time of many to the Little Carib theatre for modern dance and guitar, thoroughly enjoyable.

I was later to meet the Grand Dame of Trinidadian culture Beryl McBurnie, in her late 60's, a force to be reckoned with. She had studied dance with Martha Graham in New York City and had met Margo Fonteyn in London. After a lovely Argentine guitar concert, she had come home with us for dessert and raved over our house. A very fun evening. She was a dramatic character wearing long white gowns and floral flowing scarves. She had a sense of nobles oblige, would wave down Carlos, the Ambassador's driver if he were alone in the car, and have him take her to her next appointment. After Ed got to know her, he too was sometimes beckoned with the wave for a ride. We loved her, she was irrepressible. As she prepared a meal once at her home, I caught her at the stove, rolling an onion with her foot to "stir up the juice." The meal she prepared had calaloo soup, red beans and rice, marinated pork, in grand proportions and delicious, to thank all those who had been involved in the Little Carib Theatre's success. Beryl disliked the very mention of age.

"You are only in competition with yourself!" she said wisely.

Ed and I went for four days in Barbados, stayed at the Southern Palms Hotel. The front door of the room opened to the gorgeous sea, crystal clear, pink buildings, white sand. We rented a red moke (like a golf cart) and explored. To Pisces (Ed's astrological sign) for dinner. Had flying fish in a romantic setting on the water and reaffirmed our love for each other. Rum swizzle was the drink of Barbados; rum punch for Trinidad. Ed popped in a day or so later to the Embassy with carnations for me. Alba, my irrepressible co-worker said: "He's been seeing me and feels guilty!" I responded "If he's been seeing you, I should send him flowers!" We all had a laugh over that.

On June 3 I saw new smudge marks on the whitewashed back wall of the house and felt a burglary seemed inevitable. I asked Ed in the morning "Did the burglars come?" He said "You can't let them ruin your life." Then I walked out of the bedroom and the stereo and TV were gone. At first I thought he had hidden them. Seems they got in through the sliding door. I felt so violated and angry. Ed got to entertain the police while they took fingerprints. I went to work. Unbelievable. Three months before we had our mugging. I told Ed "3 times and we're out!" One day after the burglary we had an open house 2-6. They came, even some who weren't invited, over 40 of them. I had purchased 5 dozen won tons and 5 dozen ting sang and Thomas served the bar nicely. It was loud and lively, therefore a success. They left at 7. I set about putting our house in order, though every time I glanced at a dark corner I thought about the thieves who violated our home. Harold the Embassy electrician came to better secure the house. He was always eager to come to our house as he was fond of our maid Valde. She got to clean up all the glasses from the party and was shocked over the burglary but not surprised. Soon after I wrote a letter to the editor talking about the angry young men of Trinidad, and it appeared in the paper a few days later.

Ten days after the burglary we felt the need for Tobago's balm. He and I were the very last guests of the Robinson Crusoe, packers were coming on Weds. The Flying fish and guava pie were excellent. We were invited to sit at their table. Wanda and Kurt had both enjoyed their lives in Tobago. They used to dress as certain characters going to Pigeon Point on Sundays in their woody station wagon. As we left the next morn, Kurt sat down at the grand piano and played, "I'll see you again" - and we did, twice more.

Ed and I were both a bit surprised at the comfortable enduring warmth that had come to our relationship those almost seven years. We had each mentioned it and felt its depth. Ed said often: "Now I know what they mean by becoming one flesh!"

I found the banana trees in our small back yard entrancing. When a new bunch was ripe with scores of small tasty bananas, another was ready to shoot up and bring forth another crop. I was always bringing bananas to the Embassy for distribution. Once when the banana tree collapsed full of fruit, John and Philicia were with us to right it, and Philicia surprised us with a fine voice singing "Tree." Later she and I sang hymns and harmonized really well together. I offered a lot of wine for communion.

We took a weekend trip to see Jen in Caracas. Trinidad was only 7 miles from Venezuela's northern point. They had very low morale at the Embassy and could not figure out why we'd visit there. Try

Trinidad, I said! David from Lisbon was assigned there and we saw him a few times. He was battling serious skin cancer on his face and looked bad. Jen shared some of her pasta recipes. We dined well.

In July Ed went home to mother. The Ambassador's driver Carlos announced that he had a dog to protect me while he was gone. The dog assured me he'd care for my house and home, but I was not so sure he wouldn't keep me out as well, so I decided against it. In the meantime, I had my first guitar lesson in Trinidad by Dr. Thornhill Nicholas, a retired high school principal. He came to the house. He taught with a view to chords as well. So we'd spend 3/4 hr. on classical and 1/4 on chords for popular music. I enjoyed it immensely.

Also enjoyed the Alvin Ailey dancers at the Queen's Hall. Did I tell you Beryl McBurnie had clout?

The famed Susan Sontag came for a lecture. She at first had luncheon at the Ambassador's Residence. He felt earlier that he had to cram through her essays to present an intelligent face. But it went very well. He had an intelligent face, was a very nice man. In her lecture, she read from "I, Etc." She said she wrote essays to exhaust her mind of a subject which preoccupied her so she could clear her brain for the next project. She wanted to be a great writer people would look back on and feel was necessary. Loved Beckett as the greatest living writer. She was very charming. She read "Baby" which she felt was her best story.

Early September was the USS Radford's reception at the Ambassador's Residence. I was at the age captains find interesting. Danced a few. Lunch aboard the next day and sat on the captain's left.

A day or so later I went with an Embassy driver to visit the laid off Embassy gardener Mr. Allen. My bible at the time was Adelle Davis' book on "Let's Get Well." He had had to quit gardening because of pain in his back and legs. I was finding most people's problems was a deficiency in Vitamin C. Carlos parked the Embassy car, we crossed a stream, tip toed across the rocks and climbed up a quarter mile to his house, a plain house with a great view of the surrounding hills. He greeted us graciously. I was laden with vitamins and read from the xeroxed papers I was to give him. I turned over the vitamins and he promised he'd take them religiously for 10 days. I assured him that with Vitamin C, any he did not need would wash out. He would nod and say "yes madam!" every time I said a few words. I hoped for a success story. On my birthday September 17 Alba made me stay away during the morn to get my hair done. When I showed in the afternoon she told me Mrs. Allen had come by to thank me for healing her husband with Vitamin C. He was practically dancing around and thinking of returning to work next week! That was the best birthday gift I could have had! Now Harold wanted vitamins for his children, Vit. C. had helped Carmen's neck, Joe's wife was arthritic, and he came for a diagnosis. They were lining up! I was accused later on of practicing without a license.

One evening Alba and I went to a diplomatic gathering of secretaries hosted by the Germans. We jumped in and had a great time conversing with our compatriots. I particularly liked French Marguerite and a Japanese girl, but we all got along quite well. There was a myriad of hors d'oeuvres, suddenly it was 10 p.m. We were among the last to leave.

Ed and I learned of a direct flight to Amsterdam via KLM. Great! So in the rain we loaded up the car with TV, radio, cassette, guitar and hid them in the Ambassador's office. We left the stereo for burglar bait. I also told Alba I was going to leave milk and cookies. We took our bikes to the Ambassador's residence. At the airport we learned that the KLM plane overflew the Piarco airport because of a pot hole in the runway. I learned later that Trinidad had a huge pitch lake, had no excuse. They had been warned by KLM to repair the runway earlier, warning that this might happen. So to our dismay, instead of a direct flight to Amsterdam, we were an hour later on British Airways to Barbados, Antigua and London. We got stuck in the smoking section with no movie. We were in travel mode 17-1/2 hours instead of 6-1/2 hrs. Trinidad strikes again! Eventually we arrived in London to a baggage handler strike, and somehow made it to Lisbon. Barb and Brad awaited us and took us home to dinner. They were planning to marry in Gibraltar soon!

Since Barbara was packing out soon I bought a china cabinet to go with my Portuguese table around $200 to ship with her things and collect later in the States. Renewed friendships with Ray and Margaret, Juliet Atunes, Norm & Patricia, Portuguese friends Carmen, Helen, Judite. The latter three treated me at Celta for lunch. They said if they had asked around, all the Portuguese would have wanted to join us. How touching! Ed and I had dinner with Wanda and Jorge, recounting their Trinidadian experience, which was positive only because of Tobago.

We flitted over to Milan while on European soil. Got a picture of Ed feeding pigeons at what we called his debut at La Scala. Took a train to Venice. Stayed on the canal near the Rialto Bridge with

American Express gondoliers constantly streaming by and singing "Santa Lucia". I found it delightful. We went to Trattoria Boomerang and knew why they return, because the gnocchi and calamari were delicious! We finally talked ourselves into an expensive gondola ride to Petti Palace for almost $30. At Lake Como I bought a Modigliani lithograf 106 of 200 for $160. Ed sez: "Things cannot make you happy!" But I was pleased to have it.

Back in Portugal, Barbara told us that our orphanage was disbanding. All our wedding funds/donations did was to keep the wolf from the door for a few more months. How sad to ponder what lies ahead for them! We attempted to visit the house but it was closed. Farewells with saudades. KLM made it to Port of Spain, but the plane had to be turned around on the runway by a tractor after landing because the runway was in such a state of disrepair! Welcome to Trinidad!

To Little Carib Theatre, saw "Panomine" by Derek Wolcott, done by a terrific black actor from Guyana, Wilbert Holder. At a reception later, met Dr. Gregory Wolfe, Iris's (from Panama) friend. He said "not friend, old lover!" Small world. I believe he was a Florida businessman, travelling with Governor Graham. Iris was world renown!

Later at Little Carib: Paul Keens-Douglas "Tim Tim". A poet and storyteller. Born in Trinidad, lived in Grenada. Great. The classical guitarist played a wondrous "Anonymous". I could have listened all eve. I continued with my own lessons with Dr. Nicholas. Also later on in the month: "Three Calypsos," all very good.

More food woes. We received chickens during a shortage from a local supplier. They were thin and dried out. People could not even boil them to tenderness. Thanks to Mrs. Cheslaw for being the intermediator for our complaints, 143 chickens clucked their way back to the supplier for refunds. Quite a mad scene in the Embassy parking area! Months later after leaving Trinidad, now and then I'd get a rubber chicken in the mail from either Philicia or Alba, and of course we'd laugh and pass it on.

Ed's friend Mong, Arkansas nickname, and his wife Opal came for a visit. This time we rented a small house in Tobago. We were enchanted to see a tiny bird fly in from the window and begin industriously to build a nest in the wicker lampshade over the table. What could we do but let it happen? We ate elsewhere. Our big event of the day was to Bucco Reef snorkeling, wandering in bliss among the multi-colored fish. I got carried away by the spectacle and also by the current. I gagged and panicked, grabbed at another boat. Ed rescued me with another fellow, pulling me back to our boat. I got a bit seasick, as did Opal. I'm not a very good sailor (or swimmer).

I worked on our homemade election board Nov. 4 and was shocked that Reagan won in almost every state. The new computer world forecasted the finals too soon after polls closed. I wanted more suspense!

Sister Judy and husband Wayne came to visit Nov. 18, having enjoyed their stopover in St.Croix. I was struggling to avoid a cold, and could have given a warmer welcome. Ed took them to Maracas Beach and they were entertained/scandalized by a sexpot in a bandaid bikini flexing her muscles and other things at Ed and Wayne. They went off for a few days to Barbados. For Thanksgiving we had over our dear Freda-who-knows everything (as we called her at Embassy) and her husband Steve. Judy and I shared assignments and it went well. Then off again for Tobago for the weekend to a rented house which they enjoyed. During their stay Wayne played handy man, could fix anything that needed it. Had drinks at the Residence, about 12 people, pleasant. Another time to the Hilton to listen to steel drums, all quite enjoyable. And then off they flew for home in Colorado.

For Christmas the airlines put an embargo on the Embassy pouches and thereby cancelled Christmas for us, Bah humbug! We did not receive the stacked up pouches until Dec. 29. New Year's Eve John, Philicia and Alba came for drinks and we played Tripoli. I loved the fact that Trinidadians call it Old Year's Night, which seemed more appropriate! Ed slept and we forced him awake at 11:50 pm. Had champagne, we danced a bit, enjoyed his presence for a half hour, then John slept, and we women mused about life until 2 a.m.

Trinidad 1981

I need to tell you that I've been practicing my guitar and taking lessons. I see some progress.

I began the year 1981 with what we call a medevac for a D.C. in D.C. I sought out a bunch of friends from past lives. Many were in D.C. either briefly or semi-permanently. I was excited about getting in touch. I was there Inauguration day for Reagan and Iran handed over the hostages in his favor. I had a Portuguese reunion with David, Jim and Bob at the Pastorino house. Was Lee there as well? One ex-boss, seeing me in the cafeteria, gave a little skip, like a leprechaun. I stayed with Chicago friend Laura, who was in D.C. with her (formerly my) law firm.

Back to Trinidad 11 days later where Ed had missed me terribly but had to subdue his amorous nature for awhile after my surgery. We had a memorable occasion at the Japanese Embassy watching the film "A Spring Comes Late" about a family travelling on a train from Nagasaki to Northern Japan, following the father's dream. We endured their heartbreak and shed some tears. Home wise, I was brought back to life with our lovemaking. How compatible we are! Whenever we returned to the Queen's Park hotel for an occasional meal, the grumpy ole men greeted us warmly and we always had a good meal.

Valentine weekend brought us to Tobago with John and Philicia, and Alba & Tom. Ever since Ed and I met in Panama, we have had the tradition of writing a homemade Valentine to each other. It is sometimes pornographic, always loving.

I quit guitar lessons in February as I felt discouraged that I wasn't getting anywhere. Mr. Nicholas said "you disappoint me, man! Just as you begin to understand, you quit!" I am humiliated, first because he needs the money, secondly because I gave up on myself.

Hugh, an ex-district attorney from D.C., came to visit at Ed's invitation. I resented him immediately with his phony "sweetie" endearments to woo me. We spent the weekend at Blanchesseuse, a very charming town with a gorgeous coastline. It offered a newfound appreciation for the beauty of Trinidad, just 24 miles away to discover paradise, 45 minutes from our house.

Activities for Carnaval begin popping up with various fetes. Steel band semi-finals, watched the Queen semi-finals on the Savannah. To Dimanche Gras with 18 Calysonians singing their new tunes. Calypso King was Chalk Dust, Queen Saucy Simonetta, and King Quarter of the Moon. At J'Ouvert I got caught in a people crunch on Frederick Street and almost panicked, hated it. Scary. I drove back to Blanchesseuse to collect Ed and return for the final Carnaval parade. All agreed Carnaval was not as great and memorable as last year.

We took a trip to Coroni and the Asa Wright Bird Sanctuary. We were put into a flat bottom boat in the sanctuary just as scores of scarlet ibis were coming in to nest at sunset. What a lovely and vivid spectacle! like red ribbons on a Christmas tree. Trinis used to hunt them until 1962 for use of their brilliant feathers for Carnaval costumes. Such treachery!

I need to mention experiencing twilight so close to the equator. Trinidad was 760 miles north of it. Twilight lasted just a few minutes. When night falls, plop! As I realized that fact, I missed the leisurely, lovely moment of seeing the sunset in other climes.

Near to our house were a few art galleries. I especially appreciated the one which housed Boscoe and Jeffrey Holder's paintings. I recall a Boscoe one with a lovely Trini woman in white gown and headband holding a stark black umbrella. How I lusted after it! Jeffrey was also a well known choreographer, making it as one in New York City. The outside world seemed to find its way to Trinidad often. I gave Beryl McBurnie much of the credit.

The Alberni String quartet from Britain (one of six greatest in the world) came to entrance us and it was marvelous. Ed was soothed to sleep by Mozart. The culture was not always presented from other worlds. I was always torn by the dichotomy between Trinidadian artistic talent and the anger of the street hoods. They had lovely concerts, the fantastic display of talent shown during Carnival's costuming; the cleverness of calypso tunes, always original each year; steel drum bands; artists like Boscoe; theatre guided so skillfully by the grand dame Beryl McBurnie, who did so much for Trinidad's theatrical experience; vs. the evil, vicious (most likely on drug-induced highs) hoodlums.

I received a letter from my hero boss Hume Horan, now an Ambassador, who wanted me to replace his secretary in Yauonde, but was told of my being in the Mustang program and "was selfishly sad for himself." I would have been tempted to join him.

Ed's houseguest Hugh left finally after three weeks! I told Ed that Hugh knew he was a parasite, but made the mistake of thinking he was of the orchid variety.

Trinidadian Prime Minister Eric Williams died March 29 we

learned the next day. Also on March 30 we heard that Reagan had been shot, bullet into left side, collapsed lung, long operation at George Washington Univ. hospital. As Reagan recovered, we went to view the closed casket of P M Williams.

We went again to the Asa Wright bird sanctuary. Who would have thought nature could be so noisy! Who can handle hoot owls, tropical rainstorms, fluttering of bat wings? I slept fitfully.

Back home I was invited to an elegant party with the creme de la creme of Trinidadian society, ex Governor General's wife, etc. I had never seen such sumptuous food served, seven choices of all the good stuff.

So it was April and Ed's son John arrived with his surfboard. Once when he and Ed went surf hunting, they had been frightened by 8 Rastafarians in loin cloth with cutlasses. John quickly jumped into the car and waved weakly as they made their escape. John was easy to have around the house, cooked good healthy meals and cleaned up. He was in very sharp contrast to Hugh, who expected to be waited upon. Ed's daughter Cathy showed up ten days later and we all headed for Tobago. John wanted to take a boat, a five hour trip. I took dramamine and made it okay, but it was exhausting. The rental house was the best yet. It was Japanese style with sliding doors, a protected cove, and one of only two houses to use the beach. Australian pines, lovely view. No complaint. I was reading "Lost Horizons" and it was a good book for Tobago as Shangra la. Our view was indeed comparable to one's idea of one. Cathy and John departed together on May 7. And we became aware that we are getting "short" the Foreign Service expression for time left at post.

May 13 the Pope had been shot! We are wondering about this

errant world. The end of May we finally made it to Grenada, which was immediately more civilized than T & T. It had a new "revolutionary government" and we wondered if we had permission to be there. But all was calm entering the island. Our room on the Grand Anse had a lime tree and its own private pool. Freda's best friend invited us for drinks, went up Cinnamon Hill with a spectacular post card view with lights twinkling in the hills. Grenada was known as the Spice Island. Paradise here was a bit less than it appeared with the new revolutionary party, inflation, red tape, surcharges, no newspaper but the party paper. But we certainly enjoyed the illusion, remembrance of times past. When we returned to Trinidad we learned that we caused a near riot that we had been allowed to go to Grenada when the USIS officer was denied permission and Jack in Consular was also refused by the DCM.

We saw Wanda and Kurt a couple times in Port of Spain after we left them at the Robinson Crusoe in Tobago. Then I learned that Kurt had died in his sleep June 25, a week after he had a drink with us and they had spoken of making a visit to see us in D.C. On June 26 I noted a huge funeral at the church next door to the Embassy and did not know until much later that it was for Kurt. Wanda hadn't wanted to disturb us.

As I did in leaving Portugal, I made certain to have a get together for my favorite foreign nationals. I had a lunch at my house for Freda, Enid, Alice, Ann, Debbie, Carmen, and Jemma, with a couple token Americans. We had a lot of food, wine and a very good time. We got packed out and spent several weeks at the house of the Econ officer, out on leave.

There was a lovely guitar/flute duo at the Residence: Lisa

Hurlong/Sidney Goldsmith. On July 4 twenty demonstrators appeared at the Embassy with placards: "Down with U.S. Imperialism." I thoroughly enjoyed the party at the Residence. Some of us danced to calypso music at the edge of the pool, I had a heart to heart conversation with Beryl McBurnie.

Friends (the Habibs) told us they had 4 Rastas take over their house a few years ago, robbed them and tied them up. Recently the Ambassador and his wife both had their watches disappear from the Residence. I didn't mind the thought of leaving!

Ed left Trinidad (and me) on July 2. I worried about our car sale and clearances and penalties for nondiplomatic personnel, and odds and ends of various things to tie up before time to leave. The Ambassador would leave a month or so later than I , and was relieved that the U.S. Ambassador to Jamaica's ex-secretary would come to ease him through. Beryl opened her Folk Museum with a grand opening with lavish hors d'oeuvres and drinks, music, dancers, actors, etc. and then announced "We have come to the end of our money!" Farewell dinners and lunches were given to me, including a lovely Japanese lunch of miso soup, salad, tempura vegetables, beef and rice by lovely Yasko and her husband Floyd. I left Trinidad on July 15, with Alba, Philicia and Freda sending me off.

A lovely beach on the Caribbean Sea.

Port of Spain, Trinidad.   Prime Minister's office. 1980

Maracas beach outside Port of Spain, Trinidad- 1980

Carnival costumes were creative and dramatic, much more
impressive than those in Brazil. 1981

Carnival parade in Trinidad - February 1981

Trinidad's PM residence 1981

The infamous Beryl McBurnie, grand dame of theatre and dance.
Trinidad -1981

A typical gingerbread house on the Savannah, Port of Spain, Trinidad

Sister Judy and husband Wayne visited us in Trinidad after a
stopover in St. Croix. Also spent a few days in Barbados. 1980

Beryl McBernie, the Grand Dame of theatre and dance in Trinidad.
Was responsible for influx of noteworthy dancers, established Little
Carib Theatre with promising local talent. 1980-81

Our haven at Robinson Crusoe in Tobago - 1980-81

Bev and Ed, overlooking sea at Tobago. 1981

Old Year's Night in Trinidad with Philicia, Alba, Bev - 1980

Opal and Mong, Ed's childhood friend. Visited us in Trinidad, Brazil and Australia. Here they are in Tobago at Bucco Reef. 1980

Foreign Service Institute (FSI)

The President of the United States of America

To ——— Beverly Ann La Vigne ———
a Member of the Foreign Service of the United States of America, Greeting:

Reposing special trust and confidence in your Integrity, Prudence and Ability, I have nominated and, by and with the advice and consent of the Senate, do appoint you a Consular Officer and a Secretary in the Diplomatic Service of the United States of America and do authorize and empower you to have and to hold the said office, and to exercise and enjoy all the rights, privileges and immunities thereunto appertaining during the pleasure of the President of the United States.

In testimony whereof, I have caused the Seal of the United States to be hereunto affixed.

Done at the City of Washington this ——— eleventh ——— day of December, ——— in the year of our Lord one thousand nine hundred and eighty one, and of the Independence of the United States of America the two hundred and sixth.

By the President:

Ronald Reagan

Alexander M. Haig Jr.
Secretary of State

A-100 - FSI

I began Home Leave as I landed in D.C. on July 15, 1981. Iris, Don and Laura met me at Washington National and off we went to Bethesda. Ed showed up the next day and we went car shopping from the airport, buying a new 1982 silver Chevy Cavalier. Four days later we bought a condo at Olympus near the Landmark Shopping Center in Alexandria, Virginia: $72,500 with a condo fee of $273. At the State Dept. we ran into Charley McCaskill, Art Lowrie, Lars Hydle, Celeste Bergold and Jen DiMeglio. The State Dept. cafeteria is a mecca for reunions. Twelve days later we hit the road. To Chicago to Laura. July 29 Diane wed Charles and became Princess of Wales. It was so good to see Bev and Ben and family. Lunched with Virginia and Georgia from the law firm, along with Laura and sister Donna. In eve to see Clara and Dana and their 2 yr. old son. Dana is a kidney specialist, will join a hospital in Ft. Smith, Arkansas, and they'll start their new life in several weeks.

Onto Peoria, Joyce and Larry and Pat, wonderful rib dinner with corn on the cob. To Colorado, Dallas, Little Rock and Conway, all old haunts and great reunions, back to D.C.

On September 1 we moved into the Olympus. The condo had been owned by a member of the White House Staff and a "fun mirror" was prominent over the bed in the Master Bedroom. I immediately gained 5 distorted extra pounds and could not look up often. When in the elevator people would remark, "Did you move into the place with the mirror?" At one point our more adventurous friends (married) exchanged their bed in Maryland for ours for an overnight stay. Other than that prominent item, the apartment was nice, spacious and well appointed and we were happy with our choice. Although it was located near a main highway, it was in the back and therefore not noisy.

We set about to do our physical exams at the Department. Ed was declared in perfect shape, but he could lose 10 pounds. I too was told I could lose a few. Before plunging myself into the class for officerhood, we attended a very poignant reunion of Ed's family in Green Bay, Wisconsin. Stalwart Swedish seniors consisted of his mother and two brothers, all in their upper 80's and on their own two legs, a crowd of some two dozen family members. There was a lot of heart warming laughter in that gathering. We drove to Wisconsin in the new car with son John's surfboard attached to the roof, the one he had left behind in Trinidad. He flew it back to California from Chicago O'Hare.

On September 16 the day before the birthday I was to turn 44, I entered the A-100 course for potential Foreign Service Officers, with some degree of trepidation. At lunch breaks I took a shuttle over to the State Department to get ego reinforcement from ex-bosses and friends. My old boss Jim reminded me not to take myself too seriously. Others tried to built up my ego: I was strong, brave etc. It was my peasant secretary side of me that kept trying to emerge. I had to remind myself that I had felt strength even in that role. Two days later we had the swearing-in ceremony in the Franklin room on the 8th floor of the State Department. Ed, David, Alba, Celeste and Philicia showed up for support. After a week or so of uneasiness I gradually eased into our role playing. I was sought out for lots of questions about working in Foreign Service in general, since by then I was an old hand.

October 6 - President Anwar Sadat is shot and dies during the day. Mrs. Sadat in 1978 said she used to worry each day that something would happen. He had told her: "They cannot detract or add an hour to my life. It is already written, it is my fate."

The class spent three days at Coolfont to continue our training, a lot of role playing involved. It did much to increase my self-confidence. Later, to Leesburg to a Xerox training center, quite a sterile environment. When we were evaluated with our role playing, my group was told we had the best quality stuff (okay material) in reporting and that Jim and I were the best organized. Later, I did well on the Negotiations exercise. The A-100 course lasted 1 and 1/2 months, followed by the Terrorism course where we were shown guns to recognize, how to ram a roadblock, detailed routes on kidnapping, etc; how to be an ideal hostage!; bomb identification, a fire alarm lecture.

I learned that I would be assigned as a Consular Officer to Monterrey, Nuevo Leon, Mexico.

Pleasure-wise getaways: To Ocean City, NJ. to see Paul and new girlfriend Lil. Emily had died last year; she even sounded like her! Also in November Folger Library in D.C. had an open house with memorable vignettes from Shakespeare, actor classes, madrigal singers, a buffet. The afternoon was so pleasant, it will go down as one of our more precious moments!

Classes now began in Latin American Studies. The first day we observed starving Chilean and Bolivian Indians, and how hard up the peasants were in Colombia. Later, the oppression of miners in

Bolivia, predestined for black lung disease but accepting their fate, since they're working! Saw a gruesome movie on the fighting in El Salvador. It seemed so obvious that we were supporting the wrong faction. Another film, supporting the wrong side in Uruguay 1972. We are killing the reasonable people in Nicaragua from both ends. And there endth Area Studies.

While I was engrossed in current activities, Ed had been writing his own story, now up to 80 pages. It is a war memoire interspersed with whatever whim of his to include therein. It is not easy reading, but he's having a great time doing it.

Arnold Chacon in my class had been assigned to Honduras. So I arranged a lunch for him to meet Iris from Honduras and daughter Celeste. A very cheery lunch. Arnold - I'm projecting! - eventually became Director General of the Foreign Service. A few days later I had a brunch for Iris and Don. Then we left them to experience "the mirror" and we attended a Bach concert, string quartet and organ recital. Had a pleasing passing of afternoon. A note left from Iris and Don: "We shall return!"

Judy and Wayne came from Colorado for Thanksgiving. We had a cold walking tour of the Washington Monument, Jefferson and Lincoln memorials after picking them up at the airport. The next day off to Bull Run battlefield, to Charlottesville, Boar's Head Inn for lunch, Monticello, and the Monroe home with peacocks in the yard, and overnight in Williamsburg. We had a mini tour of Jamestown the next day, and home again.

While I resumed Spanish classes, the rest went ambitiously to the Kennedy Center, Air and Space museum, Smithsonian, tour of Capitol Hill, White House, coming back exhausted each day but fulfilled. Ed had found a huge perfect pumpkin on the road before Thanksgiving. We eventually made about 4 pumpkin pies from it. Judy and I whipped up a grand meal to accompany them. After ten days, undaunted by all the activity, they flew on to Barbados.

Nov. 30 Natalie Wood drowns off Catalina. She had been a semi-heroine to me.

Dec. 2 At the State Dept. cafeteria, within minutes I ran into Amb. Sayre of Panama, Tom Recknagel of Saigon, Gypsie from Tunis, and Margo and Stan from London 1969.

Dec. 30 to Princeton to see Wyn (Trinidad) and her mother Edith. Dec. 31 Old Year's Night was spent in a Philadelphia hotel (Bellevue Carlton) room with Jim. We were to see the famed Mummer's Parade the next day, but it was cancelled because of rain. And there endth 1981.

New Year's Day, and the Mummer's parade was cancelled until tomorrow. Jim guided us around Philly in the rain: Independence Square, where the Liberty Bell is now placed in a sterile protected spot. We lunched with him at the hotel and headed wearily home to Virginia, in bed by 8 p.m., missing the Mummers about which he was so enthusiastic.

A day or so later, we saw the movie "Chariots of Fire" - uplifting, Ed was especially enamored.

On January 13 we had D.C.'s Pearl Harbor. A blizzard stormed through the city. An Air Florida flight crashed into the 14th Street bridge, searing four cars, crashing into the Potomac with 75 passengers and 5 crew on board. On TV we watched fretfully as five people were pulled from the freezing water with six others clinging to the tail section. One of the six drowned as he nobly let others go first. The rest were entombed in the plane with seatbelts fastened. We were glued to the news for four hours. Only five passengers and one stewardess survived. On that same day a metro train crashed and three were killed in the first fatalities of its six year operation. A week later they were still recovering bodies from the plane crash, frozen in good condition.

Meanwhile, I struggled along in Spanish, knowing full well that I didn't study as studiously as my three classmates: Laurie Tracy, Roman Popadiuk, and George Staples. The latter two later became Ambassadors. We all enjoyed one another and it felt like a love fest. The Spanish teachers always bragged about how well we were doing.

Homestead weekend with Ed. Homestead is a lovely resort in Hot Springs, Virginia. We were there for a romantic Valentine weekend, along with assorted friends of Ed's. I tried ice skating, aware I hadn't been on skates for at least 20 years. I loved it, got overconfident trying a pirouette, twisted my ankle and fell. The hotel doctor thought I had torn a ligament. Ed enjoyed the Valentine celebration in the luxurious dining room downstairs as my ankle was perched on pillows and I sipped soup in bed. Upon return home and a visit to the National Orthopedic Hospital, I learned I had a broken ankle, actually the left fibula, which was then promptly enclosed in a heavy cast.

No more metros and buses to the Foreign Service Institute. Ed became my chauffeur and delivered me to Spanish class. My friends were my slaves, bringing my coffee. I began to enjoy my plight. A month later the cast was removed and a lighter brace put on. When given the final exam, I got 2+/2, all that was needed for my new job. The others deservedly got 3/3 's. We went to the El Bodegon

Restaurant for our celebration. Instructors remarked there had never been a class such as ours, so congenial, always got along, such good students! Words cannot describe the relief I felt to be out of language class!

I began the communications course. An antiquated machine was used for processing cables to and from the Department, an HW-28. It was fun to operate in a perverted sort of way. This was the end of an era. Slick communications equipment were in the works to begin a more streamlined cyberspace operation.

Joyce and Larry drove in from Peoria in April. Ed took them to the Air and Space museum, the East Wing, and later I showed them the Lincoln Memorial, Kennedy Center, Einstein statue by the State Dept., Jefferson Memorial, Illinois Representative Michel's office at the Capitol. We dined at the Old Club in Alexandria, saw Banjo Dancing at the Arena Stage, which they enjoyed thoroughly. They soaked greedily in D.C. culture on their own the next few days.

School wise I went onto my first day of ConGen Rosslyn, to deal with consular work. We were all frustrated by the disorder of the FAMs (Foreign Service Manual) guidelines for consular work. I ran into my Spanish teacher Leanore, who once again said our class had been so brilliant, two levels above other pilot classes. I gave credit to my colleagues for that praise. A week later we segued into the Citizen Services portion of consular work, dealing with dead bodies of U.S. citizens or ones otherwise in trouble overseas. The FAMs were more clearcut and uptodate. And later, Immigrant Visas, role playing for all possible scenarios of consular work.

We attended Folgers Shakespeare Library on their 50th Anniversary with puppet shows and singers with Elizabethan tunes

- lovely!

On May 28 a man went on a shooting spree at IBM in Bethesda, killing two and injuring ten. Was that a sign of times to come?

In May we had farewell dinners with our Portuguese Embassy friends and other friends collected along the way. David took me to a gay bar, the Eagles, for lunch. It was a fascinating place with waiters in black leather motorcycle outfits, great soup and salad and wine. I was one of very few females in the crowd and savored the experience.

Swearing-in ceremony at Department of State, September 18, 1981.
I kiss the days of peasant secretary goodbye and become a foreign
service officer for the Department of State (technically a diplomat).

State Department's 8th floor. Ed came to witness my swearing in as
a Foreign Service Officer, September 1981

A-100's classmates at Halloween - Washington 1981 - Roman on right later became an Ambassador.

A lovely sunny afternoon in Virginia: Portugal friend Barbara, Bev, and Panama friend Bernadine.

Iris Bergold Barnes, and Leanore, Spanish Dept. director, both Hondurans. Wash, D.C. 1989

Don and Iris Barnes, Maryland, Washington tour

Dashing John Ledbetter, roughly 1975 Washington tour

Ruth (making funny face) and Ambassador Irv Cheslaw, back in
Maryland after Trinidad, 1981-2

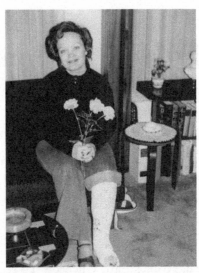

In Arlington, Virginia condo after breaking ankle(fibula) ice skating at Homesteads in Virginia on Valentine Day 1982. In midst of taking A-100 course to officerhood.

Ed, John, and Suzanne at Bill and Clara's house.

On the Way to Monterrey

We arranged to sublet our apartment to two Honduran girls. We got packed out and on May 30 left Washington in our new Chevrolet to begin a very long pilgrimage of 3570 miles.

Princeton, NJ - Wyn, Mrs. Titus, and Brooks

NYC Algonquin Hotel - Play "Crimes of the Heart" - enjoyable

Montreal, Aylmer East, Quebec - To see Aunt Irene and my cousins

Ottawa - Lunch with Ray and Margaret, formerly of Lisbon

Toronto, Battle Creek, Michigan

Chicago - Laura and Aunt Bev

Peoria - Sister Pat and lifelong friends

Springfield - Robert and Sandy and family

Cobden, Ill. - Loretta

Arkansas - Ed's mother, sister, brother and families

Dallas - Asay family (Sherrene was #2 for Miss Waco); Mary, Joe, Helen. Stayed with

Roby and Judy, Ed's niece.

San Antonio, Texas - Hilton Hotel. Turn myself into a Federal Building session with immigration officials (INS) who are the final answer to entry into the United States. We might issue visas, they decide who actually gets in. Found a helpful, cooperative group of people to show me the ropes.

In San Antonio, we also enjoyed two dinners with Ed's

childhood friend Mong and Opal, to the San Francisco Steak House, with a girl on a swing high into the rafters, and Broadway Oyster Co.

Monterrey

Monterrey

Then onto Monterrey, Nuevo Leon, Mexico, my new posting. Checked into an old gracious hotel called the Ancira. It was to become my haven, meeting Ed at lunchtime after a tortuous stint on the visa line. A trio played soothing music, we were surrounded by flowers and singing birds in cages. (They knew the music!) The legend goes that Pancho Villa had once ridden his horse into the lobby around 1910.

June 28 was my first day of work. Lots of papers, signing in. I sat in on interviews on the visa line. They projected that 3 or 4 of us should strive for around 160 applicants each per day. What a mob scene! Several days later, on my first day alone, I had 101 interviews! I gave a Durango priest a visa when he had no proof of support, a campesino family with little, a widow with a bunch of kids, all suspicious cases! And when that day ended, I felt very blah about my future there.

At a July 4 American picnic, I met Caterpillar people from my hometown Peoria, Illinois.

We moved from the hotel into our place, an upstairs duplex with the landlord, wife and son downstairs. It had a fireplace, a small balcony with a view of the Sierra Madre Mountains, and was high enough to overlook some of Monterrey's industrial pollution. The governor of Nuevo Leon lived up the hill from us, so we figured we'd have less problems with electricity and water shortages, which we heard were rampant. I soon became very fond of Maria Theresa, pregnant with their second child. When our telephone service went kaput and had been out for days, she shanghaied a lineman from his truck and brought him back to care for us. That made her a heroine in my eyes.

The Ambassador to Mexico was John Gavin, a good looking Hollywood actor. He came to Monterrey to shake hands and pose for pictures. Alba my Trinidad buddy worked in his office in Mexico City and he told me that she was a delight. I knew that. The visa line soon drove me to drink. All of us "junior officers" (I was 45 while my cohorts were in their 20's) had to serve in NIVs (nonimmigrant visas) for six months, IVs (immigrant visas) for six, and in my case I was to serve six months in Admin during my tour at the post.

I soon discovered I had an ace in the hole. I had received communications training in the Department for operating the antiquated HW-28 machine which I called the Monster. It was used for processing classified cables to and from the Department. After struggling a couple times, I learned that I had an affinity for the Monster and could quickly transcribe incoming tapes and whip up the outgoing. They soon called for me over the other fellow when classified material had to be sent from the Consul General, DEA agents and other sections of the consulate. I loved being alone in the vault with the Monster and being the master of my own fate. Gradually I was weaning further away from that dreaded visa line!

People were dying on me. D.J. wrote that her husband Paul had died of lymphoma. Reg wrote from Portugal that sweet Barbara Pie had died of an embolism after being unconscious 10 days. I went home to Ed to sob. He took the religious viewpoint for comfort, and

I took the human one for sorrow. She was 69.

In August the shock of the day was that the peso was devalued, probably 80 pesos to the $1, instead of 49 to $1. When we signed our lease, we had asked landlord Javier if he wanted U.S. dollars or pesos. He chose pesos. Now a panicked Javier came to plead, could he change his mind for dollars? I tried to plead for him, but the Mexico City finance officer would not relent. They knew a good deal when they saw one. At one point the banks became nationalized and were closed for days. We ended up borrowing from one another until we could get to our own money. America this was not! I was proud of the fortitude of the "real people", as we called them. The Mexicans at the Consulate were cheerful and fun to be around, despite the grief their government handed out to them. Many became good friends.

On a weekend trip to Mexico City, I took the diplomatic pouch. Couriers would then accompany it to Washington. We stayed with Alba and ventured to Cuernavaca for a pleasant respite. On the plane out of Mexico City homeward, we gagged at the layer of black haze covering the city. And she was training for a marathon!

In September we flew Aero Muerto, AKA Aero Mexico to Puerto Vallarta, and were a bit nervous for they were the only Mexican airline with crashes to their credit. Puerto Vallarta was our first trip to a place we would come to know rather well through the years. We visited the movie set for Night of the Iguana. Saw Richard Burton and Elizabeth Taylor houses which were connected by an over-the-street passageway. Stayed at the Bouganvilla Sheraton with a room facing the pool and sea. We were surrounded by Americans and Texans with raw accents and vowed to stay at more "real people" hotels the next time.

When our household effects were finally delivered several months after our arrival, I spent nights and weekends unloading boxes, putting guest room beds together, hanging pictures. Ed was at the ready for assistance. But now he had a new passion, creating a memoire, after a fashion. He whimsically included illustrations from Charles Shultz and whatever flew into his head as he pounded that typewriter in delight.

The September issue of Newsweek covered Grace Kelly's death on the Riviera. Ed went to Conway, Arkansas for a family reunion, his children joining from California. I went a few days later, now feeling more at home in the family with his mother, brother and sister. They are grateful to me for "taking care" of their loved one. I am grateful for all of them.

The inspectors from Washington came to call in October. Their job was to check our operations to see that they were in accordance with U.S. State Department policy. Periodically they ended up coming to the post to which you were assigned. It was my job to set up their suite of operations. I also had a brunch for them since they were a congenial threesome. My shrimp stroganoff and lemon cake were a hit. One of the inspectors Mary Ryan and I clicked. She assured me that I could shine in the Admin Cone, even at a 3 level could be Personnel Officer in Singapore or Munich, and that I should begin a dialogue with the CDO (Career Development Officer) in Washington.

During that period we awoke at home to see a herd (okay swarm) of monarch butterflies whip by the window in their flight pattern to settle in Michoacan, southern Mexico. Quite an exhilarating experience.

Ex-college roommate Margy wrote that she was setting up an ERA (Equal Rights Amendment) chapter in her county in Iowa. Feminists arise!

We had constant problems with our new Chevrolet Cavalier and made innumerable weekend trips to the border to repair or replace the rotor. The brake shoes wore down without warning, digging into the rotor. There were mysterious oil leaks and transmission fluid problems. Mr. Goodwrench was not our friend.

I moved on to Immigrant Visas in November. I sat in on Ron's interviews. He seemed downright rude to the applicants and I was embarrassed. As I began to overlook his sometimes brusque manner, we became friends. He was an ex-Catholic priest who married an ex-Catholic nun, a sweet Mexican woman, and they had two children. On the side I was still pounding out classified cables on the Monster when beckoned.

I began issuing Immigrant Visas. It had certainly less pressure than nonimmigrant visas, nor the volume. Got my first kiss on the cheek, the man was so happy to receive his visa to live in the United States. And during my term I was honored to issue an Immigrant visa to friend Lulu and husband Mar. She had earned it after many years serving the US government in Monterrey and was soon to retire to Texas.

We went to see Narciso Yepes, the great Spanish guitarist we had missed in Portugal. The experience was wonderful. I have ashamedly put my own guitar lessons aside for now.

For Thanksgiving, Chicago Laura stopped over from a Puerto Vallarta visit and we had her and our landlord family for the

Thanksgiving meal. Dini of Panama days called and will go to Amman, Jordan. We learned Reg of Lisbon died the end of November.

Had a Christmas open house, over 40 people, a success, and a bit later, a party with Mariachis, very lively. John, Ed's son arrived and the girls were wowed by this handsome creature. Then we three left for Saltillo, San Luis Potosi, Queretero, Mexico City (Anthropological Museum), a stop in San Miguel de Allende and home again. Had a turkey dinner on Christmas with some people from the Consulate. December 30 Judy and Wayne showed up with no winter clothes! They were off to Mazatlan after visiting us; it was certainly warmer than Monterrey. On New Year's Eve off we went to Monioudis' party, showing up at 11:20 pm. I tried to get high on pink champagne. Had lots of kisses from my young Visa boys.I began 1983 as Duty Officer. One U.S. citizen had died, a woman had her purse stolen with passport inside.

Took sister Judy and Wayne to Horsetail Falls (Cola al Caballa). We were out of the smog, and no one was there, making for a pleasing outing.

The DEA had to use up some old ammunition, so they took some of us for target practice at the driving range. I was handed a .38 revolver, never had a gun in my hand before and was terrified at what it could do. Yet I had nerves of steel and did very well. Only four bullets out of forty did not hit the target; most were in the critical area. It was fascinating. The DEA agent said I should take the target paper home to show Ed. I did not.

Excitement: A cable from Havana asked for assistance for one month. They asked for volunteers and Stu, Bruce and I did so. the

ConGen eliminated me; Stewart goes. When I asked later why I was discriminated against, I was told it worked down to the people they could live without. I realized it was thanks to my affinity with the Monster.

Went to Alfa Cultural Center Arte Popular of Mexico. Lovely crafts, a style show of the dresses from the various Mexican States. Lovely gowns and lovely girls.

When Ed took me to lunch at the Ancira we were treated as honored guests by the head waiter.

Mid-Feb Ed's 88 yr. old mother Woo (their nickname for her for she was always pitching it) had a blockage in her small intestine and needed surgery. We flew to Little Rock. The operation was a success. She wondered why she was to live that long. (She made it four more years.)

Ed's boyhood friend Mong and wife Opal came for a visit. Took them to Horsetail Falls and rode a burro up the hill. It was much smoother than the cart I had taken earlier. We flew to Guadalajara, rental car to Chapala, Ajijic, Jocotepec, more isolated. Paraiso Urupan, Santa Clara de Cobre, Patzcuaro, Morelia and back to Gudadalajara, flying home.

Twenty members of the Industrial War College came to call. I was responsible for doling out pesos for their dollar checks and played stewardess on their bus exchanging $100 worth of pesos. The same thing on their bus several days later, in reverse. The variety in my daily routine was sometimes surprising. We always had to cater to visiting firemen.

Ed's friend Paul Dwyer showed up and we took him to San Luis Potosi via Matehuala. Easter season, La Procesional de Silencia.

Black robed men in parade, candles upheld, Christ at Stations of the Cross, carrying huge cross, drum beat made it very moving. Dark and not much hope for good photos.

In April I made a Durango prison visit, as we had a responsibility to look out for American prisoners in our area. There were four Americans incarcerated. The director appeared very refined, very humane. It was a new facility and they seemed well cared for. At the Palacio Real Binational Center that evening they called on me as the Consul General's representative. I half read my prepared speech and Ed said I had pronounced the Spanish perfectly! It was a successful evening and I felt I had expanded my scope as an officer quite a bit in one day. (Ed had gone to Mexico City for six months after WWII in order to learn Spanish. He had been told he spoke like a native.)

At Torrejon prison the next day, two Americans were imprisoned. One had seniority of over a year, and a new one so reticent, not wanting to complain for fear of repercussion from fellow prisoners. The first one was concerned for the health of the new one. The director seemed a bit oily, giving different stories. I convinced him to move prisoner #2 to a less dangerous section of the prison.

April 18 - U.S. Embassy in Beirut was bombed: 30 dead, 3 Americans. Man drove a truck of explosives into the entrance and killed himself.

Ed returned from a trip to Arkansas and brought me a book: "Natural Superiority of Women." Right on, darling!

Visited orphanage in Monterrey with 95 children, half run by State of Nuevo Leon and half by an American couple. During our time here I made several visits, attending to urgent needs of supplies, but somehow there wasn't the interaction I had lovingly in both Panama and Portugal. It was probably due to fault on both sides.

In June Consul General Tucker wrote a glowing review on my EER (Employee Evaluation Report) written by Rivera. I read it in his presence and said "wow!" He had been very good to me. In another review for the Admin job, the CG outdid himself in his review. I kissed his hand and he was pleased, but certainly not more than I.

I was then finished with Consular, stationed in Admin, sent Bill downstairs feeling very dejected. The variety of Admin was more interesting than doling out visas. Seems they were nominating me to be Systems Manager for the new communications equipment. It would be a feather in my cap, but I wasn't sure I wanted it. The Consul General said I'd be good because I'm "responsive and responsible."

I began guitar lessons again, with Ulises Victoria, 500 peso initiation fee, 1500 pesos per month, had to go to his quarters, no individual visit to my home. For the rest of my tour, I took about 14 more weekly lessons and was pleased at the times he said "okay or fine." I felt I had made some progress but never advanced to playing "Anonymous" my favorite guitar tune.

We took the single gauged railway from Chihuahua to Los Mochis across Mexico's Grand Canyon, larger than the U.S. one in Arizona. It was a fascinating journey of stark beauty. We stayed overnight in the Copper Canyon lodge on the brim before continuing on the next day. On the train we met two girls who worked in Los Alamos and had known Barbara White's father Jessie

White. They informed me he had died several years before.

From Los Mochis on the Pacific side we had the brilliant idea to return to the states to visit Ed's children. We flew to Tijuana, took a taxi to the frontera and experienced culture shock entering California. No one would make change at the bus depot for needed lockers, would not take travelers checks or credit cards, were extremely rude to all of us. We took a bus like migrant refugees to L.A. and Ed's daughter Cathy rescued us and took us home. The next day Cathy went to work in Santa Monica, we had a good lunch with her and she delivered us to the airport. The PSA flight at Oakland made a fast turn. We were told a small plane was 500 ft. above us and 500 ft. across, too close! We were also told air controllers were switching at that time. So that reassured us?

John met us at the airport and gave us a tour of Oakland and San Francisco, then to Marin County where Suzy lived with Stan, an architect in California's Who's Who. They had a spectacular view of the Bay in Sausalito. After a lovely dinner, we were told that Suzy and Stan had plans to go to Lake Tahoe the next day. John took us to his place in Berkeley, visited Napa Valley and Calistoga the day after.

On the 4th of July we took a plane from Oakland to San Diego, taxi to border, feeling we were going home again and welcomed. We arrived in Monterrey quite weary from our journey.

Back to my tour in Admin, I had U.S. State posters framed, put into the lobby and stairwell, considerably brightening up the place.

Ed went home to his mother's 89th birthday celebration.

I went to El Salvador for Laurie's (my FSI language buddy) wedding to Greg from USIS (U.S. Information Service). It was like old homeweek. Stayed with Philicia and John from Trinidad days, also saw Bonnie Lincoln (Trinidad), Jane and Ken Bleakley from Panama, George from language class. Went to La Mer restaurant for Laurie's bachelorette party, lived it up, too much food.

On the Wedding Day I had been violently ill during the night, from both ends and my vomiting was accompanied by gunshots, since they were fighting over the hill. Rooster crowing added to the chorus. Pasty me meekly survived the wedding ceremony, held in a lovely garden. Everyone rode in armored cars. A Salvadorean hosted us at his lakeside place. The volcanic lake was clean and clear. I noted the Americans here had become close friends, unlike us uns in Monterrey.

Ed returned from Arkansas to see family and the dermatologist, a 12 day separation. We often walked up the mountain in the early morn, watching the sunrise. I had an Admin lunch for my Mexican friends with Swedish meatballs and lemon cake. Was unhappy with the gravy but they were very forgiving.

On yet another border visit for Chevy repair, we collected Mary of the Peoria Big 4 at the San Antonio airport, and took her on the river cruise. We had dinner with Ed, Mong and Opal and stayed for the first time at the Menger's Hotel, famous place where Teddy Roosevelt had organized his Rough Riders. She and I visited the Alamo and she was pleased to swim at the hotel. Back to Monterrey. At her first moment in the market she was jostled and her wallet lifted out of her purse, losing $100 worth of pesos. Since I had forewarned her, she had earlier removed her ID and traveler's checks. She had been initiated. Ed and I had been robbed four times (twice in Trinidad), once in Portugal and once in Mexico (Taxco), when we had visited from Panama. Did more exploring and shopping and sent Mary off Sept. 8.

I had been intrigued by the television series based on Colleen McCullough's novel "Thornbirds." A girl in Australia in love with a Catholic priest. That made me recall the time in Tunis when I necked with a 6th fleet chaplain!

Somehow in September I turned 46! (while I think of myself still being in the 30's). We celebrated with lunch at the Ancira. Later in the month John blew in from Baja and Tijuana. While camping with friends unknowns ripped off clothes and fishing tackle from the group. On landing here, John immediately got in touch with Carmen, whom he'd met on a bus to Monterrey some months ago.

Off we went to Real de Quatorce with John and Carmen, lunching at Las Palmas in Matehuala. It was San Francisco Day and we could not drive up to Real, so had to take a bus with the real people. The next day we drove to San Francisco, Mexico and encountered a beautiful area of pine trees, pristine loveliness. Had a picnic under a magnificent pine tree with John and Carmen billing and cooing. Clear blue skies, clean air. Back to Monterrey's smog and filth. Will be glad to leave before we develop black lung disease. John went off to San Francisco, CA with Ed dropping me at the Consulate before heading to the airport. John said: "I love my wicked stepmother!"

In October we drove to Harlington, Texas for the Confederate Air Show, where scenes of WW II were reenacted. Ed was reunited with his B-17. At the same time, yet once more, our lemon car was worked on. To El Cadillac Bar in Laredo for lunch, which was a legend in Nuevo Leon. Wonderful bolillos!

I learned that I'm to be assigned to Sao Paulo, Brazil. Will have a two month conversion course from Spanish to Portuguese, plus Admin and GSO courses. So now, officially, I have the short timer's attitude! CG Tucker told me that Sao Paulo was great, lovely food and restaurants, good climate, good exchange rate, fun and cheery people. Called John Monoudis in the States re a bounced check. His wife Irene said the only thing she missed about Monterrey was Ed and me. Called Aunt Bev in Chicago, and she's divorced from Ben. She said she had one good year and eight of misery with him.

The maid's daughter Martita told her mother I looked like a muneca (doll). Great for a 46 yr. old to hear from a 4 yr. old!

Oct. 24 - U.S. troops invade Grenada. I cannot believe they are going to screw up that lovely little island! Reagan is unbelievable! Ed sez "Nobody has a monopoly on human folly."

Oct. 27 - Ed saw the herd of monarchs coming through at home. But they had a rest stop near Monterrey. A couple days later, our landlord Javier took us to their ranch outside the city, 35 minutes away, with Ma. Theresa, and the two children. Hundreds of monarchs were perched in the trees. If there had been sun I could have won a prize in National Geographic. It was a lovely back to nature experience. We visited their cows, chickens, collected eggs and weeds.

At a Halloween party I wore a Flashdance dress and grey wig hat and danced 2 hrs. straight. "She's a Maniac!" was now my theme song.

In November we flew to Mexico City and onto Oaxaca, staying at the Victoria Hotel. Drove to Mitla, Zocalo, Merida, having lunch with my nemesis, Ed's ex-girlfriend now in charge of the Merida consulate. We met her fiancé Don and had a pleasant lunch. I was on the defensive at first but then decided to like her. I was happy that she had more wrinkles on her face than I did! Back to Oaxaca, flew to Mexico City and back to Monterrey.

There was a card party to benefit the Episcopal Church. I participated in a poker game with a Greek, Taiwanese, 2 Swiss, 1 Dutch, 1 Mexican, 1 Puerto Rican and myself. I was corny, we laughed a lot and all felt like old friends when the evening was over. Regrets for me that I met them just as I was leaving!

A new Consul General came to town. Martin Heflin, brother of famous actor Van Heflin. The staff instantly felt easy with him.

Dec - Judy of DEA gave me a going away stag (doe) party. No boys allowed, and we laughed like school girls. We had other farewell dinners. Ma. Theresa and Javier had a lovely meal for us.

Farewell at the Consulate with Larry Rivera giving the speech. I gave one in Spanish about how I'd be Mexican if born again because they are pretty, courteous, nice and loco.

I returned to say my goodbyes at the Consulate, got all teary eyed and had to dash out. I felt so close to the nationals, more so than those from the U.S. When we had an occasional happy hour after work, with music, the Americans had to have a drink to relax enough to dance. The Mexicans were out there on the first beat.

We packed our lemon of a car and headed once more to Laredo, lunched at the Cadillac Bar, onto San Antonio to stay overnight with Mong and Opal. Parked car at airport and flew to Denver where it registered -18 degrees. The skyway was frozen so we had to walk out in the snow. Had 1-1/2 hr. wait for luggage. Sister Judy and I started singing carols as tempers got hot. The Stetson clan was there at the house: Robert and Sandy, Robert Jr., Robyn, Cindy, Greg and Stephanie. Ed's son John called unexpectedly and showed up in a taxi from the airport. Some in the crowd got upset by Judy's list of rules, but twelve people enjoyed a delicious turkey dinner on Christmas Day with a caroling session afterward. The day after Christmas we took John to the airport in the morn and later Robert left alone for St. Louis.

Wayne had been nervous with all the noisy kids around (five in Robert's family) and wondered if he'd get his own bed again, as the entire family of 7 had taken over their bedroom. The ski gang of all five kids were gone all day until 5 pm. They decided to leave early the next morn, gave the bedroom back to Wayne and Judy, and slept on sleeping bags on the living room floor. Early bed for all. And off they went. Sandy called to say they arrived in St. Louis at 11 PM, two days later, with only 100 miles of bad weather from Denver. So we had a day with the four of us, got hair done, did some visiting, to Goodwills. To Skipper for dinner of clam chowder and lots of good fish.

At -15 degrees we flew nonstop to San Antonio, and were met with a pork roast by Opal. Our Christmas gift from Chevrolet was that the car now needed two rotors. How many disasters for this new car, the Chevy Cavalier? We never again bought an American car, since we also had enough problems with the new Buick Skylark in Trinidad. (When it landed in Trinidad, we received a "recall" notice from the Buick dealer. Thankfully, it regarded just seat belts.)

On New Year's Eve (Old Year's Night) we drove to Dallas. The Mizes had just pulled in from three weeks in Europe and we dumped on them as houseguests! Ed wanted to be with his niece.

I'm alarmed that Texans (even liberal Joe) had a fascination for guns. Roby gave Jennifer a .22 rifle for Christmas. Where are we headed?

Sacrifice for Choc Mu (spelling) Mayan ruins, Chichen Itza, Mexico 1983

Ambassador to Mexico John Gavin visits Monterrey Consulate 1982

A trip to Mexico City, 1982.

John Edwin Ledbetter and his father, my dear husband. Mexico City
1982

Detour to El Salvador for Laurie Tracy's wedding, 1982. George Staples and Bev.

Philicia and John Collins, hosts in San Salvador, friends from Trinidad and Tobago, 1982

An unplanned trip to California after riding single gage railway across Mexico's Grand Canyon. Ed and daughter Suzanne, 1983.

Ed and daughter Cathy in Santa Monica after that railway trip from Chihuahua to Los Mochas 1983

John in Mexico, 1983

Burro ride up to Horsetail Falls, Monterrey, Mexico 1983

Thrilled to give friends Lulu and Mar Abdu an Immigrant Visa to the
U.S. for over 16 years of government service. 1983

Judy and Wayne's house in Englewood, Colo. Christmas 1983

Leading to Brazil

We were to do our usual pilgrimage: Dallas, Conway, Ark., Illinois and D.C.

Upon arrival in Dallas, I flew alone to D.C. for my Spanish test and got the required 3/3 in order to attain tenure. Thankfully that is over! Saw some friends briefly and flew back to Little Rock. Ed was waiting for me with a cardboard sign "Hooray Miss Poopsie, Conquering Heroine, I love Her!!" You might wonder about the nickname Poopsie! In Panama we had seen the movie "Pajama Game" and in one sequence during the song "Hernando's Hideaway," a man with a candle in the dark was looking for his "Poopsie." We thought that hysterical and thereafter Ed used it often. On the trip to Illinois, a surprise, as sister Pat's eldest daughter got in touch with her and announced that Pat was now a grandmother. She and I went to visit mother and son for a touching reunion.

While I visited friends and family in Chicago, Ed took a bus to Marinette, Wisconsin to reunite with his aging uncle. Wending back to Washington the end of January, we stopped at the air force museum in Dayton and spent a wintry night in Granville, Ohio at a lovely inn. The snow began to fall in lovely clusters and we thought there would be no nicer place to be snowbound. The owner's black cat adopted us, and came into our room to visit. The next day the snow eased and we drove out on snowpacked roads, and arrived in D.C. that night, now the end of January.

We moved into a townhouse with three bedrooms and a requisite fireplace in preparation for my several months of training before Brazil. During a medical visit at State Dept. I discovered I was hosting a souvenir parasite from Mexico: a round worm which took six pills to chase away. Another fascinating facet of life in the State Department's Foreign Service! We dined with various friends from various postings, learning that Iris' ex had been named Ambassador to Nicaragua.

I discovered that there was no conversion course available from Spanish to Portuguese, so I had to struggle along with beginning Portuguese. There were several men in my class to slow me down, causing some concern.

On March 9 Ed turned 60 and friends treated him with a special cake and special meal.

We still had the problem Chevy, which acted up again to the tune of $200 plus. We learned that Chevrolet had a suit filed against them by the Justice Department and the Dept. of Transportation. What about us?

We heard that FSO Robert Homme, an acquaintance, was shot in Strasbourg, France, but wounds were superficial. Where is one safe, if not in France?

Iris and Don joined us for drinks after Don, translator extraordinaire, met with Secretary of State Kissinger, the Honduran Prime Minister and a Congressman. Later on, in his retirement, the walls of his garage sported a rogue's gallery of official photographs with Presidents (at least seven) and Kings. Don was seated between the two principals, placed slightly in the background, trying to look invisible. His parents had been missionaries in Argentina and he grew up bilingual.

In April the entire Portuguese department took the metro to the Jefferson Memorial to view the splendid cherry blossoms on a beautiful day.

On a Friday the 13th I received the required 2/2 in Portuguese. Met the entire American gang from Portugal for a lovely lunch at the Alpine restaurant.

A few days break to the San Francisco area. To Suzy's house with the spectacular view of the Bay. To gather in a group at Gaylord's elegant Indian restaurant on Ghirardelli Square. Then to dine a couple days later at a chic French restaurant in Napa Valley, and onto Stan's place in Santa Rosa. The hot tub was a new thing (at least to us), intriguing. Stan gave me a glass of champagne to sip, bubbles for the bubbles.

On Memorial Day Ed and I paid our respects at the Vietnam memorial in teeming rain. It was quite touching, despite the camera crews hovering. We met Iris for lunch and had martinis and enjoyed ourselves, drinking to our two great husbands who made us so happy, lucky us!

Before our departure to Brazil, we visited Jim O'Donnell in Cincinnati, fed corn to his menagerie of mallards and Canadian geese. Dashed to Peoria to see old friends. Peoria is fast becoming more attractive than the days of my youth. Went on the Julia Belle Swain riverboat for 1-1/2 hr. cruise with perfect weather.

We unloaded our lemon Chevy Cavalier for $3000 in Arkansas --good riddance!

After visiting again in Dallas with Ed's loving niece Judy and her orthopedic surgeon husband, crusty Mary Nelson and sweet Joyce and Ray, we were Miami bound and points southward to Sao Paulo, Brazil.

Brazil

Sao Paulo, Brazil

We landed in Sao Paulo June 10, 1984 with a torn up garment bag, though the clothes appeared to have survived. The biggest shock was seeing Sao Paulo from the air, like a gigantic graveyard with mammoth tombstone skyscrapers spread out as far as the eye could see, covered by the eery mist of pollution. The population of Sao Paulo itself was around 13 million people! The next shock was to note the grey dreary apartment they intended for us, with absolutely no charm, and a lot of oppressive sleazy furniture. We were both so depressed, ready to turn around and go home (wherever that was!) It took the Consul General 11 days before he agreed I could find my own place. In the meantime, we grew even more depressed by the dungeon.

The visa section was in some ways worse than Mexico in that you never had any relief during the day. After interviews in the morn we had boxes of passports to process for tourist agencies which took the rest of the day.

My boss, the head of nonimmigrant visas, was Leslie Rowe. She and I were both untenured officers, but she had come in mid-level and I was a junior officer (yes, at age 46!). She had been Director of the International Office at Tufts University in Boston. Her husband Ted had been the Director of the International Student Office at Boston University. Ted found a job at the Consulate in serving as the Community Liaison Officer, and also coached high school basketball at the International School.

Mid July we moved to our apartment on the 9th floor of Monsao Fragonard, Almeda Fernao Cardim, Sao Paulo. It was a modest but stately building a few miles from the Consulate. We were ecstatic to be out of the dungeon across the street from the Consulate, which was to become a transient apartment only. Ed and I eventually discovered a divine Hungarian restaurant up the street. We drew even closer together in our struggle to survive our new surroundings. We found another Chinese restaurant nearby, with very tasty moo shoo pork.

I had lunch with a tourist agency head, who spoke of the Korean mafia. They lied about their relatives in the states. And how do you possibly track down so many Kims? The high percentage stay in the U.S. when they land with tourist visas.

July 28 was our 5th legal wedding anniversary. We dined at an elegant Japanese restaurant called the Suntory. The bill was over 47,500 cruzeiros or over $50. Ed had to go home for more money. This was before credit cards became so ubiquitous.

I had been in the country less than two months when an event occurred which was to become Leslie's and my biggest headache. A Los Angeles attorney came in with a suitcase loaded with Iranian visas. The Iran/Iraq war had waged by then for two years and wealthy Iranians were doing their best to escape being summoned to fight. The next week a NYC attorney came with her bag of 15 plus for Iranian visas. We were stunned. In granting visas, the study of the case included assessing ties to the country where the application was proffered. Number 1: these Iranians had no ties to Brazil. It should have been a cut and dry case for refusing the visas. Leslie and I refused them. It became known that the head of the

Consular section had frivolously given visas in his prior countries of assignment. They knew who and where he was and had followed him to Brazil. So the attorneys got to him and even though it was not in his providence to issue visas, he would sneak down and issue them on his own in off hours. So, we would refuse and he would issue. We went to the Consul General with our complaint. He was told to stay out of visas, a directive to which he did not adhere. Leslie and I at that time were both untenured officers, fighting an uphill battle, but we were resolved as we were in the right. The situation went on for months. The boss would come down to interrupt Leslie in her duties, and Beverly often had to do the interviews.

I took a diplomatic pouch to Rio. To the Teatro Municipal for a program with half ballet and half variety show, some charming, some not worth it. We took an enchanting bonde (tram) ride with real people. The Brazilians were a lively brand of people, so enthusiastic and open!

Seasons were switched near the equator. It was cold the end of August and we had no central heating.

A straggler Iranian student fainted when I turned him down for a visa; had to usher him into my office to recuperate. We had received a cable from Hamburg stating that the boy's father feared for his life if he returned to Iran, which gave little chance of his returning, as they were immersed in the Iran/Iraq war. We were in a no win situation. We weren't finished with blockhead (my nickname for him). He gave visas to Iranians that Leslie, myself and even he had earlier turned down. He was driving us insane. I told the CG I would rather have a direct transfer than work with him. He told me not to do anything hasty. The next day blockhead said he was injured that I had gone over him to the CG. I said how could I go to him when HE was the problem? He said he'd try to do better. In the midst of all this angst, I believed I was in the early stages of menopause, with night sweats, etc. Grand!

We bought a 1984 Volkswagen Voyager. When we went to collect it VW was having a party so we were greeted with brass bands and clowns, a nice welcome!

One weekend six of us were flown by a private company jet to a chemical/mineral company's inn in the lovely countryside. We planted trees for the environment, watched the explosion of chemicals into minerals (can you tell I've lost the background material?) It was a lovely weekend. The Brazilians were very gracious people.

On September 17 I turned 47 years of age, how did that happen? There was wine and cake in the visa section. I got along very well with the Nationals (we used to call them locals in the olden days!) Jose Mario, Fabio, Frances, Edna were all visa assistants. I grabbed our live mike in the afternoon and sang Strangers in the Night with an Italian accent. They appreciated my sense of humor!

I attended a Bamberg Orchestra concert with Witold Rowicki of Poland directing. He was fascinating to watch with his subtle directing, did so much with a small flick of the finger! They presented the New World Symphony. It was so exciting to be entertained by genius. I floated home at 12 midnight.

To Embu for the weekend and ate in a lovely restaurant President Figueredo had eaten in the day before. Perfect day, lovely view of the valley, delicious food.

We have appreciated the great optimistic spirit of the Brazilian people, despite economic difficulties. Many live for Caraval, saving their money for exotic costumes. (In many cases they lean toward "lack of" over the exotic.) The Brazilians are attractive, often effervescent, and fun to be around.

Ed went home to mother and I plotted with Mrs. Rose from church regarding a cat she told me about, having been dumped on the streets by his owners when they moved. She had talked him up, saying how gorgeous he was. At her place a very motley creature awaited me. I immediately took him to the vet for wash, flea removal, clipped nails, rabies shot. I retrieved him the next day, looking 90% better. He was petrified entering our apartment, tried to hide behind the dryer. I gave him catfood and milk, he knew what to do with the litter box. I pet him, he gradually relaxed. Suki was a name that peeked out of my cranium.

Ed had taken a LAP (Lineas Areas Paraguaya) airline to the states, so on his return to Brazil I met him in Asunsion, Paraguay. At dinner that night I felt we were surrounded by Nazis that had been hiding out in Paraguay since WWII. Coming home, Ed accepted Suki better than I had expected, though he said he was first in getting the attention around the house! Suki was basically a chicken cat. The slightest movement sent him running away, but he did like music. So one night I mentioned to Ed: "Suki doesn't get frightened when we play classical music." His quick response: "Would you then call him a long-haired cat?" Funny!

Soon the Inspectors from Washington State Department came to investigate our Iranian visa problem. So we untenured officers laid it on the line vs. our boss. An inspector informed me that the boss's actions were indeed questionable.

On November election night at the Cultural Center, Reagan won in a landslide. Mondale had only D.C. and Minnesota to his credit.

Several weeks later we took an Argentine airline to Buenos Aires, staying at Hotel Colon. The Chiguin restaurant served sole florentine, absolutely delicious. I noted the Argentine men over 40 found me attractive, one attempted to follow me when I didn't have Ed's protection. We met up with Gail, also in B.A. at the time. She was the Cultural Affairs officer for USIS. Went to La Boca in the Italian section for a 5 course dinner at Spadavecchia for just $10 each. A waiter led the conga line in a noisy dance throughout the restaurant. The Italians were raucous, the waiter thought I was a Brasiliera. We watched a lovely couple doing the tango on the street.

The next day we went to the flea market and I ran into Taylor Blanton (Panama days) assigned to Ecuador but at a consular conference in B.A. I bought 30 year old German silver plated candlesticks for $100, dipped 4 times over brass. The taxi driver told us that he had a brother and two friends taken by the military in 1976, and were never seen again, joining the thousands of others as "desaparecedos?" (the disappeared). He too had been arrested but they had let him go. He said people could now say what they think in Argentina, but the economic situation was horrid. That evening I went to the Opera "War and Peace" by Prokofieff, three hours long. A $3 ticket put me in the upper upper balcony, but the charming usher moved me closer to the stage during the 2nd act. After the opera, completely exhausted, I met Ed to eat at a Chinese place.

Ed had been in Buenos Aires after WWII and remembered the

Cafe Ideal, an old elegant spot where an orchestra played as one enjoyed tea and crumpets. He found the place; one could sense the old world charm, a small balcony extended from above for the musicians. The waiter said the orchestra had stopped playing at tea time just ten years before.

Home again and Suki was happy to see us. He then had parasites and we had to tackle him to give him the meds. A bit later we went to see Bibi Ferreira, who played Edith Piaf. She sounded just like her. It was a terrific play/concert, giving vignettes from Edith's life with four husbands. She died in 1963. Ed especially loved her voice of longing and angst and I too became intrigued.

In December Luis, the jewel man, gave me a Columbian jade ring given to him by someone in Miami: my commission for Rosita Marley's order. I had connected him with her on one of his visits to Washington.

To Campo do Jordao, the Toruba Hotel, gated with a guard and a big black dog. It cost 250,000 (over $100) for room and board for two. (An aside: The poor Argentines had to suffer an alarming rise in the exchange rate. During our first six months in Brazil in 1984, the Spanish peso went from 74 to the dollar, to 205 pesos to the dollar.) There were too many courses for dinner and we ended it with a 1000 meter stroll midst enchanting moss laden trees. Ed recited poetry by his favorite Emily Dickinson. We were quite content with nature and our lives, so much in love. He had been so much comfort to me in my dealings with blockhead. He had his own project, happily at home working on his war memoire and having Suki as a companion.

The DCM from Brasilia came for individual interviews with

those in the visa section. After hearing my complaints he said it sounded as though I was more correct in making decisions than was our alleged boss. He assured me that the boss would definitely not be writing my EER (Employee Efficiency Report). I had thought about seeking a direct transfer but political officer Donna said it would not be to my advantage. That's what they expected of women. Cut and run.

Mid-December at a party, I met George Little, the language institute director, at Jim Dandridge's USIS party. It was the beginning of a long friendship between the two of us.

My sister Judy and Wayne flew in on Christmas day. We drove them the next day to the San Sebastian beach area with lunch at the Gran Portal hotel and a few days later a trip to Sierra Negra and Hotel Pavoni. Quite a scenic area, had a tasty lunch. Ed and I walked for 45 minutes, it was so peaceful. For Old Year's Night Ed and Wayne had barbershop shaves. Ed went to bed at 9:15. Judy, Wayne and I played cards til 11 pm. There was a modest buffet, free champagne and Panlidone. We welcomed in the New Year midst Sierra Negra's appealing innocence.

1985 - Brazil

Home again to Sao Paulo.

Took Judy and Wayne to Guaraja and to Casa Grande, a 5 star hotel. They'll stay four days on a honeymoon. We had heavy rain 2-1/2 hours there and 1-1/2 coming home in a pea soup fog. Next day blockhead did 3 and I did 185 interviews, such partnership! Later, Ed took J & W to Rio and I flew. Hotel de Bret gave us a suite, the best in the house with a view of the ocean. Went to a Samba show, topless, lots of color and feathers. The famed Rio robbers took our spare tire and tools. We had offered nothing more.

We celebrated January 9, Judy's 42nd birthday with breakfast and gifts. We left them in Rio and drove home. They took a bus back to Sao Paulo a few days later. Took them to Embu on Sunday. Wayne wanted to buy all that Brazil has to offer, he was a compulsive shopper. It was a complication to find a box large enough for his loot. They left January 15 and were charged $73 excess weight.

I finished with my Korean profile and the alleged boss pronounced it excellent. Leslie is pregnant and nauseous. We had a surprise baby shower which Francis and Sonia arranged.

The Inspectors' report was mealy mouth with no substance to it on blockhead's mealy mouth actions. It frosted me to no end, especially when they had voiced support for Leslie and myself. Donna of Political was pregnant at the same time as Leslie. Bossman wrote a memo, hiding behind our 27% refusal rate. Leslie lambasted him and said she'd written a memo of her own with more appropriate statistics, ergo he gave all visas to Iranians which we had refused. He had undermined all that the FSNs have been taught regarding bad cases.

Had a consular corps lunch at a French restaurant, meeting a Brit, Canadian, German, Venezuelan from the 25 in attendance. It was a pleasant two- hour diversion.

On a weekend we went to Joyce and Bert's sitio for lunch with their neighbors. Their city place is just down the street from us.

Work with "the boss" was pure torture. He found any excuse to avoid working with visas. My workhorse mentality made me work when I saw a job to be done. The CG asked me to lunch and grilled me about blockhead. I told him that he was constitutionally incapable of saying no. He remarked that he was on pins and needles waiting for the January statistics regarding Visas. I told him I was trying to balance them; I refused 100 to his 7. How nice it would be to return to the world of decent, bright and interesting bosses, to return to the days I looked forward to going to work!

Ed and I took the classified pouch to Porto Alegre and met Ed's old friend Dona Haydee Leao. Her 78 yr. old brother and wife took us to a German restaurant for a congenial evening. After WWII Ed had spent a few months wandering Brazil and had met her back then. His Portuguese was better than mine. The next day we went to Gramado via rentacar. Bought an antique bellows for $6.36. But, sez Ed, we don't have a fireplace. We will! I countered. And we did. Back to Porto Alegre and the flight home.

On Valentine's day I had some aggressive visa applicants and was aggressive right back. One cousin said "I fought for you in Vietnam, remember that!" I said "I did too, sweetheart!"

The CG had a farewell reception, as he was about to depart. Met members of the Consular Corps.

Went with Francis and Antonio Carlos to Rio. Met Laura (from Chicago) at the DeBret, who was not happy with the comedown from the Sheraton. Gail, her sister, Diane, Les and Ted, Louis and Donna and I gathered at the beach. To Club 1 for dinner, the good food and music soothed us. Back to hotel 1:30 a.m. Leslie has named it the Debris since she saw it at Carnaval time when no one did his job properly. They lived only for the action, who needs to change the sheets? Ed and I are fans, as the DeBret had always been good to us.

And on to Carnaval in Rio! For the parade we had little tables set up in front. The parade was disappointing, raucous, not nearly exhibiting the same talent as that of Trinidad. They would have about two hours wait between parading schools, making it quite boring. I called Ed in Sao Paulo to tell him that the parade was a fiasco and he said he had seen me in my yellow Rio shirt on TV.

Laura and I flew back to Sao Paulo to Ed and Suki. Laura and I gave the latter a bath and counted 30-40 fleas. He tried to claw his way out the window. Rinsed and dried him and he looked fluffy and in less anguish, so we were friends again.

Laura, Ed and I went to Iguacu Falls and stayed at the Cataratas Hotel, which faced the falls. It was filled with German, French, Brazilian, Argentine and American tourists. Ed and I walked the falls trail and they were lovely, a surprise at every turn. A few days later, back to Sao Paulo and Suki. Laura left for Chicago a few days after our return. She certainly helped Brazil's balance of payments with her shopping sprees.

In March the new CG arrived on the scene and reassured Leslie that she and I had been heroes in the Iranian crisis. He said we wouldn't be the channel for them to enter the U.S. while he was here. Finally! support for our side. Dealing with what's his name and our Iranian background, I've been generally depressed and even entertained thoughts of quitting altogether. I had lost the old zest I used to have and thought I'd never lose.

We went to St. Paul's Episcopal Church for Steven's baptism. Met older ladies who knew Reg and Barbara Windsor when they had lived in Brazil. It was touching. To Gail's for champagne and lunch. Felt friendly with the help of the bubbles.

Watched the MASH farewell and got depressed over the camaraderie they had developed during the Korean war. We didn't have that in Vietnam.

March 9 Ed's 61st birthday. The nice cotton shirt fit him and he loved the Isaac Stern record.

Now Francis is pregnant! This place is contagious!

CG sat in on some interviews, an Iranian and Korean lady. It began slowly at work, then exploded into disastrous cases, 6 evangelist musicians, a playboy bunny showing all her wares in magazines, liars whose own mothers admitted they would stay 2 years, an East Indian who was turned down in three places, one for mental retardation. Unbelievable! Phone checks proved useful. Lots of phone checks in Visas told us lots of people had left their jobs, heading for the land of milk and honey. I refused 14 in one day and there could have been more. I would never resign myself to the drudgery, especially doing the work of two. A few days later I finally gave in on a case, and the man sent me two dozen roses.

Watched "Choices of the Heart" which gave the background on the social worker who was killed with three nuns in El Salvador in 1981. It was well done, so depressing, and really caught the flavor of the place.

Ed's son John was in Peru and we hadn't heard from him, were beginning to worry, especially as we heard about the terrorist activities of the Shining Path. He and a friend were there with surfboards, seeking the Big Wave.

Lunched at Oscars with Earl, Leslie, a Canadian vice consul and Canadian INS woman from Buenos Aires. A pleasant, good time.

Dorothy Magee, the Personnel Officer in Brazilia, came and we hit it off very well. Lunched at St. Peter's Pier. Talked of her ex husband Charley and D.J. and Saigon. As I drove home, a boy thrust a dozen roses at me and said "that man back there is in love with you." I looked in the car behind and it was Fabio. I put them through the sunroof and shouted, "Que romantico!" He smiled and that was it, tender. I took Dorothy to the Italia building, 41st floor, with a NYC kind of view and then to the Cado Hotel. Delicious. We had a good time together. She's going to Paris as PER.

Boss man showed up at 10:30. I walked away and let it be all his. I was so angry I went home to report to Ed that I had called Peru and talked with John's contact who said that John and friend were wandering in Peru and John expected to come to Brazil the second week of April. It was a tremendous relief for both of us.

End of March Earl gave me an introductory tour of the General Services Operations (GSO). It seemed so organized and tidy. Then we were off to Rio. At the rentacar agency, we had to sign that we'd pay 10% of the cost if the car was stolen in Rio. Signs of the times! We met Iris and Don, now of Bethesda, Maryland, at the Lancaster Hotel. Took them to Grottomar for delicious food, and introduced them to caipirinhas, the Brazilian drink. Next day we took them to Pao de Acucar, foggy on the second level, then Club 1 for a nice dinner. Then to Tijuca waterfall, watching hand gliders land onto the beach. We left early and they stayed in our room awaiting their plane home in the evening. It was a nice reunion.

April 1. Boss was upstairs so the NIV unit gang and I were more efficient, as usual. Ed's son John and friend Rob with backpacks and surfboards blew in from Peru, earlier than expected. They had tales of close calls with the Shining Path terrorists.

President-elect Tancredo was dying. He was very popular with the populace, an honest man. He was the first civilian president elected in 21 years since they had a military coup in 1964. When Rob read his stack of love mail, he planned to pay extra and go home early. Took them to La Trainera restaurant for a feast and they loved it. Rob is 25 and fell in love two weeks before they left California. John is 30 and in good shape. They had a terrific experience, got some good waves and Machu Pichu was wonderful. Ed was happy to have his boy home with him for six weeks.

I was duty officer as it was up in the air whether Tancredo would be sent to the States for medical treatment. Took Rob to the airport to join his love in the U.S. She cost him the price of what he sold his surfboard for in Peru.

Saw movie "Passage to India." Absolutely beautiful, aroused a curiosity in the country I never had before. The scenery was spectacular, fine acting, awestruck, better than the "Jewel in the

Crown."

Took John to our NYC view at Edif. Italia. They rejected him in thongs and we went to buy shoes and return for a nyeh nyeh. The next day he took a bus to Rio to visit a friend he'd met at Berkeley.

Had a happy hour which everyone needed.

We left for Rio. On the map we spotted what we thought of as a short cut. It was smooth going for awhile, but then large boulders appeared in the road, it began raining and there was no turning around. We plunged forward, dodging craters in the road. I think we prayed a lot. When we got down below, no one believed that we had actually traversed that road. Stayed overnight and thought the worst was over. The next day as we went along the ocean road, it suddenly was not there. We stopped and at the dropoff was the ocean. Turnaround, then a flat tire, which the two of us managed to change. This is not my imagination! My diary verifies our adventure. Along the road to Rio we bought some equipment to wash our mud -caked car under a waterfall. We finally made it to our DeBret Hotel in Rio; Suite 1102 was quite welcome!

The next day we collected John from his friend's house and went to Corcovado and Pao de Acucar, and headed north. In lovely Petropolis we went to the old hotel Quetandinha where FDR had signed a Treaty of Friendship with Latin American countries during WWII. It was a huge sprawling place like the Homestead back in Virginia. At the Hotel Margarida on a hill we checked in and had a huge chalet for the three of us. Went through Dom Pedra's Palace before settling in.

To Ouro Preto, a colonial town of churches, rain. Stayed at Casa do Ouvidor, nice. We were hounded by little kids who wanted to be our tour guides. Then the long drive to Brasilia, Brazil's capital. Checked in at the Bristol Hotel. The morning papers reported "Nao ha esperanca for Pres. Tancredo Neves" (no hope). I went for lunch with Dorothy from the Embassy to a nice French restaurant with delicious fish, and some laughs. At the airport I trapped Ambassador Ascensio so I could say hello to him from Iris. He was pleased and said he'd seen Harry recently and he had gotten fatter. Ascensio should talk!

We flew from Brasilia to Salvador, leaving the car at the airport, with Tancredo still hanging on. Our 3 star hotel more resembled a surf shack. There was no air conditioning but a strong breeze from the Atlantic. Went inside three lovely colonial churches, gilt and friendly flowers. The treat of the day was dining at Ondina restaurant with heavenly "peixe maqueta" Bahian style with coconut milk and hot sauce. It was a meal well worth all the calories. A wild and windy storm blew up like a typhoon. Rain poured through the bathroom windows, the roof leaked steadily at the foot of the bed. President-elect Tancredo Neves died that night and many places were closed to mourn. They gave us a dry room when I screamed for one. We drove in a rental car north to the ex-capital of Bahia Cacholira, peaceful by the river and took a ferry with the car back to Salvador. We decided after the last scene to spoil ourselves at a 4 star Grand Hotel Bahia on the bay. And in that 4 star we endured the Chinese torture treatment with the rain dripping on the A/C above our heads.

Took Varig to Brasilia and the VW dealer to collect our car. They had replaced the muffler which had been damaged on the Cunha-Parati road disaster earlier. We were glad to be back in our own car. On the road again, now headed south. Viewed an extinct volcano, stopped at a pousada at Rio Quente. John dashed off to the thermal pools. An older woman had her clutches on him, asking for swimming lessons. Several pools, water falls and babbling brooks. Later I saw Ed outside viewing the stars. At 6 am I went with him to the thermal pools and jumped in with my cotton dress. Others were there taking the cure. One woman crossed herself as she leapt in. I loaded up my handbag with pears and cheese and off we went, headed for home to Sao Paulo, arriving at 8:30 p.m. Pearl had babysat Suki while we were gone.

The funeral for President Tancredo Neves, an honest man, was the largest in Brazil's history. More than two million people viewed the coffin in its procession. He died just three months after his election. The Brazilian people truly grieved.

Stopped by the Consulate to hear of visa problems while I was gone. Put me in a depressed state. I wanted to walk away from it all, leave the Foreign Service rat race. Such a thankless job officerhood had been!

To a feijoada at Dona Zila's. They are customarily held on Saturdays, using all the leftovers from the week. But what tasty leftovers, and always washed down with caipirinhas! Earl, whom I will replace when I move to Admin, had his mother there, a Honduran. She had lived next door to Iris and her two sisters in their childhood.

I was sick most of the next day. Then to see "Killing Fields" about Cambodia, our bombings there, and the Khmer Rouge killings. It was a true story of a NY Times journalist and his assistant. So tragic. Millions died.

Over the weekend we took Suki to George's beachhouse in Guaraja. There was no surf for John, it was calm and lovely. Suki was terrorized. Bahian shrimp was delicious, John surfed a day later, Suki got comfortable in his new surroundings. Next day home again in fog.

On a trip to Embu on a beautiful day, I bought a cedar? sofa table for $145. At Otapecerica da Serra we had wonderful sole with spinach, had an afternoon visit at Joyce and Bert's sitio. A few days later John and Ed went to Ubatuba and found perfect surf. Spent the night. When they returned we went to Suntory restaurant where John devoured eel and sushi and it was catastrophically expensive. Later a treat at La Trainera for great sole singapore and to Earl's farewell party. I will replace him as General Services Officer, GSO for short.

On Mother's Day John gave me a homemade card with a tender verse which brought tears to my eyes. To Gail's brunch. Leslie and Ted's kids clung to John. Then we took him to the airport. I told him he was the only one of our guests, no matter how long he stayed, always left too early. The girls: Liliana, Pearl, Sonia, Giselle are sorry John had left. I told them they had their chances and blew it.

A letter from Canadian cousin Irene said that Aunt Irene had died April 14 of kidney failure and brain tumor, about 80 years old, so sad. She was my father's sister. I had seen her just four times in her lifetime. She was a sweet, generous soul.

On May 17 a horrid disaster occurred just outside the Consulate building. A cement truck lost its brakes and careened down the hill hitting and causing to crash 21 cars. Two people were killed. A taxi driver was crushed under the cement truck right outside the gate of the Consulate, plus another man up the hill was thrown out of his car. It stunned everyone. Each one of us could have been out there during lunchtime. Christina had been pinned against a wall as the truck headed toward her.

I went with Donna to pick up James Ferrer, my old boss from Lisbon, taking him to the airport. On an official visit, he stayed just a few days and she had kept him occupied. I got to visit with him in the VIP lounge for a drink. The CG was also there headed for D.C. When he asked JF why he didn't spend the weekend, he said the family (meaning Dolores) would have killed him. I gave him a hug goodbye.

My dreadful nemesis had said I was to fill in on visa work even as I served as GSO. I have been fighting that. He talks out of both sides of his mouth pretending to be supportive of me. I feel I'm in my own fantasy where my alleged friend and enemy are the same person.

I listened to my childhood friend Jackie's tape. She had MS and was then blind. Her tapes always cheered me. I felt ashamed that I had eyes but did not see and she had such a sensitivity it was amazing. She saw so much beauty in her world of blindness, hope in a handicapped body. She even made me nostalgic for Peoria, and that in itself was a great feat. She had attended our high school reunion and told me what everyone was up to in great detail, while my other friends remarked only that they had a good time.

Another tortuous day in visas. Blockhead was up to his old tricks of killing time, showing up only occasionally. I took Pearl and Fabio to lunch and said it was only right that the three workers in the section dine together. A day later Ed and I dined at Chaplin's. He'd been so supportive, this year especially. I would have gone crazy without him.

Ambassador Ascensio had a book signing "Our Man is Inside." He was a victim of a terrorist takeover while attending a soiree. It lasted several days. He and his wife were pleasant people. Later on Ann Patchett's "Bel Canto" novel was based on that event.

Finally, it was my first day to turn myself into Admin. I was terrified that the visa unit would find me and drag me down there. I hid out as much as I could. Leslie called to say there were 40 people down in visas at 8:50 a.m. and the boss hadn't shown up yet. She was currently working in Citizen Services and he was in charge downstairs. I had lunch with her and Nancy and all three of us agreed we had survived a tough year. Leslie rued the day she asked for an extension and would have to bear him for another year. I began to relax in the afternoon, but I still looked around the corner. I didn't want to know how they were doing. I called Dorothy in Brazilia and she said she had worked hard to support me and my rights in Admin, that the DCM was in on it as well. She told me she wanted to spend her last nite in Brazil in Sao Paulo and go out to dinner with me.

On my new assignment, I'm called the General Services Officer. I manage the maintenance and supply problems of the Consulate and its 35 apartments housed by Americans. I buy whole households of furniture and charge it to Uncle Sam, have around 40 people working for me. As I said when I switched over to this job, "I would rather be the Consulate's housekeeper than the nation's gatekeeper."

It had been an interesting posting. As far as Americans at the Consulate were concerned, they were replenishing the earth. We have had five babies born to Americans, all from matched parents, natural births. Then the adopted cases add up: 3 to single parents, and 2 to a married couple (my friend Leslie and her husband Ted). That is an astounding story. They had intended to adopt in Brazil, but while they made preparation, she became pregnant, and when they went for the adoption of a girl 4, the social worker informed them of the existence of a brother, 5. To make a long story short, a childless couple had 3 children within 5 months! Their family upon arrival had included just two cats.

Several days into my Admin tour, bones were discovered, alleged to be those of Josef Mengele, the famed Nazi, according to the newspaper. The "Angel of Death" had been the Physician in charge at Auschwitz. He selected those who would be gassed immediately, who were worked to death, who would be guinea pigs for experiments. He was particularly fascinated by twins. Admin chief Arnold, the CG and USIS all went to meet the bones. In the meantime, Ed was off to the airport to collect Father Aires and Jorge Lagido from Lisbon.

Mid June I attended a curry luncheon given by the Canadian Vice Consul for a British Vice Consul in the Trade Commission. It was nice to have a group composed of other than all Americans.

John called to say his mother was in London with cancer of the mouth and didn't have much longer to live. Suzanne later called Ed when she had joined her mother in London. He then decided to support and join her there as well, $2100 worth!

I had a half-hour appointment with the CG and kept wondering when the boon would be lowered, but he was Mr. Congeniality, what could he help me with, etc. It was almost a suggestion that I could go over Arnold's head. I didn't believe there was much regard between the two of them.

After Ed left for London, I flew off to Rio for the weekend to meet Leslie and her sister Nancy . We ranted about our grievances with the head of the consular section. Despite the subject matter, we had a good time. To Mediterraneo for dinner, always pleasant. Pearl babysat Suki. We lunched grandly at the Hotel Copacabana Palace by the pool. Took Nancy on a wild bus and taxi ride with a bonde ride up to Sta. Theresa. She reneged after that on the cable car to Pao de Acucar. Went to a piano bar for batida de coco. To Corcovado and to the Sunday artist fair. A good weekend with fun people.

The latter part of February I flew to Brazilia for several appointments with Embassy people. Stayed with Dorothy, went out to dinner. She was always fun to be around, we were solemates. Ed returned from London, his ex-wife Estelle was still hanging on, and was shipped off to a California hospital.

Leslie and Ted treated us at an elegant Indian restaurant called Govinda, with delicious food.

End of June I pitched at a softball game: the Consulate vs. the Marines. Did not mention the winner, so it most likely wasn't us!

July found me in a hunt for new warehouse facilities. The current one was archaic and dirty.

Les was fretting over having just a possible two week leave when she had her baby, since Donna bragged that was all she needed. The two officers are due at the same time.

I picked up Dorothy at the airport here, a stopover on her way to Paris. She, Ed and I dined at C'adero and later returned her to the airport farewell.

I blackmailed the consular boss and said I wouldn't sit in for his vacation unless he wrote position descriptions for Fabio and Pearl so they could get promoted. He finished them at 4:30 p.m. that same day.

We had our first auction at the warehouse with a very good auctioneer. Made in the neighborhood of 170 million cruzeiros (divide by 8000). Took the gang to lunch at a churrasqueria for 310,000.

Talk of starting a cooking group with Vigdis, Heather, myself, Lee and Fred. We named it SPCA (Sao Paulo Culinary Assn.)

To hotel to greet CODEL, Congressman Alexander from Arkansas, 13 people, 7 crew on AF plane that carries 80. Also Berkman from Dept. of Energy.

Ed had been active volunteering for the Cheshire Home. To an Italian restaurant with a professional pianist playing the guitar. He played Anonymous for me, and we spoke of the difficult financial times in Brazil.

We had our first SPCA meeting at Fred's place. He made okay Chinese food, but it was too long between courses.

On August 24 - 7:50 a.m. Leslie called to say her water broke. I went to collect the kids and brought them home. Paulo and Danielle set out to search through everything in the apartment. Paulo was five, Danielle, four. Ed took them one by one to his publisher, AKA as the xerox place. That wore him out. We decided we were too old to be parents, we could just rent a kid. Someone else took over for lunch. Leslie delivered Jacqueline Dieffenbacher Rowe in the evening. When we went to see Leslie the next day, Luis was there and announced that Donna too had delivered last nite, a son. What a shocking coincidence! I planned the announcement for the State Magazine, two FSOs delivering on the same day! Not to be outdone for attention, Arnold called to say that ex-boss man would probably be medevac'd. (Sent back to the States.) Such a self-centered hysterical wimp! Unbelievable!

On August 26 I met with the CG. I was now Acting head of the Visa Section, we must all pull together, wear two hats, etc. Dennis and I did the visas, along with our ever efficient staff of nationals.

Aug 27 -To the Maksoud Plaza for Florida Governor Graham's delegation reception. Ex-boss man went off to Medevac land in the U.S., cause unknown.

Staff help arrived from Brasilia to cover me for my planned vacation to Tunisia, Spain and Portugal. On September 1 Ed and I took a DC-10 to Madrid on Iberia Airlines. Upon arrival Iberia provided a free 5 star Hotel Eurobuilding through their Madrid amigo program. We went to a flamenco place that evening "Corral de la Pacheca." The next day we flew to Barcelona and onto Tunis on a DC-9. I had chosen the Amilcar which had been elegant 20 years earlier. We got a dumpy room with a nice view. Dined at Les Dunes for fish and beef medallions, which cost $30, stateside prices.

Soon, a visit to the Embassy. Saw several who recognized me. Larbi, the driver told me that Dorothy Wahlgamott had died in 1982. Sidi Bou Said was now loaded with tourist stands, the tea house I'd known was a tourist trap. I got a boot clamped to the tire of our rental car! Progress had hit Tunis! Ed walked away in disgust. I then had to find the police station, pay the ticket, find someone to remove the boot. I picked up Ed walking downhill. Later, I found a favorite restaurant Chez Slah and Slah looked exactly the same to me. I had calamar doree, delicious, and the owner looked good at 63. Had the sole, wonderful flan. He bought our wine. I was comforted that some things stayed the same. Ed and I were friends again after a wearying day.

I took him to the U.S. cemetery outside Tunis. It had always been a restful spot with rare green grass back in the olden days. And it was still that way, very peaceful, with lush green grass. Onto the Carthage ruins and wouldn't you know they were rebuilding them, at least putting columns upright that were lying down 20 years before. I found another hotel Megara, which was charming and 1/3 the price of Amilcar, and had a private balcony. Ed was patient in the souk as I purchased a rug, silver hand of Fatima, puppets and a djellebah for him. Back to the Embassy and Hedi, my old pal, showed up. A Tunisian doctor had screwed up his cataract surgery and he had been blind for two years, but was getting his sight back. He had finally married a Tunisian after his two Belgium women. In the evening, Hedi, Sonad, and their boys 7-1/2 and 4 years came to the hotel for drinks, and we went to Sidi Bou Said for dinner. Hedi had been born in 1923, one year before Ed. He reminded me that Tunisia in WWII had six months of fighting on its soil. The next day Hedi and family sent us off at the airport. It was great to see him once more.

We flew back to Madrid, our trusted Hotel de Vega, and also Margaret Higgins' apartment. Received the gossip from Monterrey. Hal and Rosita were there for a conference and he treated us at Club 31 for lunch. With all the goodies we ordered, the bill must have been equal to the national debt. We all flew to Sevilla to the Alfonso XIII, a five star hotel, done in Moorish style with lovely fountain and patio. We had lunch at poolside with the Marleys. Had a city tour the next day and went to a flamenco place in the evening. To La Dorada for a fantastic meal of clams, smelt, mussels, fish, all delightfully tender. That one was our treat.

Then we boarded a bus for Portugal. On the way to Beja, Ed noted a sign for a pousada (state-owned inn). We got off, taking a chance they'd have a vacancy. And they did. The balcony overlooked groves of olive trees, an endless stretch of the Alentejo plains, no telephone poles or other signs of humanity in sight. We devoured alentejo gazpacho, pork chops, lemon tart. The waitress looked like my idea of a commie, stiff and proper with sensible shoes, black skirt and mustache. The Alentejo area was the last stronghold of the communists after their brief six-month revolution.

The next day we made complicated negotiations for a rental car. The man Mr. Soares drove a Renault 5 to us from Beja and we had to return him back to Beja . He told us that Prime Minister Soares would dine in Beja that day. He'd be the next President of Portugal, but was no relative. We then headed for Portimao on the ocean in the Algarve region. Suddenly it had become crowded and looked more like the Costa del Sol in Spain. Waiters then spoke English, who can you trust? The Delfin, 4 star, was huge, but had only a suite free for $105. We took it. Ed was about ready to become disgruntled, so it was in the nick of time. There was an odd assortment of people, mostly Americans. Where were the good old days when we were the only ones?

Then, heading north to Setubal we got the Pousada Castle's last room, a monk's cell. It turned out to be fine as we were sound proofed from a noisy wedding party on the terrace. Dined on amejois cataplan, quite good. Ed had goat. As I looked out on the terrace at the wedding party, a goat carcass with head was staring mournfully as they picked his body clean.

The next day we stopped at the Pousada Palmela, which was only six years old and sterile. Well, Ed and Thomas Wolf both said you can't go home again. I was very disappointed in that one. We even had a rude waiter at the bar, in my beloved Portugal!

On September 17 we arrived in Lisbon. Ed called Jorge and made plans to meet him. I felt deserted on my 48th birthday! We had a blowup and he stormed out. I jumped into the mini and took a meandering route to Alges, where we had lived 1976-78, over to Belem and our favorite Caldero restaurant. I had a wonderful birthday lunch of amejois espanol, casal mendes wine, peasant bread, and a dessert mixture, all perfect. I figured we came into this world alone and would die alone, so I'd better figure out how to enjoy myself alone. After my return at 4 p.m. Ed went out for 3-foot gladiolas and we used the bidet for a vase. We declared a truce and were friends by the time we went to bed.

The next day we met Jorge and the three of us went to Sintra. The weather was lovely and we had a good lunch at something dos Arcos; sole for Ed and myself. Went to the Capucho monastery with tiny cells in the Sintra woodland, enjoyed it. We drove to Pena Palace but did not go in. I loved the ancient stone walls, moss, sunlight in the trees. Later, back in town, we went to the British cemetery to cry over Barbara Windsor's headstone 1910-1982. Back home to make love, a celebration of life. Later in the evening we three went to Sr. Vinho fado. Jorge insisted on waiting for Maria da Fe who came on after midnight. She had a good strong voice and I loved it. Ed had never been an afficionado but had to be polite. Home at 1:30 a.m.

I loved so much that Lisbon hasn't changed all that much in seven years, you could still find the old places. Sameness is comforting.

9/20 - Ed woke me to say that 1/3 of Mexico City had been destroyed in an earthquake. The early reports say that Avenida Reforma was greatly affected. I wondered about the Embassy.

I lunched with Carmen, my Embassy pal, and we had a good time. She said I had been very popular here and was considered to be "one of us." I was quite touched. Wanda, Jorge's girlfriend, had us for dinner. I received an Amalia Rodriguez record from them for my birthday. I recalled attending a function where Amalia sang the first week I landed in Lisbon back in 1976. It was at an economic conference held at the Sao Jorge Castle in the Al Fama. She had come up to me and sang and wanted me to sing along, but I had no idea how to do it. Only later did I learn how famous a fado singer she was.

Ed and I lunched at a favorite seaside restaurant called the Saisa. Had a tasty veal cutlet, mussels as an appetizer, a gorgeous day, and the waiter even remembered us from before! In the eve we visited our British friends Norm and Patricia Wilson in Cascais, a suburb of Lisbon. Norm had had a heart bypass in January. Pat was very interested in Brazil. I felt no loyalty to my job or Brazil when my soul was home in Portugal.

We wandered the Al Fama, the old section of Lisbon with the

narrow streets and laundry stretching across the pathway. In the late afternoon we drove out to the westernmost part of Europe and found Carmen and Marinho's weekend house at Rochal Cabo da Roca. Marinho was in his lavish rose garden, had a fantastic variety. He called out the names of each of them for us, for which he was justly proud. The adorable house is in 4 layers, an eagle nest midst the mountains and lighthouse. One could climb to the rooftop and survey the kingdom beyond: old windmills and monasteries, isolated homes in the vales, and to your left, the Atlantic ocean. Carmen wanted us to experience the place, even before electricity was connected. They left us to return to Lisbon. We lit candles, sat before the fire and savored the experience. The place had a wonderful connection with nature. It looked lovely in the morning, first the sun, then fog enveloped us, and it cleared again. It could be a candidate for House Beautiful with the profusion of plants and flowers.

Before we left Lisbon, I picked up Carmen one day and we went to Albefeira and the Crystal factory. I bought Acores glasses, Evora highball glasses. It had a leaded crystal reputation almost equal to the famed Waterford of Ireland. We lunched in Nazare, took a lot of pictures, having a thoroughly enjoyable day. We noted people gathering grapes for harvest and bringing them down the hill in an overloaded truck.

Back to the Embassy, I saw more nationals I knew from before. It was great to see the drivers from the olden days. I ran into Jose Tenreiro of the ECON section, now retired, at the airport as we were leaving. Splendipity! He had seen his brother off. We hugged and exchanged greetings and off Ed and I flew to Madrid.

To our hotel Lope de Vega overnight. After check out we moved our luggage to Margaret Higgins' apartment and hung out there. I discovered Ed's sports jacket was missing, called the hotel and it was there. I took two subways each way to recover it. I was weary upon return, and Ed walked in two minutes later! Then Varig had screwed up and didn't have Ed's name on the passenger list. The flight was full and we had to wait until the last minute to get cleared for the flight. Made both of us quite edgy! What a miserable night it was! The flight left Madrid at 1 a.m., which meant they served dinner at 3 and movie at 5 a.m. We were squashed in the middle seats when we could have made our seat selection early if they hadn't screwed up. It was a long night to Rio, stayed on the same plane to Sao Paulo. We hid out all day. Suki was home and was so grateful to see us he almost flung his little paws around our necks. Slept 11 hours. Suki had been unbelievably affectionate, wouldn't let us out of his sight. It was nice to have an appreciative child.

It was also nice to be liked by my staff, lots of welcome back kisses. It was Secretary Day so I took Vera and Cristina to lunch. My GSO work included signing leases, getting pictures framed, doing inventories at Embassy personnel's houses, estimates at furniture places. So much less stress than visas and you know who. Leslie's mother was here, friendly. We went off to the fado "April in Portugal."

We had lunch at the Jockey Club. They had older male runners to place our bets. I picked a horse at random to win and he came out second. Ed bet to place and won, all a lot of fun, and ate delicious shrimp on rice.

Ed and I had a disagreement. Soon after I announced that I

could only find happiness if he took me for a ride in the country, and it was to Itu. He agreed. Driving out of the city I cheered up considerably. We had wonderful gnocci at a humble Italian place, bought an oratorio (mini altar, spirit house) and paid one million (or $100). The Brazilians use it in which to place religious objects. On the way home we bought a new fruit "nespera" and it was delicious.

Saw "Paris, Texas" with Gail, a powerful movie, with lovely scenery around Big Ben National Park. It was directed by a German with a French actress.

Off to the beach with Ed, Suki and Sarah Rowe; walked the beach with her. She was very talkative and sweet, said "cripes" like my mother used to say. For dinner we braved the gales to go out. Had a good meal of salad, spaghetti, shrimp bahiana, strudle, splitting it all. Sarah and I played gin rummy. We learned that she and Ed had been in Miami the same time at the end of WWII. Gail was at the beach in another place and had gone stir crazy for three nights, thereby welcoming our presence. Sarah almost got in trouble way out in the current; a lifeguard came to warn her. Later we accidentally found the best restaurant in town called Il Faro. Delicious crab, shrimp baiana, sole. It was a lovely day. Ed bought Sarah a beach mat gift, then Gail got her one in a different color. Gail, Sarah and I had wine at Gail's and then to a chicken place. I especially liked Gail today.

Sarah and Ed had an early morning dip. Later she and I played cards. A lovely day, we took off before 10 a.m. Suki was glad to be home again.

Learned that Aunt Melba died after 3 weeks in the hospital with cancer. We have missed a lot by not enduring the daily trials with our relatives, not really knowing them. She was the wife of Mom's brother Ted and made the best Finn bread.

October. State Department and other U.S. agency personnel were sent pins to wear with purple to remember all the victims of world terrorism. "Let Peace Take Root" (Fat chance!)

To Schenker to sign our contract for the new warehouse facility I had searched for. It was night and day from the old seedy place to new and clean. After work I went to tea at Francis' place, being the only American of eighteen women. She had stuffed crab and various desserts. It was show and tell for her baby's room, with everything done to perfection.

To Dona Zila's feijoida. I was half zonked by the time we ate her delicious food.

Ted and I will update the Post Report. Arnold agreed eagerly. Fred Sackett had to say disparaging things about Ginny, Ed's ex-girlfriend. An opportunist. Maybe this is the time to say that the Brazilians add a "gee" sound after the initial "d". So we had Edgie, Tedgie, and Fredgie!

On Halloween I was offered the GSO job in Rio. No thanks I said. Frances had her no-name, no-father kid. Sonja said both mother and daughter were beautiful, and Antonio Carlos was excited as well. Ed and the CG were both Julius Caesar at a party. Ed was superior, which deflated the CG's ego, who spoke hardly a word all night. A few days later the Trezises had a big event, and were the ultimate hosts. The CG joined my table and would not have if Ed had been there. So we listened to him. Others remarked to me on how great a Caesar Ed had been.

Bernadine of Panama fame has Nizar as a Jordanian boyfriend.

We are happy for her.

My first day of Acting Admin Officer. I handled things quietly, efficiently. Arnold always stirred up a hornet's nest around him.

November. Ed and I worked the Christmas booth at the church bazaar, a first. In the eve to the Marine House feijoada. When we walked in Dennis remarked : "Here come the beautiful people." Nice.

To Atibaia, a clean, wholesome town. I bought an arreojlos rug made in Portugal for $76, much cheaper than it would have been in Sao Paulo.

The staff meetings seem built around puns. We women are usually above it all. The CG loves to have a captive audience, but he has a certain charm.

Ed and I are so content in our love for each other, we don't need the outside world. But somehow it is always leaking in.

I got sick with flu-like symptoms, stayed home in a ragged housecoat, dripping and sniffling. At the end of the day in walked Ed with a handsome Hollywood actor. He's here to star in a Brazilian production as Halley of Halley's Comet. Later as I healed and became more presentable, I squired around Kale and his actor friend Charles, a good looking black, lively and funny, who would play his sidekick in the movie. We became quite compatible and were always laughing. The girls in the office were thrilled when the two of them visited me, those handsome Hollywood actors. In 1986 Halley's Comet was due to come around again, 75 years after its last visit, alleged to be seen by the naked eye. So it was a topic of conversation.

Leslie and I lamented having "no brains" to guide us as

untenured officers. We had grown close in our common struggle against the nonpolicies of our supervisor. Where were the bosses of yesteryear? I wondered. She had had no history in foreign service in order to bring forth better examples.

Ed went off to Arkansas for Thanksgiving.

The Annual Marine Corps Ball had always been a main event in our lives overseas. I went alone that year and made up a dance card. I made certain to collect on those who signed it: Ted, Dennis, Dandridge, Art T, Vera's fiance, Randy, Luis Flores, Arnold, Dachi and others! I felt like the belle of the ball! We officers took Marine Guard Duty for them so they could enjoy their big event. My shift was from 3-4 a.m, so I went wearily to bed by 4:30 a.m. Suki was not amused. He yelled a lot for me to wake up to tend to him. Eventually he gave up and joined me. I talked with Ed and he still loved me. His mother told me that she was going to kidnap him.

Thanksgiving Day. Gail delivered a 27 pound turkey in her son Stevie's stroller to cook in my oven at 9:30 a.m. She lived a block up the street. I wondered how it would work out with Hollywood meeting the diplomats. I picked up Kale and Charles. They were both instant hits with my gang. Gail was an animated charmer. George Little was enamored as well. Visits to my house to check the turkey. Leslie and her brood were two hours late. Producer Sara DuVall came later, all in time for the feast. It was a magically fun time, a real love fest which will go down in memory. Donna and Luis, the Dickmeyers, Rowe/Dieffenbachers, George, myself and the two actors. Hugged and kissed and they were grateful for the dinner. Ed called, stuffed, and had his own good day.

I worried with Jerry Rosenblum (IRS) over his kidney stone.

With the help of Adelle Davis, I prescribed mega doses of Vit C plus B6 and a lot of exercise. He thanked me for my concern, was to have surgery on Monday, which his wife fretted about. I took Kale and Charles to the airport for Rio. They would stay a few days at the Director's apartment. Charles is 29 and Kale 36, full of life.

December 1. It was christening day for godchild Jacqueline, with Ed becoming a godfather by proxy. Gail, with her Stephen was doing the same, feeling a bit of a hypocrite in her lack of spirituality.

The first news of the next day was that Jerry had walked up and down a bunch of stairs during the weekend, followed my prescription, and in the shower passed the kidney stone the very morning of the planned surgery. They were ecstatic, cancelled the surgery, and his wife gave me all the credit.

Enjoyed the Brazilian Chamber orchestra at Maksoud Plaza.

I had dinner at Tatini's with Kale and Charles. They had the hotel and restaurant in an uproar because they were actors from California. A fun eve. Kale told me that actor Christopher Jones had died of pills and liquor. I had met him in Peoria twenty years before at his Irish cousin's wedding and we had hit it off. He told me he was the only Christopher Jones in the NYC phonebook, and to look him up if I ever came to town. I am sorry I never did.

Gail and I went to the English Cultural Center's version of "Hair." It started out sluggish but energized quite a bit and was generally enlightening.

Dec. 6 - The Award ceremony I was in charge of went well.

Magda Rosenblum brought me an African violet and homemade wheat bread, thanking me for healing her husband. Sweet.

The next day I oversaw the Foreign Service Officers written

exam. Six had been scheduled and three showed up.

Kale took me live Christmas tree shopping. We sang kookie Christmas songs there and back, fun. Charles came to visit on his way to a movie.

I had the idea of a trip to the Amazon, but it was a no-go, as it filled up fast.

We had a meeting of the SPCA at Lee's. Great cucumber soup, too strong a fish salad, beef bourguignonne fine, dessert was divine, pears in triple sec.

Gail and I, Kale and Charles dined at a Japanese restaurant. We had a great deal of fun and were hysterical in the car coming back home. They are impatiently awaiting the go ahead on the Halley Comet filming. Staging is set, costumes etc., but the operation seems to have financial problems.

Donna, Ted Kennedy's advance man Greg and I lunched at Papa del Rei. I took notes on Administrative needs. Kennedy will come January 9 with his sisters and two children; it is not a Codel.

Took Kale and Charles to Praca Republica and they went crazy shopping, were there three hours. To a Portuguese place for lunch.

Ed returned. It took forever in construction traffic to the airport and back again. We came home with short tempers.

Dec. 20. Farewell to Kale and Charles, returning to California. At the airport Charles filled in the departure paper's "occupation" blank with STAR. I told him, no in Portuguese it was ESTRELLA. He filled that in, and we had a laugh over that. The movie project had gone broke. The Director had overextended himself in setting it up: staging and costumes bought, then it collapsed. They had even talked of putting me in as Halley's mother! But I would have had to have had him at age 13!

Dec. 24 I gave perfume and liquor to my staff. Got hair and nails done. Candlelight service at church. Gail's dinner with George and Irene, great shrimp and French champagne.

Christmas to Leslie and Ted's. Ten adults and four children. Gail came back to tell Ed and me how we were a wonderful couple and she loved us very much. Was she in her cups? The spirit of the day shone brightly and the food was delicious.

Dec. 28. We took Suki and slept over at Munoz's house. They were gone for the holidays. They had A/C in the girls' room, it was very hot outside. So we took advantage of the A/C.

Dec. 30. Wine and cheese at the POL section.

Dec. 31 I went with Mike Delaney to Viracopos to deliver the classified pouch and pick one up. To the El Dorado with Ed for a pork dinner with scalloped potatoes. I took a bottle of champagne to Les and Ted and played Tripoley, a quiet welcoming of the New Year.

Finish Brazil

My excitement Jan 8 was to head for the airport to collect Sen. Ted Kennedy and his two sisters. I rode in the lead car with Chris, his aide, acting as his translator in Portuguese. After collecting them and getting them into the four car motorcade, "Mas despacio" was my main call, slow down! Chris moaned over the sirens and sporadic gaps between cars. I rode in my first motorcade! I was home by midnight after they were settled into their hotel.

The CG was pleased to accompany the Senator and one sister as they called on the Mayor. One elected to stay in Brasilia and Gail was upset as she was to have been her charge. It was a two day rush and I received a kiss on the cheek from Dachi for a job well done. Chris saw that I got a pix taken with Kennedy but the rest missed out.

On January 28 the "Challenger" blew up on take-off, including the woman schoolteacher who had been chosen among 11,000 applicants, with her students and parents watching. Such a tragedy.

To Rio February 7 for Carnaval. Laura and Aunt Bev came from Chicago, as well as Jim from Cincinnati. I flew over, and while in a taxi from the airport, I got trapped by a mass of humanity from the Transvestite Ball. To the parade at Sambadrone and spent most of my time in line for the bathroom with a bad case of the runs. After three such trips I left them and took a taxi to the hotel. The next day rain and its downpour did not stop the parade. Jim became more obnoxious as he drank. He kept calling my aunt "Blanche" because he had been told she once starred in "Streetcar Named Desire." She was not amused. The two of them came back to Sao Paulo with me. Aunt Bev returned to Chicago a few days later and Jim went on to Iguacu Falls a few days after that.

End of February Brazil's cruzeiro became a cruzado; knock off 3 zeros.

In March I had the Modigliani print framed which I had purchased at Lake Como. Cost $10. I was told that the print (106 of 200) was worth at least $1000 now. I paid $170 in 1979 during our trip to Italy.

My favorite hobby at home seems to be picking off Suki's fleas.

The SPCA met at Heather and Jim's place. Had Greek food: Oozo the works, quite tasty.

Ed awoke on his 62nd birthday with "stinkin thinkin", no recognition from his children.

March 11 - The East Asia Bureau is strongly recommending me for Canberra, Australia. A shocker. Suki would be nine months in quarantine, six months in Hawaii and three months in Sydney. I do not want that assignment.

March 27 - To Curitiba: Araucaria is a 4 star hotel. Vila Vehla is 90 kilometers away with strange rock formations. Passion Friday services were on TV throughout Brazil from the Vatican.

March 30 - Bought souvenirs for Dannie and Paulo from the town they were born in - Curitiba.

April 1 - April Fool joke for Jose re assignment to do lots of work. He almost killed Vera and Cristina, then me.

April 3 - A bomb on a TWA plane exploded over Greece, four were blown out of it. Libya strikes again.

April 8 - Dachi is basking in the publicity he made for himself over Josef Mengele. Mengele had drowned in 1979 off the coast of Brazil and was buried under an assumed name. The body was exhumed in 1985. Records show that he landed first in Paraguay in 1959, and later moved to Brazil. Dachi (as a former dentist) identified Mengele's dental records, confirming that it was indeed the famed Nazi.

Went with George Little to a mime celebration with Peruvian portrait painter Marolino. Had done portraits of Lynda Byrd Robb and Ingrid Bergman, for which he charged several thousand dollars.

April 11-12. To the beach for an overnight and to watch Halley's Comet through binoculars. Gail and Donna, Luis, Trezise, Ed and myself, Les and Ted coming late. I recall a vague flash of light across the heavens. But mostly we lay in the sand and sang a lot.

April 15. Reagan bombed Libya last night.

April 16 - Bomb threat at 8:58 a.m. USIS was to have 60 students in for a USIS film. A Libyan demonstration was scheduled for 10 a.m. Guess who was acting Security Officer? We cancelled the USIS plans, called Arnold to come in. Then I had to go with Israeli experts to meet the U.S. expert re Mengele. Daniel Goldman to meet David Marmell. Goldman admitted he wasn't yet ready to admit the corpse was Josef Mengele, despite the evidence.

The news said Muammar Gaddafi's adopted daughter was killed in our bombing, and two badly injured. Depressing. So I picked out more fleas from Suki.

April 17 - Had the shocking news that Joao Rocha, a Consulate chauffeur, died last night, only 30. He had been fragile from an insect bite he had as a child which poisoned his system, and weakened his heart. I went to the hospital where they had laid him out, with a gauze over his face to accept the leaking fluids; cold hands, so young. I sobbed a lot, hugged his wife, talked with his mother. From there a long trip to the cemetery, then to a chapel for a five-minute service, then to follow the rolling cart to the burial into concrete slabs, opened like muffin tins waiting to be filled. Four hours of anguish. It had been Arnold's job to do, but as often occurred, it was foisted upon me. We collected 3 million cruzados for the family, or $3000.

April 18 - Ted went after Chinese food and was stuck in traffic an hour. We watched "Boys from Brazil" in recognition of Josef Mengele.

April 22 - The Justice department is questioning Ed for visas given to Nazis while he served in Frankfurt 1954-56.

April 25 - We have had bomb threats each day after Reagan bombed Libya.

Apr. 26 - Gail and I went to see "Ran" Japan's King Lear, and it was very well done. "Man seeks suffering more than he seeks peace."

Apr. 30 - The Russians have had a nuclear meltdown near Kiev (Chernoble) and the world is in panic.

May 1 - To Jose Mario's wonderful house in Cotia. It is high up, tastefully furnished. He designed it himself. Balconies and great views. I met his friend Rodney who told me: "Voce nao tem espirito Americano, tem espirita Latin America." I will treasure that.

May 4 - Lise Rose (my Suki contact) showed me a Russian icon. The woman wants $1700; it is a good investment and very lovely.

May 5 - Ed and I went to Oscar restaurant and found the spot on the wall where I wrote "Nos ficamos?" (will we stay?) on 6/24/84.

And here we are two years later.

May 6 - Gave Lise Rose a check for $1500 for the Russian icon: Black Madonna of Kazan. A Russian princess wants a face lift.

May 8 - The Trade Center got a couple of calls from an Arab named Youseff stating that General Walker would be shot today. He is Kadaffi's No. 1 target. General Walker is the UN Ambassador for the United States.

May 9 - Had my farewell Happy Hour. Alfredo and his wife made hors d'oeuvres and the prepping. At 5:20 p.m. my Admin group pulled out a farewell gift, a brass sculpture of a couple entwined (Ed and me) "because we are always hugging each other." I was told that no American had given a farewell for the staff, and I'm glad that I did it.

May 13 - A pouch run to Viracoos. In eve, stopped by Les and Ted's. Farewell to the kids.

May 14 - Gail and I had planned a farewell lunch for Leslie, and the guest of honor forgot! Ted gave her a guilt trip re responsibilities to the kids, but she would have come late. I went to see them off. Gail was incensed and pouted. Leslie and I were friends for life, after what we endured with blockhead. There wasn't much of a display of "saudades" since we'd soon see them in the Washington area.

May 19/20 - Packed out.

May 24 - Farewell to Poopsie (Ed's nickname). He was headed back to the States before I was. Donna and I went to Iguacu Falls. Beatrice from the Governors' office met us plus several ministers of Tourism. Charge Watson from Brasilia joined Donna and me to fly to Argentina. I bought a nutria jacket in five minutes for $250. "What else do I get" I asked. He answered "Me!" He was a kid of

30 yrs. Watson is nice, Donna got a harp for her kid. We three had dinner, easy conversation. Donna is always "on." It was a John Whitehead visit, Deputy Secretary of State. Wes Eagan from Portugal days was with him and said that Ferrer would be coming to Brazil. I didn't know in what capacity.

May 29 - Leslie and I both got tenured! Lunched with Dona Zela, Cristina and Ann. Jim Dandridge was at the next table and bought caipirinhas in honor of my tenure. The Japanese sewing ladies gave me free mending because I was leaving. I was touched.

May 30 - Arnold's farewell party for me. A lot of drinking going on.

May 31- To Rio to see Brazilian friends I had met in Monterrey. Went out to eat, she nagged him all nite.

June 1 - To airport for 10 am, 11, 12 noon flights, no luck. They then announced an extra flight at 1 pm. The waiter ran in to get me checked in. A smooth flight back to Sao Paulo. Brazil played Spain and won 1-0. Had a quiet evening with Suki.

June 2 - To an avant guarde rendition of "Carmen" with Gail and George. Enjoyed it visually set-wise, but did not always understand the diatribes.

June 3 - Dachi gave a spiel in the staff meeting about how wonderful I was, said everybody loved me. I should have had a recording! Later I went with Magda Rosenblum to see the official story about the ones who disappeared in Argentina. It was very poignant. I sniffed and Magda cried.

June 4 - Vera, my secretary, gave me a very sweet card about how I taught her about life and dealing with people. Poopsie called from his mother's house and misses me.

June 5 - Arnold gave me a rushed EER. Had a farewell lunch at Chaplain's with Cristina, hugs from two favorite waiters. I cried a lot saying goodbyes. Got bumped up to first class on plane, I thought, but it was business on top of the 747 Clipper with plenty of room for Suki in his cage. He kept quiet as a mouse.

1984 in front of Consulate. What am I in for?

Leslie Rowe, Chief of Visa Section, Sao Paulo, Brazil, 1986.

Yours truly, Visa Officer, Sao Paulo, 1986

Rio de Janiero, Brazil from Pao do Sucre.

Queen Elizabeth 2 Round The World Cruise 1986

Rio de Janeiro, Brazil.   Gail, her sister Diane ,myself seeing George
off to London on the QE 2.   Champagne sendoff!

Gail Gulliksen, Ed and myself, Halloween 1987

A weekend in Buenos Aires, 1987

Arnold Munoz, me, Lou Flores, Sao Paulo

you are
my
sunshine

Hollywood comes to call with Kale Brown, Charles Mc ? to make
movie on Halley's Comet.

Kale and Charles, in Brazil to make a movie on Halley's Comet. 1985

A Thanksgiving day love-in at Gail's. 1985

Our adopted cat Suki, left abandoned on the street by departing homeowners, 1987

Leslie, husband Ted Dieffenbacher at christening of Jacqueline, my goddaughter, Sao Paulo. 1985

Christening of Gail's son Stephen in Sao Paulo, Brazil

Gail and Leslie with Stephen and Jacqueline.

A trip back to Tunisia to see friend Hedi Benamor and his family.
1985

Paulo with Fredgie, Political Officer and friend, Sao Paulo. 1986

Aprez Brazil

June 6 - Ed and Paul Dwyer met me in Miami. Drove to Key Largo and stopped at an Italian place for dinner with horrid service. The next day I was so sad to have to send Suki off to John on an Eastern flight. Our arrangement was that John would take over his care while we were in Australia. I felt like such a rotten mother. We took Piedmont to Tampa, drove down to see Iris and Don in Nakomis. Visited Ray's parents in Tampa and flew to Washington, D.C. To the International Club with Hal and Rosita, his treat. Kevin, ex-producer of Milton Beryl and a mother of a congressman joined us. A metroliner to New York City, stayed at the Mayflower Hotel. Met Kale and his ex-girlfriend Helen Shaver, a Canadian who was raised only seven miles from Aylmer, Quebec, my father's birthplace. Ed and I walked in Central Park, to Kale's apartment to watch tapes of his soap opera "Another World." When he was first hired, he told us he would get $1000 per episode. To a Chinese place for lunch, Bloomingdale's and Alexander's. In the eve Ed and I went to the Russian Tea Room, opened the menu to $30 entrees, and walked out. Kale had breakfast with us the next day, we shopped some more. On checking out, we discovered that our now rich actor friend had paid the hotel bill.

A train to Washington, D.C. Car rental places were sold out, so a taxi to Pavonis. Were settled into our "suite" in the basement. Dinner out to an Indian restaurant. The next evening the Marins were invited to dinner and came late, which riled Jack. Ray's sister

307

and brother-in-law from Puerto Rico were nice. Ray and Margaret had loved their Canadian assignment to Ottawa. Jack was tipsy. He acted hostile in the morning refusing my taking a shower while Liz was asleep. Ten minutes later he announced it was okay, but by then I was dressed and ready to go. After our medical exams and lab work at the State Department we returned to their place, packed up and sneaked out, leaving a note. Moved to Quality Inn in Arlington. Next day to visit Kathy in Reston and met Jim Devine for the first time. A lunch with Barbara Morrison who is now a GS-15 and loves Pete. Saw Iris' daughter Celeste at the Department and she's been interpreting at the White House, spent $200 for a white blouse when she interpreted for a Spanish general. She's on a real high. More people to see, Norma Price of Tunis days, Louie Hebert, Tunis, Ann Kramer, Lisbon. The State Department cafeteria was a general circus of meeting a variety of people from a variety of postings. Talk about a high! It was fun and stimulating. Introduced Kathy to Paul and Patti Hoffman from Brazil, as they were also moving to Reston.

Then to Chicago to see Laura and Aunt Bev, Peoria/Washington, Ill. to stay with Joyce and Larry. Joyce asked "How are my two favorite people in the whole world?" Seeing sister Pat, I saw someone with straggly long hair streaked with grey, no longer the lovely auburn, weighing over 200 lbs. She is better on the inside but worse on the outside. Some day she'll match. Joyce and Larry's daughter Jane came by with her child. They're all in heaven. Ed and I offered to buy Pat a house. She said no thanks, she likes the company she gets at the YWCA. At Vonachens Junction with Ed, Phyllis, Mary and Joyce, I ran into Rita Moody, who chastised me for not keeping in touch. Another day the Big Four went to Happy Hollow, Johnsons' cabin, to spend the night. A lot of laughter over old times.

Took a bus to St. Louis to see Robert and Sandy, dined at the Po Folk restaurant. Rented car and met Loretta in Cape Girardeau, Mo. Drove to Conway and to the nursing home to see Woo, Ed's mother. It was sad to see her with ties to her hands since she was always attempting to undo her colostomy bag. She looked so pitiful. To Ed's sister Emily, to his brother Bill and Clara's new home. We stayed in Woo's little green house and it was empty without Woo. She cried in pain and was not her usual cheerful self. Ed was very hurt to experience the changed scene.

I flitted off to Dallas to see Joyce and Ray, Judy and Roby, Joe and Helen. Took my aged friend Mary Nelson back to the Dallas Country Club where we had met and worked together. We were greeted by a happy staff, white and black.

Then a flight to Denver and met Ed's later plane from Little Rock. Ed said the worst day of his life was saying goodbye to his mother. Both of them cried. Sister Judy and Wayne met us and took us home. We were there three nights before heading to San Francisco. John met us and took us to his home at Half Moon Bay. It was so great to see Suki again. He rolled over to show he remembered us. He seemed to be a long time outside, but he returned to sleep on our bed. How wonderful to have him cuddle and sleep on my legs like old times. Suzy and Stan came down and John treated us at the Chart House. The next day we had to bid farewell to Suki. I sobbed a lot. I wanted him so much to be with us! We spent the night in Sausalito at Suzy's place with a great view of the Bay. John took us to meet Betty Webster, a fascinating person. He had rented a room at her big place in Berkeley Hills when he attended Berkeley and she became a surrogate mother.

Onto see Joyce of Panama days who lives in Los Osos with husband Bob and three cats. Bob was in San Luis Obispo job hunting. Stayed overnight and Ed's daughter Cathy came after us, taking us to Santa Monica for lunch and her place. David came over later, has nice teeth and looks like Donny Osmond. He's a few years younger than Cathy. We all went to a seafood Greek restaurant. Chatted, a pleasant time. Cathy sacrificed her bed for us, still smokes.

Heading for Australia

The next day we were off on Hawaiian Air to Honolulu, on our way to Australia. We stayed at the Ilikai Hotel, now a Westin. I fulfilled my promise I had made in 1967 on the way to Vietnam that the next time I would return with my husband. At the PX I glanced through a TV mag. Kale was mentioned as an up and coming soap star.

On take-off day July 18, the plane was delayed and we returned to the hotel room for more sleep. At 2:30 a.m. we headed out of Hawaii on a Continental DC-10. Soon Friday was wiped out of existence and we were cheated out of 24 hours passing the International dateline. Continental had a pub open all night. I slept perhaps an hour during the lost Friday.

It was six hours from Honolulu to Nandi, Fiji. Fiji has over 300 islands, 100 inhabited. The Regent Hotel was lovely but we simply could not get into our room. Twenty minutes turned out to be 2-1/2 hours. Breakfast was a shocking $10 each. "Bula" is hello, "Binaka" thank you. Men wear skirts below the knee and women wear long skirts. It was a gorgeous setting, with boats on the water. We walked the beach, collected shells. The people are attractive with nice smiles. The male Fijian singers in the evening were not always on key. Ed went for an early morning dip in the Pacific ocean. I bought some local products: sarong dresses for gifts, placemats, a wooden bowl for salad. We watched the sundown ceremony with guys on drums and young kids running after the oil lamplighter runner as he lit scores of oil lamps. Ended our three day visit without taking a single tour. How shameless! Our hotel bill was a national disaster. We left and collected on the first breakfast Continental served from its L.A. flight to Melbourne. The flight was both late and rough, running into strong headwinds and a jet stream to boot. Our baggage was the last to arrive and we were dashed past customs and to the TAA flight to Canberra.

Australia

Australia 1986

We were met by the Administrative Counselor Paul Sadler and Personnel Officer Al Nugent. They delivered us to the temporary quarters, quite decent, at Kingston Court. Paul had us over in the evening. He has a lovely place with lots of paintings and sculptures, a large wooden horse, a real showplace with elegant taste. He's a good friend of Dorothy Magee, is much too creative for a normal Admin type.

Ambassador Lane's secretary is Ardith Miller, who had been Ambassador Russell's secretary back in Tunis. I lunched with her; she has worked in more stimulating places, thrives on war zones. In the eve we dined at Nugent's house, another charming place, where we watched some of the Royal Wedding: Fergie married Prince Andrew.

Several days after our arrival, Canberra had its first snow in a decade. Yes, it is July but the world had turned upside down! We are in winter. The snow lasted about a half hour and was on the ground until the afternoon. We ordered a new Mercedes 190E. What are we doing? I'm panicked as Paul was attempting to get us into newly built houses, mostly intended for single secretaries and communicators, the DCM sez. The eight houses are much too small for us and who needs to live in a commune? Are we to endure the repeated agony of our landing in Brazil? Paul offered us his house while he is on home leave. At least we'll have a lovely nest for a couple of months! He had a party for us with chicken pot pie and four luscious desserts made by himself! He's wild, showed the pool and the grounds we're to care for, and his imposing British four poster canopy bed! Cannot wait!

Watched "Crocodile Dundee" to get a glimpse of the real Australia. Half of the film was in NYC, but it was entertaining, and we saw a bit of the Outback.

We dashed to the local zoo to see kangaroos. Saw an emu but didn't have time to check on the koala bears. I noted that the interviewers on TV were very aggressive, even combative, and were annoying to watch. The weather forecasts in Australia were funny. They didn't use technical terms mentioning some front or other. It was either "mainly fine" or "unsettled." I have found that Chinese restaurants were more tasty than some of the Aussie cuisine thus far. Wrote a letter to my Canadian cousins. Pat had been in Canberra with the Canadian High Commission.

Australian farmers had a demonstration in the morning over U.S. wheat sales to Russia, and dumped a bag of wheat on the Chancery's lawn.

The Aussie dollar was worth 62 cents of the U.S. dollar.

As the Leasing and Contracting Officer, I have over 200 homes throughout Australia I need to ride herd on. We had 60 government leases in Canberra, plus over 10 government-owned places, the Ambassador's Residence atop the list. The USG had recently purchased an additional ten new homes. Guess who has to oversee getting them decorated, furnished and inhabited? Mon dieu!

Workwise, I was doing the work of two General Services Officers, as the Supervisory GSO had not yet arrived. My days got progressively more frustrating, signing purchase orders, work orders, meeting after meeting, revamping transportation schedules, receiving calls from D.C. re the Art in Embassy collection due to arrive soon for the Residence. A house has been reserved for soon-to-be boss Lynwood Dent. Now to furnish it! In between were frustrating questions about leases and contracts, furnishings, etc. I was finding out early on that the Aussie male did not like to take orders, let alone from a woman. So I worked on a different approach: "What do WE have to do today?" (It took about a year for them to accept me, somewhat wholeheartedly!)

In the midst of this introduction, the Ambassador's wife Mrs. Lane had a coffee for Prime Minister Hawke's wife, to which I was invited. I had to regret, much too much work! One evening Judy Jones, a political officer, invited Ed and me to a dinner for a woman senator from Western Australia and another representative. They were pleasant people. I was quite surprised to be served a cold meal, like a picnic, on what turned out to be a very chilly evening!

Paul, the Administrative Counselor, spent USG money very lavishly. He had a whole section of the warehouse filled with expensive materials for upholstering furniture, not very practical! He had what we used to call high-falluting ideas. In Brazil we had to beg to buy paper clips. Here, it's Rumpelstilskin, spinning out more gold. Paul's an amazing character and we liked him in spite of his flamboyant ways. Before he left for home leave, he showed us his friend's house at 94 Endeavour, a perfect honeymoon place for us, lots of charm, fireplace, family room, two bedrooms. We were quite enthused, was there hope?

In the meantime we checked out of Kingston Court, loaded up our air freight and a ton of boxes and moved into his home, hauling them up the stairs and down and around. I sorted our clothes, washing, hanging them, moved a desk into the back bedroom for Ed's study, getting all things in order if only for two months. I felt if I could accomplish that, I could somehow get my life in order. So I sorted for my life! A cute little cat came to our door wanting in, but I wasn't falling for it!

Went to see Marcel Morceau, the mime. His talent showed way up to the S row. Saw Ambassador and Mrs. Lane down in front.

Watched fantastic American Ballet do Triad, very sensuously done; and Paquita, quite lively and interesting. Mikhail Barysnikov opened with a more modest Les Sylphides.I gathered over $19,500 worth of checks and mailed to bank for Deutschmark exchange for our new Mercedes. Our past experience with new American cars and their myriad of problems set the stage for the feeling it was time to spoil ourselves. The new Supervisor is due so I moved from his office to my office at the other wing. So the Dents arrived and seem pleasant. His wife and kids liked the house chosen for them; he reserved his comment. Ed and I had a delicious meal at Baci Italian restaurant in Philip territory. Next day when Lyn Dent showed up, I was pleasantly surprised that my workload would be diminished. He gave the impression that he'd be on top of things. He told me I was the third person who had said "I like Paul Sadler in spite of himself."

Ed's mother Woo had her 92nd birthday. Ed and I visited the town of Bungendore, 100 years old. The woman in the bookstore got excited when I asked her if she needed books. I'd give some when we unpack. The countryside is vast like Texas with places "fur and far between." A nice experience. A French painter had said of

Australia: "It has a vast metaphysical sky." How true. We saw newly sheared sheep in bright blue nylon wind jackets.

Met Bill Martin for the first time. He and Ed both went to Berkeley; he is considerably younger by at least 30 years. Went to Batesman Bay for an overnight. We had the best food so far in Australia at the Anchorage Restaurant. Saw a dead kangaroo on the side of the road. In Mexico it was usually a horse.

Some Aussie expressions: G'day mate! lay-by is layaway; script is a medical prescription; chook is a chicken; bludger is a loafer; garbo is the garbage man; one uses clothes pegs, not pins. And it goes on.

After two months of housesitting the Admin Counselor's place, moved into the cozy home at 94 Endeavour, complete with fireplace and lawn to mow and rose bushes to tend to, some growing to enormous size and quite lovely. Then there are violets, sweetpeas and plum trees to keep alive.

Had the Art in Embassy unveiling, selected works by well known artists on loan from various museums in the States. All were placed in the Ambassador's residence, an elegant Georgian mansion on the hill above the Embassy buildings. One was a Caitlin painting entitled "Three Peoria Indians." Mrs. Lane was excited when she learned I was raised in Peoria. She was from Lincoln, Illinois not far south of Peoria. She said "I knew there was a reason I liked you." Ambassador Bill Lane was a political appointee, publisher of Sunset Magazine and Lane Publishing. They as millionaires were accustomed to the individual attention that money brings, but both were affable and good natured.

On September 24 I picked up our lovely thistle green Mercedes.

Drove like a dream.

Made our first trip to Sydney in October. Harpoon Harry's food was very tasty, perch and sole. Had a harbor cruise where lunch was served on a 1-1/2 hour tour. The car presented us with a flat tire and we drove back to Canberra without a spare.

Aside from the daily frustrations at work, I added major dental work to accompany the stress.

When a political officer was to leave post, I discovered their dog had urinated in about every room with carpeting. The damage was over $3000 and they refused to pay. We withheld their tickets and they stomped off to buy their own, to hire an attorney, etc. Add that to a typical day of frustration: balance real estate agents, attorneys for property to be purchased in Melbourne, dissatisfied tenants in Canberra, for one reason or another. We were also trying to finish off newly built government-owned properties, with tile, electrical, paving, appliances, furniture, curtains for the windows. I had about 60 leases to keep track of in Canberra, plus furniture and maintenance for those, plus some 20 government-owned properties, not to mention warehouses. A full plate, as the Brits would say.

After two months at Paul's house it was time to check out and move into our own at 94 Endeavour (we lucked out regarding the small government-owned places). On the day of our move, Ed's sister Emily called to say Woo was in the hospital and was not expected to make it. We made plans for Ed to go home for the funeral. Woo died November 7, several days after Ed had arrived home. I accompanied Paul to the Marine Ball the next day and danced with the GSO gang: Henry, David, Peter. Sat at #1 table with the DCM and others. The Marine Ball activity eased the recalcitrant David and Peter relationship with me.

Melbourne Cup day is cause for celebration throughout Australia. I stopped in at the office party midst my unpacking at home. My champagne glass kept getting refilled and as the afternoon progressed, I was certainly in my Melbourne cups!

Two weeks after Woo's death, I planted a lilac tree in our rented yard in her memory.

--The Pope came to Canberra November 24. 100,000 sedately organized people came to the mass.

Had my first experience with the aggressive Australian flies. They attacked us as we walked in our neighborhood; that first experience was not enjoyable. There was more to come.

--Cary Grant died at 82 in Davenport, Iowa.

December I delivered English language books to Mrs. Angel's bookstore in Bungendore and she was excited to get them. In turn, she gave me a book of Aussie poetry.

We went to the British High Commissioner Leahy's home for a meeting on Cheshire Foundation. They support a leprosy home in India. Ed is on the Committee, having met Cheshire himself in England.

Paul told me he is ready for retirement after 40 years in the Foreign Service. He's fed up. It didn't take me that long!

Ed and I sawed off 1-1/2 feet of the Christmas tree, put it in a bucket of water, and leaned it against the wall. The smell of pine was marvelous.

One evening we went to see the Aussie comedian Barry Humphries. He was so vulgar Ed left before half time, which surprised Colleen/Roger, Steve/Chris. In the second scene he was a dead man musing over his memories; it was good. When he was Dame Edna it didn't do it for me. His spittle flew over to those of us in the front row. The Aussies love him.

One afternoon Arlene came to my office and said she'd rather retire than live in Swinger Hill or Fisher. It made my day, this job is so rewarding! I had of course gone through the same thing! And came back a winner. At home I hassled with Ed over the tree, and balanced it in that bucket against the wall and decorated it. I thought wistfully about Suki our cat knocking the balls off the tree in Brazil.

Mid December Ed and I dined at the Red Hill Cafe Provencal, authentically French, delicious.

Had a Christmas brunch at our place for a dozen of us which was a success. To midnight mass at St. Paul's Anglican Church, seeing the Dents and the British Leahys.

On our first Christmas in Australia, we arrived too late for food at an open house. We were starved by 4:30 pm and tried McDonalds, which was closed. We ended up at Rex cafe, a veritable bus stop, discovered we didn't have money and told them they had to trust us, it was Christmas. Ed went to a Wespac bank and returned to pay the bill. We walked a bit by the lake, saw a movie in eve. Little Lord Faunteroy was heartwarming.

A reminder: December is summer down under. I hung the laundry outside in the back and it was dry minutes after it hit the line. I loved the smell of the outdoors on the sheets.

We went to Dents with Paul for delicious turkey and coconut cake. Had a pleasant time outside by the pool. One time they had the most deadly brown snake on their patio, not that day! The Australian attitude is, do not kill it, it is only passing through!

A few days after Christmas Ed and I in our swanky car headed out to Melbourne. Ed wanted to stop at Merimbula about 3 p.m. but I said it was too early. About 5 we found Orbost, and a humble hotel called the Commonwealth. He and I were bickering by them since I had passed the more romantic spot. Toward the end of the eve he recalled his mother telling us fights had to be settled before bed time so we retired, snuggling. The next day we had a leisurely drive to Melbourne and landed at the Hotel Windsor, over 100 years old, charmingly Victorian. Melbourne is Victoria London, then a modern plaza with waterfalls, NYC. There are Greek and Chinese sections around the corner. A very nice place, would seem to be a perfect posting. End of year sale at Myers Dept. store, I bought an $18 Italian silk tie for Ed for $8.

To Fanny's for dinner, served on Limoge china, with absolutely heavenly food: gazpacho beyond reason, veal and cheese, pasta divine, chocolate tarte. It was $105 aussie dollars with tip (62 cents = $1 US). One of my more memorable meals in life!

To the Consulate for money and chat with Tom Young at Admin. He knew Munoz, Goldberger, did not gossip. Talked about the Philip Island penguins. Later we took a tram ride to Menzes at Rialto, with a lovely courtyard bar, a woman playing classical music on a baby grand, a very soothing setting. We walked back up the hill to our hotel.

On New Year's Eve we learned that the trains and trams would stop running at 8 p.m. because of holdups and violence, and the city would not let the drivers carry "trudgeons." Melbourne had theretofore seemed so perfectly innocent. We awoke to a rainy day which dampened thoughts of the botanical gardens, so we checked out and headed for Philip Island. It was a 1- 1-/2 hour drive to the Sundowner motel, very basic after the glorious Hotel Windsor. The crowded town was Cowes. Tried to eat at the best restaurant, the Jetty, but they were filled up. We were even denied a take away barbeque chicken, all were spoken for. So, cheese and crackers and onto the Penguin Parade at 7 pm. Saw a film, were harnessed behind barriers with the Japanese rushing to all the good viewing spots. The fairy penguins began to show up at dusk, tiny little guests at a black tie function on New Year's Eve, 18 inches tall at most, staggering up the beach with full stomachs to feed their kiddies in the bush. All humans clamored for photos, a most unique experience!

1987 Australia

On New Year's day we headed home from Melbourne on Princes Highway 1, lovely back roads, lush green foliage. We had a delicious lunch at Lakes Entrance. Stopped at the Seaview Hotel, Edin, New South Wales. A brief walk brought clinging flies. We had never been in a spot with such demanding creatures. At home Patrick, the owner's cat showed up, had been missing for five days. Mr. Humphries, Carol's father, collected him once again. After the Poulsons had gone on to their new assignment for the Australian Foreign Service to Tuvalu, an island in the Pacific Ocean, Patrick had been sent to live with his grandparents, but kept returning to his real home. The return to work was not rewarding, not much done while I was gone. Lyn was disgusted as well, plus he had the Lanes to himself now since the departing Admin Counselor had turned it over to him until his replacement arrived. Why do I take this job seriously, I should laugh. I do, but it is an hysterical one.

Paul had an Admin reception for the new people, about 30, elegant pates, salad, ham, spring rolls. The Marines had a barbecue and Ed and I went. Vic remembered me from a party in Tunis, another telephone fellow from Bonn had passed through Lisbon and met me, small world! The Dents and Lanes joined us at our table. Ed recounted our fairy penguin adventure.

I have to state somewhere that I have a very passionate, caring husband, no complaints! We went for a picnic, hovered over the food as the flies attacked. People do not linger at picnics, eat quickly and pack up the food and run.

- -Watched Don Quixote ballet on television with Rudolph Nureyev; most energetic. He was stupendous.

-- Paul Sadler had us over for dinner. He had received cards from both Dorothy Magee and David Lambertson, who had said Canberra was a favorite post. He had been a DCM by then, was a boss in the political section of Saigon. I had received letters from Vera and Cristina in Sao Paulo on how they missed me and the new GSO was a jerk.

--We went for a picnic but ate in the car when flies attacked. To Robertson overnight at a hotel built in 1924, Ed's year of birth. Had huge fireplaces, plain rooms, but a sense of romance prevailed. There was a wedding party, a bush band. We danced in an empty ballroom. We then commenced an amazing tour, to the beach in Kangaroo Valley with a stop at the Kiana blow hole. The Moss Vale antique place had a lively Brit, about 65, playing the piano. I bought silver plated skinny coffee pots, very unique. To the White Horse Inn, Berrina for lunch. We had an enjoyable day, in tune with the universe and each other.

At the house we mow and weed often, a lot of work. Watched a program on Nureyev and Margo Fontaine, with comments on a woman and a man half her age making exotic, sensuous dance moves together.

Paul helped, rather taught me how to make plum jam. We had two small bushes which burst forth magnanimously. We sweated profusely in my small kitchen.

To Colonel Waggener's for Australian/American Assn. reception. Ed was talking to Mrs. Lane when Jean T. interrupted as he was telling a story. A very rude moment. I beckoned to him and we left before the program and speeches.

When I was on the phone with DCM Teare, he said Lyn and I had made a difference since arriving, it was apparent all the way around. Nice to have one's work appreciated, it was very rare.

February 1 and 98 degrees down under. Paul brought his Bryn Mawr friend here for dinner and stayed five hours. Three of us devoured 2 bottles of wine and champagne. She had lived 25 years near Amalfi Drive in Italy.

--U.S. Dennis Connor won the America's Cup in Perth, Australia. We never got to Perth.

We were introduced to Nugents' cats as they sought homes at their departure. One timid black cat with white socks, whom they called B.C., came to me and she was ours. Her name was immediately changed to Timida.

Got a Japanese silk painting for $350 from a man I met at a picture framing place.

--On Valentine's Day we drove to the Blue Mountains, 3-1/2 hours to Katumba at the Felton Wood guesthouse. The hotel had a fancy dress dinner, sparklers and hats, like New Year's Eve. The people were so outgoing and friendly, unlike the general feel from those in Canberra. We then drove to Mt. Victoria.

--I attended a lunch with other diplomats from Britain, Sweden, Ireland, Greece, Israel, New Zealand, Nigeria, Burma, France and the Philippines, 16 of us. It was so enjoyable to have the international flavor.

--Had a farewell dinner for the Nugents, which included Bob/Jean Kepler. Jean had been Marine Guard Carl's second girlfriend after myself in Tunis. Chicken divine recipe and strawberry shortcake.

--The Embassy warehouse auction brought in $40,165 aussie dollars. Interesting but exhausting. I reported in the staff meeting that we had lured them in with quality items but most walked out with junk.

At the end of February we met Ed's ex-relatives in Sydney: Jut Castleberry, Betty and John Miller, Bob and wife. All are California affluent. Stayed at Park apartments. To Cyranos restaurant, great service and food, all very pleasant. Jut is charming and attentive, Betty has hang ups, Ollie quite natural. Bob looks like Ronald Reagan. We had another good meal at the Waterfront restaurant, a most congenial evening. A fond farewell, kiss on cheek from Jut. Arriving home, Timida gave us a lecture on leaving her and a souvenir poop in the living room.

--March 7 was a gorgeous day. After the fish man at the market told me to have a pleasant day, I suddenly felt I liked Canberra (after seven months). Ed and I went to a flower show, walked about.

--March 9 was Ed's 63rd birthday. I gave him a navy jogging suit and flannel nightshirt. No cards from his kids, which hurt. Two came a week later.

Timida loved to have me comb her back, went into ecstasy. In some ways she was more of a character than Suki, more expressive. Suki was arrogant in his territory, with his tail up straight. Timida never had her tail up, she either stalked or skulked.

My daily work life was fraught with frustration and I often felt it was for naught. Ed's life was richer with his interests, Cheshire Foundation, and his writings. I ate in frustration and was gaining weight.

--To the Tipsy Gypsy Hungarian restaurant. The owner's wife is enormous with a pretty Zsa Zsa Gabor face. (I learned later they were third cousins.)

--An Embassy contract employee died at age 50, found in his hallway with a comb in his hair, readying for work. He was a friend of Letty, frightening.

--In eve with Steve and Chris to see "Run for Your Wife", a British farce. Cleverly staged and funny.

--Saw "Peggy Sue Got Married." Cried a lot. It was about high school arrogance and how we felt we had all the time in the world to achieve whatever we wanted, but then somehow we never stop to think about what it was; so it slipped away and we never did it. I sobbed quite a bit going home in the car. I who felt I was a writer and never followed through.

--Paul and I went to the shops at Hall and had lunch. We felt easy with each other and he was certainly lively. Ed came to join us at Paul's as he heated up a spinach dish for dinner.

--Secretary's Day. Lyn and I took Steve and Letty to Yarralumba to a Chinese Restaurant.

--To Garden City motel with the Consular Group of Russians, Arabs, Lebanese, Egyptians for Gambling Night, went with Steve and Colleen. At the roulette wheel I'd scream if I won a chip. The Arabs and Lebanese took to me. I bought a Mercedes key chain with my earnings and won a meal for two at Sinbad Lebanese restaurant. A fun eve.

--End of March a group of seven women took the train to Sydney to see " Cats." The general effects were great, but I felt it drag at times. It was disappointing. Another disappointment occurred when we saw "Starlight Express" and they had to stop the show to clear up water on the ramp, breaking up the entire continuity of the production.

For an April Fool joke, Andrew put a black widow spider under a glass on my desk.

To Brisbane to check out the new Principal Officer's possible home, a charming Victorian style. Security officer Rick checked it as well; all looked good. Any main city out of Canberra is enticing. Canberra with its parliament people was stuffy. Anywhere out of Canberra I note that people are more openly friendly.

One day when I threatened to leave the job, Letty suggested I ask for a transfer to another Aussie post for my last year rather than get out altogether. As two years approach, I am ready for another posting. Three seemed insurmountable.

On Easter, no church but went on a day trip to Cooma, then Thredbo. Tunafish lunch picnic by a dam, a lovely day. Went for Devonshire tea, scones with strawberry jam and cream, tasty. Watched glider planes. Ed, the former pilot, would like to try them.

Three hours in a dental chair as he redid one-fourth of my mouth, prepared for a three-crown bridge, lots of drilling. A new crown bridge will cost me $1365 U.S.

Ed and I went to the British High Commissioner's house for Cheshire Home discussion. Aussies and Brits, lots of friendly people.

In May we flew to Christ Church, NZ to meet John. Had to buy a ticket at last minute, as we were given to believe we'd have a free flight there on a military plane. We went to Mt. Cook State Park in

New Zealand. It was lovely and eery at the same time. Ed felt we had arrived at the end of the world. Lake Waka was lovelier than Lake Como or Lake Geneva, pristine and innocent.

To Milford Sound, a scenic drive. We learned that 38 sailors were killed on a US. boat "accidentally by Iraq." We settled in at a wog (Aussie slang for European) place for the night.

We met John again in Sydney. Dined at Bayswater Brasserie with wonderful food, congenial service. Took a military C-141, equivalent of a 727 back to Canberra.

Back home John made fish and salad, went the next day to the National Gallery, enjoyed it thoroughly. He later got close and personal to kangaroos and was thrilled. Next day he took a bus to Brisbane for a job interview with an American company who would exhibit at a special fair there.

Lyn went on a U.S. Presidential visit to Venice. I had many balls up in the air: several moves, Colleen and Letty both sick, Ron's father on critical list in Tasmania, plans for Secretary of State visit.

To meet John in Sydney. The New South Wales gallery had nice works by Australians; I liked Grace Cassington Smith's works. John's job fell through. He now plans to meet Emmanuelle, a French colleague, for a weekend in California wine country. His interest in her has been much enhanced by their separation.

Had a very large weekend for Paul's farewell at Ranelagh House in Robertson. Colleen/Roger, Wes/Candace, Steve/Chris, Paul and Pat, Ed and me. We dressed kookily, I wore my grey wig hat, Ed a beret. Colleen wore a sheet and an old wig of mine. Pat and I sang a duet to Mr. Sandman and my lyrics for Paul; it went over big. Also more switched lyrics to Wild Colonial Boy. Wes did a mock country team thing, cute. All but Ed drank heavily. I sang Louisville Lou. Tried a seance. Pat cried for her mother. I was sick, with Colleen taking gentle care of me. What a disaster, she took a tablecloth into the bathroom.

A lot of big heads around the breakfast table the next day. Ed's cheery talkative state was annoying; he was so healthy and liked rubbing it in for the rest of us.

There was an Admin lunch with representatives of other countries at the Scottish Club. Talked with a Burmese who was afraid of returning to Burma for his next assignment. The political situation there was very tenuous.

Soon it was the Secretary of State George Schultz's visit to Sydney and we went down to the hotel to set up the control room a day before. Defense Secretary Casper Weinberger was also in the party. I saw Rust Deming from Tunis days. Ed came down via train for overnight. A fellow from the Sydney consulate told me that my foreign nationals really liked me! My hard work of campaigning had paid off - took a whole year! Two to go, can I survive my longest tour of duty? Did not meet the two dignitaries. We packed up and flew back to Canberra.

Made shrimp stroganoff for Paul's farewell dinner. He gave us a lot of goodies, leftover liquor, a cutting board. He finally admitted that I could cook. Ed said Paul was the end of an era. He was certainly a colorful character.

Squash with Colleen and Steve, strenuous but fun. Foreign wives of Americans make more demands I have found. I gave a speech at the new Marine house: "Welcome to Semper Fi Fraternity house. remember no drinking and no girls in the room after 11 p.m!" That brought some laughs.

To one of our landlord's sheep station. Had lovely 1200 acres and 3000 sheep, 24 kilometers from Yass. We spent 3 hours, she asked us to lunch for the future.

--My college roommate and C.J. friend Margy died May 14, 1987 of cancer, her husband Rich told me in a letter. So sad, she had just become a grandmother.

Took a drawing class with no direction given. A vase with two flowers. I felt alternately depressed, intimidated, smug that other drawings were as bad or worse than mine, frustrated, am I a quitter? Went to bed in a funk.

July 28 was our 8th legal anniversary. So Ed smashed the Honda and miraculously escaped with a scratched left hand and strained muscle. To bed early to cuddle Ed on the right, Timida on the left.

I had a yelling match with Lyn who wanted Mrs. Ramage (the new Admin Counselor's wife) to enter the warehouse after I had refused her. Most likely looking to butter up his employee evaluation from her husband. We have rules, no one gets to saunter into the warehouse and choose their own furniture. He later apologized.

I later had Beverly's Basic Brunch for the Ramages (Paul's replacement), Wes and Candace, Lyn and Carol and Ed.

Met new Kate of B&F (Budget and Fiscal). Liked her right off.

August 16: a "harmonic convergence occurred, nine planets aligned for the first time in 23,000 years. "It's our only chance for world peace if only we can all get tuned in!" someone said.

Had a wine and cheese at the Residence. When Ambassador Lane had remarked "I'm glad you can enjoy the Residence after all your work on it" I mentioned he never invited me. Of course a week later Ed and I were invited to a buffet dinner with a pianist to entertain. I was ready to accept but remembered we'd be in Cairns.

Ed's cousin Betty Hayes and her husband Bill came for a 3 day visit. We gave them our bedroom and took the sofa bed. Took them to an Indian restaurant and to the British High Commissioner's the next night. High Commissioner Leahy raved about his days at Yale and the girl he left behind. Also took them to the Tipsy Gypsy, with wonderful stuffed cabbage; we gluttonized on a chocolate crepe for dessert.

The day after they left, September 3-10 we were off to Cairns and the Great Barrier Reef. It was an eight hour trip changing planes in Sydney and Brisbane, so it was not very handy for us. The climate was much warmer than at Canberra. We snorkeled on the reef, went on glass bottom boats at Green and Fitzroy islands. When we went to an underwater observatory we saw a wide cross section of sea creatures: gigantic clams the size of boulders, fish of spectacular color and size, and at least ten species of coral (spaghetti, brain, boulder, leather, Christmas tree, to name a few). We were guided by a very informative fellow. Our first meal there was Coral Sea trout for Ed and Burrumunda for me, both good. To Port Douglas, Island Point restaurant was reminiscent of the Robinson Crusoe in Tobago. So of course we loved it, food was splendid, huge crab and Coral Sea trout. Home again, to Timida's scolding. Back to winter at 10 degrees centigrade. The trick: double it (20) subtract 10% (2) = 18; add 32 degrees: 50 degrees farenheit.

For my 50th birthday Ed gave orchids and balloons: Happy 50th! My cake had "It's your 50th - accept it!" Steve's friends, Colleen and I had a birthday lunch at Tivoli. Steve had earlier filled my office with black balloons that said: "50 and over the hill." By then, since the age was blown, I decided to have a Happy hour the next day. Over 40 people unloaded onto our small honeymoon cottage. I was delivered a balloon-o-gram, a lovely arrangement of five helium balloons with a champagne bottle for ballast (from my secretary Steve). Then in the middle of the party in walked a gorilla with an ape-o-gram and another bottle of champagne (a first for both!). He read poems by Colleen and Steve. I had catered food for $170 with some luscious hor d'ouevres, received lots of cards and flowers, and it was a great success. I even followed Ed's footsteps and went to bed before the last stragglers had left. I figured 5-11:30 p.m. was long enough for a happy hour, so 3 or 4 remained to close the door behind them.

A week or so later we went again to see Mrs. Snow at her sheep station, this time for lunch. Guess what she served? Lamb chops! And I later weighed in to find my eating so ravishly had added up to 66 kilos!! (make that 145 pounds). Ridiculous!

To the National Gallery to see Old Masters from the Phillips Collection in D.C. It was like going home since I'd seen them before, felt comforting. Renoir's Boating Party was so alive and lovely. At lunch hailstones as big as golfballs battered the windows.

A day's respite to Milton Park Inn near Bowral to a posh country inn with a fantastic garden of lilacs, camellias, wisteria. A wedding party was there with a bride in a gorgeous gown of three tiers of satin.

The Ambassador gave a farewell dinner for Ardith. I sat on his left. We had a singalong at the piano and it was a pleasant sendoff.

To Bolshoi Ballet, so thrilling. As we walked out, Ed said he was tired from all that leaping.

I steal lilacs whenever I can. October is spring, remember!

Squash with Colleen. I beat her 2 to 1.

I took Ardith to the airport. She looks forward to Baghdad after an uninspiring time in Canberra.

Kate and I went to the Philippine National Day banquet. Letty was the lst Vice President honcho and was gorgeous in a gold gown and emeralds. Had lively folk dancing and a fashion parade.

I was disappointed not to be on the promotion list. Ed wrote a consoling letter to me which said I was his golden girl and Timida and he loved me. It was sweet and touching.

We attended a black tie event at the British High Commissioner's with some 80 people for the benefit of the Cheshire Foundation. I bought a watercolor by Lady Anne, a garden scene for $95- 30% goes to the foundation. We had pate, the typical beef wellington, and lots of other goodies.

At home Timida had found a hammock for herself, snoozing on the screening over the back patio.

Halloween night. Tried the New Shanghai Chinese restaurant: marvelous chicken cashew and scallops stuffed with crabmeat.

November 1 - To Burra where Ed worked the Cheshire booth in a Mexican hat and poncho and sold raffle tickets. Netted $700 for the lepers in India.

Nov. 3 - Melbourne Cup Day - It is a day when no one even makes an attempt to work, but we gather there to bet and party. I brought two cases of beer, invested $11 in the races and recouped almost $8. Others brought chicken and cole slaw. Steve won the largest amount.

Colleen and I went to the Canberra Labor Club function. We collected on dance promises with about a dozen males, drank moderately, and had a very good time until past 1 a.m.

Ed and I went to the Thai Embassy international function. Baba our new Hungarian friend had flower (petunia) pictures on display at a gallery.

At the staff meeting at the Embassy a few days later the Ambassador asked if I could walk after all the dancing I did at the Labor Club. He also said I reminded him of a burlesque star named Bubbles, all effervescent. I told him he could call me Bubbles. Others snickered and the DCM looked askance.

Glancing through my diary from 1987 I noted blank pages where I never went back to fill something in. It was entirely unprecedented! It must have been that I was so harried in the day to day operations of my job as housing officer, fielding complaints, searching for furniture, having curtains made, measuring potential spots to rent, doing leases, etc. I hardly had time to reflect. So much of it was same same with perhaps a different name. Ed was so supportive of me I so looked forward to weekends and undivided time together. We caught up on lovemaking, went on picnics and other excursions, dashed off to a weekend in Sydney, made other journeys and enjoyed our cat Timida.

The yearly Embassy auction of used government-owned furniture brought in $37,215.

At Thanksgiving I made two Thanksgiving meals, one on the day and one on Sunday. Colleen, Steve, and Ardith's replacement were there for Thanksgiving, and Bill and Ann and their children came for Sunday, both events featuring turkey, cornbread, waldorf salad, sweet potatoes, dressing and pumpkin pies.

December 1 was the first day of summer.

To the Canberra fair with Colleen. The roller coaster was terrifying and fun. Some kookie kid wanted to cling and speak to an American. I had not had such a good time in a long while.

The Dents had a Christmas party. Bob Arthur was a friend of Lars in Trinidad. I hadn't known that Lars had been there.

Ed worked a Cheshire booth again, raising $362. I am so happy with my loving, generous husband.

The Salvos (AKA Salvation Army) came to sing carols. The band was on a flatbed truck, the singers in a bus. It was touching. Want to speak Australian? We have milko, posto, abo, salvo, arvo (get it?) Fair Dinkum!

Mid December Colleen, Letty and I took Gino our painter to lunch. He confided about his rotten marriage, frigid and gloomy. It was hard to imagine, as he had always kept such a cheerful demeanor.

Colleen, Pat and I ate at Tipsy Gypsy. It's a BYOB place and we emptied 1 red and 1 white. I bought Baba's petunias painting for $220 to give to Ed for Christmas.

Ed's daughter Suzy and her friend Stan came Christmas eve from California with a stop first in New Zealand. I made my old standard, shrimp stroganoff.

Christmas day, Ed was happiest with his long white hose for his shorts, was now a real Aussie! To Colleen's for dinner. Later, a family walk up Endeavour Street. The day after, we took Suzy and Stan to Tidbinbilla (I love Aussie place names!) nature preserve. Saw a wombat on the side of the road and a bunch of emus who came to beg, some kangaroos, a stop at a waterfall. Dashed to Ginninderra for lunch. Took them next day to Wendy Snow's sheep station. She was terrified of having a barbie since the earth was so brown and parched and the grasshoppers had eaten her grass. We went down to the river and some abos had been drinking. Some wanted to start trouble, but they finally went off. It was beautiful there by the river.

We took Suzy and Stan to the airport for their Heron Island adventure at 5 a.m. Back to bed with Timida. It was absolutely wonderful to sleep until 9 a.m. Timida latched on to another bird and we scolded her and she scolded back and left at our ingratitude. Several times earlier she had come to us with an offering in her mouth. It rained steadily all day.

End of year, I was depressed over my weight gain, yet certainly did find solace in food. Suzy called to report how lovely it was at Heron Island. They watched turtles laying eggs and were having a wondrous time.

1988 Australia

New Year's day we passed the three hours to Sydney in good moods. Met Suzy and Stan there at Park Apartments with a harbor view. They ranted about Heron Island, sea turtles and all the birds of nature in a general uproar. To Hyde Park for oysters, New Year's good luck omen. Made love, a wondrous way to begin the new year. It was rainy in the late afternoon. To Cyranos, good meals. Went to the Sydney Opera House to see "Carmen" by Bizet. It felt stiff when the entire company was on stage but they did warm up and did a good job. Carmen had a fine voice. All enjoyed it. Went across the harbour bridge, then to the Queen Victoria building for champagne taste and to Paddy's market for beer pocketbook. To Bayswater Brasserie, lovely food, rain. Started playing Geographical Pursuit, a lot of fun; all have become relaxed with one another. A few days with them in Sydney, then farewell. Suzy said I was wonderful. Home again, Timida lectured us for leaving her, she had never been so chatty!

Ed and I went to the Tivoli restaurant. Tibe gave me a bottle of Spumante for New Year's. Did fire safety telegram, lost in power shortage, and had to do it again. At home Timida lay in her screened hammock.

Colleen and I went to the Lakeside Hotel regarding rooms for Codel Shalby, made them switch to the refurbished floor. Lunched there. The Princess of Tonga was at the hotel and we saw some of her entourage. Then to Marine House Happy Hour. Turned myself into weight loss place. Have never been so fat! Ed and I went for a food farewell dinner, celebrated my diet by splitting a heavenly dessert.

Took a U.S. congressman's wife to lunch at Hill Station where others had gathered. She asked me the name of the purple flowers along the roadside. I didn't know, but it was pyracantha! I'll never forget it now.

Went camping in Karangra-Boyd National Park with Kate, Lois, Linda. It rained, got wet, had big breakfast and went to Jenolan Caves. The Orient Cave was gorgeous with lovely formations like an ice palace, a perfect site for a science fiction movie. Later played cards called Pitt (corner on market wheat). Got loud and crazy and broke down the last of remaining barriers between us. Liked them all. Lois was in the army and is one of ten children. Linda was married to a communicator for six years and walked away with nothing. Rain. Colleen had sneaked a rubber spider into my sleeping bag. Sun peeked out first time in days and the flies came. Home mid afternoon feeling dead, soaked in the tub. Ed welcomed me with roses, Timida came to say hi.

Got hair done and went to the farewell dinner for Sir John and Lady Leahy; all Brits and we two Americans. Sang whiffenpoof song with John and Peter, ex-Yalies. Two days later, to their farewell reception for 800 of their closest friends, as I mentioned to him in the reception line. Saw Ambassador and Mrs. Lane. Some British came to visit as well as a fellow from the Dutch Embassy from my Admin group. His wife was a Japanese prisoner in Indonesia for over three years in WWII. What a story she had to tell!

Working on inventory reconciliation. Lyn was over for raging rigatoni and talk of office.

Ed and I went to Dr. Nugent re his prostate, plan surgery for February 24..

Saw "Fatal Attraction" a real cliff hanger. If I had seen it in Chicago in the 70's, it might have changed my life style there.

One day Janice walked in with a black eye and pretended she had hit a cupboard. I felt helpless. What easy way does one approach spousal abuse? Had a letter from John saying he wanted each set of parents to lend them $17,000. He's a real dreamer.

Colleen and I went to Yacht Club for an Inner Peace Movement lecture. They herded us into different rooms in chaos. Told us that the 20 minute lecture was free, the next 1-1/2 hr. cost $3 and the next day's workshop was $11. Sounded fishy to us, so we left before the $3 charge. Put some coins in the pokeys (slot machines). The boys in the bar wondered if we had found inner peace.

I had noticed that a hub cap was missing on the right rear tire of the Mercedes. Later at the Yacht Club Colleen and I had lunch and were in our cups. We were parked next to a similar Mercedes from the Russian Embassy. Colleen thought she would steal one of his hubcaps for my car, and somehow managed to work it off his wheel, dashing back to mine for a quick takeoff. Half drunk, we were both hysterical. It was just a few weeks later that the newspaper reported a crash in Canberra by a Mercedes from the Russian Embassy. We felt a bit vindicated somehow, for that car had been totaled.

Feb. 14 - Exchanged our Valentine poems, a tradition we cannot lose.

The QE II pulled into Sydney Harbor, had a TV short on it. It reminded me of being on it in Brazil when several of us saw off

George Little. Had champagne in the lounge for his sendoff to Britain. Ed and I went to Bungendore for lunch at the Carrington, lovely meal, a special place. Lyn, Ramage and I took Greg O'Regan of Prime Minister and Cabinet office to lunch at Seasons restaurant, good food and environment. I enjoyed being the only woman and felt my ego massaged. He and his wife have ten children!

I went to Dr. Greenman, woman doctor who reassured me that Dr. Nugent was an excellent doctor. The DCM's wife, when she heard earlier of Ed's planned surgery, said: "I forbid you to be operated on in Australia!" She was ignored.

Workwise, I was frustrated over inventories with past disasters. Worked on position descriptions. Redid David's. Lost just four pounds in a month. Watched winter olympics, ice skating by Russians. Katrinka is only 16 and Sergei 21. Gold medals.

Blackberry picking in February in my upside, downside world. Went with Linda, Kate and Lois at Urialla Crossing, thorny and bramble bush. We ouched and howled and swore a lot, all the while stomping to keep the snakes away. Heard some rustles and there were a lot of wombat turds. To Muambiggie River for a picnic, waded a bit, and home again mid afternoon. Made blackberry cobbler, very tasty. Janice was raised in Tasmania and said snakes love to hang out in blackberry bushes. Nice!

Checked Ed into Calvary Hospital, luxurious like a Hilton, private room. Ed had a wonderful attitude about this operation so I didn't fret either, at least until the next day! I stayed three hours and met Colleen at the Diplomat Hotel for potpourie textile show. They showered us with champagne and we selected a lot of material for A $12,000. Colleen will cut it down tomorrow when the agent visits the office. Had meatballs and chicken and partook of two brandy alexanders. Timida came in to snuggle with me all nite and was very loving.

To hospital at 8 and Ed was in surprisingly good humor and a pleasure to be around, a lovely positive attitude. So I putzed, played cards, read, brought him some flowers: "To the man I love" and went to the bank. I sneaked wine and sandwich to the bathroom since he had to fast. They rolled him off at 3:00 p.m., seemingly cheerful in his gown, paper pants and blue cap for surgery. His friend Russell hung around a lot and I was annoyed and tense, wanting the experience all to myself. He finally left and I walked to the window with the lovely view and wept. I told myself I wouldn't fret for two hours and did pretty well, but at 5 the suspense killed me. They finally rolled him in at 5:30, pale looking with a pint of blood and saline solution drip. He was cheery until the spinal wore off in four hours and he felt pain. Everyone was attentive and terrific. Dr. Nugent breezed by and I thanked him for taking good care of him. They gave him a shot for the pain. I went home exhausted at 9:10, leaving him with Russell. I love my darling! Timida was hungry and waiting for me.

Feb. 25 - I awoke at 2:30 a.m. fretting. Prayed a lot, went to pick up Timida from the sofa for comfort. Back to sleep til 6. Dialed his number at the hospital, and was so glad he felt better. He said he was suffering at 2:30 a.m. Psychic? I was there after 7, stayed til 9 and went to work. Lots to catch up on. The hospital and staff were phenomenal, cheery and willing, no real sour pusses. I was back at 12:30 for an hour and he mostly wanted me to snurgle as he dozed. Visitors in morn: Peter, Russell, and Bill. Dashed home, started wash, clothes in dryer as I got my hair done, dashed back and Ed wondered where I had been, already spoiled. I dashed back, no dinner. He could go for a walk, pushed his "constant companion." Ran over to hospital at 6:30 next morn with a thermo of coffee. Poopsie loved to be pampered. Stayed til 9. From 6 p.m. Colleen and I had our Yacht Club initiation. They offered wine or beer, a few token "bickies". Commodore chatted, we broke away, had drink in bar and went to Tivoli. I felt I was playing hookey. Called Ed and he had been asleep. Home at 10, Timida slept with me all night. Ed nagged me to get there. Spent 8 hours on 3 different shifts. His bag is now urine yellow, gone from blood to rose to yellow. He's progressing very well, taking Vitamin C and calcium on the side. I went to see "Last Emperor" a true story.

Feb. 28 - They took out his catheter at 6 am. I kept thinking earlier that I'd have so much time to myself, but it hadn't turned out that way. I ran back and forth, take home bloody laundry to wash, needed to return at his whim! He'd been spoiled by his visitors and his loving slave. Timida purred to him over the phone. All is well sez Dr. Nugent, he could go home tomorrow. - Ed and I walked in Telopea Park. Served him chicken sandwich and chips in bed. He loved the pamperage and slept much of the afternoon. In eve we went to Stewarts' barbecue. They had USIS inspectors, total of 20. The chief had been in Panama with us. The Stewarts are the perfect hosts: great lamb, veggies, ice cream, cake. Had a very pleasant eve; Ed was sociable.

Mar. 9 - Ed's 64th birthday. Lunched at Yacht Club. Dinner at Dutchman Jenson's house with Ed. Pleasant.

Colleen and I took Don Ramage to lunch to talk about

Bangkok. He was very forthcoming. Also suggested that I have a hardship tour before retiring so I can take advantage of differential pay. Recommended China. Annual leave is reimbursed at differential pay.

- Something got lost in the translation. Laura and Virginia from the Chicago law firm came to Australia and we were to meet them in Melbourne, I'm not sure why, but we did, took the train. Went to Fast Eddys and Fanny's. We flew back on two different flights. Dropped Ed and I took them to Rehwinklers animal spot: kangaroos, sleeping koalas, wombats. To Bungendore to Carringtons for an enjoyable lunch. Went on a buying spree, Laura with her hats. I even bought one, looked good in it. Virginia looks but doesn't buy, Laura buys several at once. Back to Ed and clams and spaghetti.

Went to the British High Commissioner's for tea. Laura and Virginia were dressed nicely and when we arrived we were sent to the back door. Men were varnishing the floor in the main part of the house. Scones and tea were good, we stuffed them down. Took them to see our American Residence. To Lakeside Inn for dinner, their treat. Ed stayed awake and the scenery at night pleased them. They thought Canberra was lovely. Took Laura and Virginia to Tipsy Gypsy and they bought some of Baba's paintings. Next day they went on to Sydney.

Mar 18 - Andrew Durham, art conservator at the National Gallery, came to check out our Art in Embassy paintings at the Residence, as I located them for him. Spent a pleasant two hours. Then to Ed for a fast bite and I got a bus to Sydney. A four hour ride, met Laura and Virginia. We had an Italian meal and Laura was addicted to the pokeys (slot machines). Walked through the Chinese Gardens at Darling Harbor. Lovely design with waterfalls and pagodas. Chinatown beer and wine and dim sim. Paddy's market. In eve to see "Nine" at Her Majesty's Theatre. What a lovely surprise, it was wonderful. Based on Fellini's 8-1/2. Huge and voluptuous women corrupting young boys. Everyone was terrific. The all Aussie cast will go to Broadway. Took bus home. Ed met me and missed me. Laura and Virginia leave tomorrow for Hawaii.

To my art lesson with Baba. Chaos reigned as Baba and Stefano screamed awhile. Her theory of art: think of the bulk, the core of something. Visualize it, and draw it with your eyes closed. It worked better for me than when I tried to intellectualize or draw from view. I was there for 5 hours. She said that ten lessons were all that's needed for a foundation. I could then pursue it on my own. She had quite an ego.

Mar 26 - Colleen and I headed out for two weeks to Manila, Hong Kong, Bangkok, Malasia, Singapore. An Aussie acquaintance of Colleen's had arranged our hotel and we arrived in Manila to a very sleazy bar girl hotel with a dingy dirty room. We checked the beds and found dingy linens and escaped to Sehalis Hotel, 5 star but down at the heels.

- Called our Kepler friends from Canberra now transferred to Manila and spent a day and night with them. Lovely handicraft center, museums, lovely church which could have been in Spain, Mexico or South America. To lunch at a seafood restaurant where you chose your own crab. It tried to crawl out of the shopping basket; live fish flopped in the bag. Quite dramatic, but ate well at $10 per person. In eve went to a lovely Japanese restaurant.

- Learned that the Embassy was on alert because NPA (New Peoples Army) promised to kill an important Embassy person this week. Bob got us a bullet proof van to transport us to the airport for Hong Kong. Grand Hotel, Kowloon side. Drink at the Peninsula Hotel.

- Half day tour to Stanley market and Aberdeen to see water people living on crowded boats. Bought a sapphire ring and gold bangled earrings for $500 US.

- To Wong Tai Sim Temple to have our fortune sticks read in a very small alleyway. Assured us that health was good. To American Consulate and got passes to the China fleet on the Hong Kong side. They assumed Colleen was American. Peeked into Mandarin Hotel, still elegant. Also to Hilton where I had stayed 20 years ago. It was no longer the tallest building, now dwarfed by others. Had a wonderful martini and food at Jimmy's Kitchen. We were relaxed and happy and ate there again later on. Shipped our shopping goodies to Australia at China Fleet.

- We were the only Occidentals at Fortuna restaurant with a houseful of chattering Chinese. Quite an experience. One man dropped face first into his plate of food. No one was alarmed.

- At the airport we were offered first class and executive upgrades to take an earlier flight. Colleen took first but we ate the same food and had the same attention. A nice Japanese man was next to me and his adorable daughter Fumi came to visit. It was a wonderful 2 hr. 15 min. flight to Bangkok. Letty from our office in Canberra came to our Asia hotel with flowers and dragged us out to shop before we had time to decompress. We met her entire Philippine family, it seemed. We went to dinner at Tam Nak Thai, the world's largest restaurant, very lovely with ponds and pavilions, bus boys on roller skates in constant motion, ordering done by computer stations. Fifteen of us were in our group. I have never sat down to a more exotic display of food: flamed chicken, poached fish, Thai dishes, all delicious with lots of sauces, mango, sticky rice, at least fifteen selections served promptly and with flare.

- A sweet Thai girl in an attractive uniform took 8 of us in a minibus for the Royal Palace tour the next day. Quite a few halls and wots (temples), all very spectacular in Thai, Chinese, and Cambodian styles. It was 97 degrees farenheit, dripping humidity. We sat in the Buddhist temple minding not to place our feet toward Buddha. We spoiled ourselves later with massages, manicures, pedicures given by gentle, lovely women.

- Took peasant class flight to Singapore, with orchids and free liquor. To the York Hotel in Goodwood Park for dinner, an old elegant hotel. A seahorse as an ornate butter sculpture was poised over the buffet.

- Had breakfast at the zoo with an orangatan, homely creature with an orange bottom. He didn't care what you did to him as long as he was fed first. Got our picture. We then had very fine Russian stroganoff at the Balalaika restaurant in our hotel. We meandered to the Raffles Hotel for the signature Singapore Sling. Ate at Palm Court and the crab and spinach crepe was delicious. Went to visit Jerry and Magda Rosenblum at their security-laden apartment. He had been IRS rep in Brazil. Their walls were filled with her paintings; she's quite talented. Jerry gave us a downtown tour and tips for income tax filing.

- We rented a car and off we went to Malaysia. It was a bit tricky shifting with the left hand and driving on the wrong side of the road! But we did it. Found a shop with the perfect wedding dress for Colleen's daughter, to be wed soon after we arrived home. $135 US, all hand done. At the main border town we had to shi shi in an Arab-style two footer. Colleen was repulsed. Back to Singapore, we devoured rigatoni, salad and margarita at the Hyatt, having had no lunch on the road.

Next day in the Indian section of Singapore with the exotic smell of spices in huge baskets and a surly old Indian man in a shop, I looked for a Malacan cane for Ed. Had no luck so bought an opium pipe of silver and blue and white porcelain, still on my coffee table today. But it has never housed opium during my reign. Goodwood Park's Chinese restaurant dinner was both elegant and delicious.

Going home the next day was fraught with inconvenience. We sat on the Quantas plane's runway 2-1/2 hours as they fixed a suspect gauge. Slept restlessly on 6-1/2 hour flight to Sydney, arriving two hours later than estimated. Dear Ed and Colleen's clan met us in Canberra. It was so great to see him once more. At home I needed Ed to hug and snurg (our name?) and he kept at it the entire day.

We had our sexual fling, sorely in need. Timida was attentive, kept coming around to make certain I was really back home. Blustery weather.

- Back to work. Colleen and I collected six boxes from the APO and dug into them at my house at lunchtime. It was Christmas all over again! We had a new data entry person, Christine Bird, an American married to an Aussie. She's a figure skating instructor by night.

- Had the Martins to lunch, a roaring fire.

Apr 23 - attended Colleen's daughter Tina's wedding. Ed spoke to the father-in-law in Greek and was a hit.

May 1 - On May Day we both labored and cleaned the house.

- Ed and I weighed 85 kilos and 65 kilos respectively, which translates to 187 and 143. Decided we needed to carve off a few pounds, a community project.

More and more I note blank pages in my diary, unknown in past diaries. I attribute that to the general frustration at my work, always rushing to another project before one had been completed. I was harried constantly by those dissatisfied with their housing, requesting various repairs, or some even chose me to vent their own frustrations. I should have hung out a shingle! My blood pressure shot up, the Embassy nurse was nearby.

-- A farewell Happy Hour for secretary Steve. I will miss that character!

- In mid of night Ed narrowly escaped disaster as the light fixture in the kitchen dropped and exploded into a thousand smithereens as he was about to enter the room.

Baba had an art lesson in Telopea Park with some of her Jewish friends and me. One worked on watercolors. I concentrated on leaves, felt I was getting somewhere. Stephano took me home.

Timida is back with us after disappearing five days; I don't know when she returned! She now nestles with us each night.

- Another Embassy auction. I bought old fireplace antirons from the Ambassador's residence for some future fireplace.

- Colleen, Linda and I went to Tipsy Gypsy for wonderful stuffed cabbage. Stefano looked pale with his enlarged heart; wants to sell the restaurant.

- To Canberra Theatre Center to see "Giselle" by the Australia Ballet Company; did a lovely job of it.

- Drove van of trainees from the Dept. of Defense to briefings by our administrative sections. We lunched at the Tivoli. I became the old comedienne from my past and entertained the troops. An Indonesian fellow said as they departed: "I admire your driving!" What a laugh! An enjoyable two hours.

- Nice crisp air that I love. Stole a branch of red berries for the dining room table. Ann and the kids came for lunch.

The first part of June we moved to 14 Aland Place, Fadden, as our Australian foreign service landlords were to return home before my tour had ended. The vet had overdosed Timida's tranquilizer for the move. She was like a zombie for several days and it was scary. Lyn Dent went off several times to work on Reagan visits, leaving me to tend the shop.

- Unpacking to make the place a home. Timida likes the warm family room in the sun.

- Timida has become anxious to explore the jungle next door. We are next door to a forest preserve.

June 21 - The shortest day in Australia is the longest day in the U.S.

- Hung 14 pictures on the wall, finalized the nest.

- Weekend lovemaking. To Carrington restaurant at Bungendore for lunch. Angela sold her bookshop and it certainly is not the same without her.

- Ed asked me, Colleen, Lyn, and Linda to lunch and we all ended up at a Vietnamese restaurant - enjoyable.

- Had an open house from 4-8 pm which lasted until 11 pm with the diehards. Liz, Colleen's daughter wants to babysit Timida while we're gone. She told them later that if anything happened to them she'd see if I would adopt her. Quite a compliment.

July 4 - The U.S. shot down an Iranian passenger plane with 290 aboard. The Ambassador called for a moment of silence at the 4th of July reception.

- Timida has been sleeping next to me on top of the down comforter, never getting under the covers. She is so precious to us, the child we never had.

- Had a brunch, 12 of us. As I heard the gossip undertow I thought of the pettiness of the gang at the Chancery, sticking their heads in unwanted and unmerited, and got depressed. My very least loved posting!

- The Foreign Service that has offered me the travel I needed certainly has not measured up in other needed respects. Conrad informed us in a staff meeting that the Macarthur rapist would strike again in three days, I asked does he telephone in his schedule? Got some laughs over that.

- Inspectors here. When interviewing the FSN's Peter told one of them that I was the only ray of sunshine in the office, that I livened things up (referring to the American duo). I heard of his comments through Colleen, so of course I was swayed to the Aussie side a bit.

- To fortune teller at Colleen's house. All were impressed by Ann Bishop's pronouncements. Many hit head on.

July 19 - Sign on Residence lawn: "Yankee murderers, Imperialists OUT!! " A symbol indicated the same person who had damaged South African cars earlier.

July 23 - We took a bus to Sydney, staying at the Park Apartments. Went to see "Les Miserables" at Theatre Royal, great seats in row G. Really appreciated the fine voices.

July 24 - We are in the midst of Australia's 200th Birthday Celebration. We became miffed with each other and he deserted me; I meandered on my own. The fireworks over the Harbour Bridge were lavish and unending.

July 31 - Took the Russian icon I had purchased in Brazil to "Love or Money" crew at the Hyatt. Was told it was worth between $5000-$10,000 Aussie dollars, and that it was especially lovely.

August 11 - Goodbye to Timida for now. Bill Martin will catsit as we head to the States for John and Emmanuelle's wedding in Berkeley, California.

Aug. 14/15 - We are house hunting with Joyce Ford in Los Osos, California. Saw a couple, made up two offers. Had to sign releases to acknowledge that "yes, we know Diablo Canyon nuclear plant is down the coast, and the San Andreas fault is just over the coastal range, and we won't blame California when they both erupt!" Oh yes, another disclosure regarding Indian reservation artifacts!

- Whirlwind real estate deal went through with female realtors Joyce and Marie, lender/Pamela; and broker escrow officer Barbara. All females, how could we fail? Ed could not believe that we had done it! We took the Amtrak train to San Jose. John and Emmanuelle met us and took us to Palo Alto. Emmanuelle, French and mignon, is lively, an active vital person, tiny, probably size 3.

When we were reunited with Suki, he gave a cool greeting but later joined us in bed and was wildly affectionate and so loving that

I almost cried.

- Emmanuelle's father Bernard, a pediatrician, seemed to be very nervous and smoked a lot. Renee, Emmanuelle's mother, was the pharmacist in La Haie-Fouassière, a no-nonsense type of person. Ed surprisingly seemed to get along well with Bernard, lack of common language didn't hold him back. Nina, a Filipina married to Rene, was nice and served as interpreter. Thus, a celebration of the Frogs and the Hogs.

- Hogs came from Arkansas. (Their college football team is the razorbacks?) To a seafood restaurant in Oakland with Betty, Renee and Bernard, John and Emmanuelle, Bev and Ed. I learned later and awkwardly that it was to be our treat. All were on their best behavior.

Aug 20 - A lovely wedding ceremony in Berkeley's Rose Garden. Met Estelle, Ed's ex for the first time. Her only words to me: "I owe you a lot." (Because I write the alimony checks?) She is 69 and looks 90.

It was a lively reception with a typical French wedding cake of sticky balls stacked into a pyramid. I had first seen the like at a wedding in Tunisia 1966. Dancing was lively. Emily's grandchild red haired Travis was a wild break dancer who kept everyone in stitches. He might have been six. The French siblings observed the American antics. I danced with anyone. The ones I knew had a wonderful time. It was a successful meeting of the hogs and frogs!

- We learned of a real French farce. The wedding couple had been turned away from their hotel because they neglected to make a late-late reservation; then were turned away at two other hotels and ended up sleeping in the car. After reporting all the drama, they flew off to honeymoon at the Biltmore in Santa Barbara. The French crowd went their way and we enjoyed the Arkansas crowd at Giovanni's restaurant that evening.

Aug 22 -   Ed and I flew from San Francisco to Washington, D.C. Stayed in Crystal City near the Washington National airport.

- Ed was nominated as Guest of the Day with a split of champagne and a basket of fruit, He went to a Capitol Hill meeting with Hal. We later met Jack and Liz at an Indian/Cambodian Shiannok restaurant with luscious food.

- Joined Hal and Rosita at the International Club. She can be a bit of a shrew, ordering him around. They both interrupt people's conversation. In eve to Gail's caipirinha and onto an Afghan restaurant, quite delicious.

- Ed and Hal went to State Dept. I went to Reston to see Kathy, Jim and Meg who will go to Geneva in October, marrying beforehand. She always lifts me up.

- Ed had money stolen in the motel, plus my Olympus camera was gone with all the pictures from the wedding in it! Onto Chicago where Laura picked us up in her new El Dorado. Met Aunt Bev Enslin at a restaurant and Ed was chatty at his only event with her. Later Laura and I went to Ann's house in the woods with Bev and dinner with Ann, Scott, Chris, Jean and husband Sid. Had some laughs.

- To Greek restaurant with Laura and Ed. Joyce and Larry had to cancel the trip to meet us in Chicago because of rain and flooding. Larry as waterworks head had to fix the mess. She was all upset and we had a long phone chat.

- Flew to Denver, met by Judy and Wayne and a salmon cookout dinner.

- Endured a lumpy sofa bed. Ed off to a noon meeting. Wayne was making a summer shed for his Texas Longhorn bull Ole. He had him and a woodchuck eating literally out of his hands. Judy made a turkey meal with all the trimmings.

- They had 14 adult peacocks and 8 of their kids wandering on their land. He had a landscape business and a load of saplings growing on the place.

- Judy drove us to the airport for the Billings flight. Second cousin Sally and husband Terry met us with their 2-1/2 yr. old grandchild Amber, a bit of a terror. We learned that a Delta 727 had crashed in Dallas while we were in the air. Visited with cousin Joanne and her husband Bob with the Interior Dept. There was animated talk about the Yellowstone Park fires and the rotten policy of the Park Service.

- Drove to Red Lodge and Roberts to visit Uncle Ted, Mom's oldest brother. He drove his four-wheel drive fearlessly through a herd of cattle to daughter Joyce's house, where second cousins paraded in and out the wazoo! I couldn't help but feel Mom would have had a happier life in Montana with her relatives than being isolated in Peoria, Illinois with just a few of us.

- Tracked down cousin Barbara in Red Lodge who took us to the Roberts cemetery where Mom was buried in 1964. Lots of sobs. Back to Billings Northern Hotel and dinner with Sandy, Ione's daughter and her well-to-do husband Jerry. Dinner was somewhat strained.

- Sally and Terry took us to the airport in Billings and back we went to Colorado to Judy and Wayne. Off to a Mexican restaurant. All went to see "A Fish Called Wanda." It was terrific, a blend of

US and English humor.

- Labor Day picnic chicken/steak cookout, potato salad, deviled eggs, salad.

- I'm impressed by Judy's talents, healing nature within her. Her "spirit guide" stated she had been a healer in other lives. They took us to the airport and I had a wonderful sense of peace on the flight. I'm certain Judy gave me a surge of healthy energy. Flew to L.A. and Cathy picked us up and we waited for Joyce who took us to Burbank. There we signed escrow papers for the house in Los Osos.

- The Burbank smog is worse than L.A. Lunched with Ken Karst, ex-law school classmate of Ed's, now UCLA law school professor. They were a pleasant, down to earth couple. In eve Cathy and David met us at Bobby McGees. It had a kookie atmosphere, served by Miss Kitty, Houdini, Little Bo Peep. I called it my Disneyland; enjoyable repast.

- Spoke with Ambassador and Ruth Cheslaw and Paul Sadler on the east coast. They all said we had to stay with them the next round. Cathy took us to airport. Strong winds, had to lighten load. We volunteered when they offered two free RT domestic flights plus stay and meals at Sheraton, plus business class from Honolulu to Sydney! That sold us!

I cannot believe that I had blank pages in my diary from September 10 through to September 23 which included the overnight in Honolulu, the business class seats to Australia, and my own birthday September 17, turning 51 years.

Sept 23 - Dr. Ingram, the dermatologist removed stiches from my ankle area. The biopsy said it was Bowen's disease.

- A kookaburra visited us on the back deck. It has a crazy cackle

I've tried to imitate. We watered the lawn at 94 Endeavour. The lilac sprig in Woo's memory is budding again.

Sept 25 - Had dinner for the Martins. There was a curtness in me I almost did not recognize. (Menopause strikes its onery head?) I talked about there being no perfect marriage. Ann asked "Is that directed at me?" since they were having problems. I said it was directed at all of us. In the evening we went to a Cheshire gathering at Jack Thurger's house where I spoke with Major General Bakhis and wife Shiva. I enjoyed her very much; she was gracious and kind. Said that November and March were the ideal times to visit India. August had monsoons. A drunken uncle said I was beautiful and wanted my phone number. I cannot abide by full-fledged drunks.

- I'm definitely going through a bleak period. Every call I received one day was from a "whinger" a perfect Aussie term for whiner. Rosie J called to say Dick didn't like attached houses. I told her it was too late. Victoria called to complain about furniture, Mike H to complain about his landlord, it went on and on and I couldn't get any answers out of Don R. It was so exasperating. The beauty shop rejected me and I had to go another and she was a disaster and I could hardly keep from screaming. Finally she did it in a passable chignon. To APO to hear their grievances about letting Ray go and somehow I was made to feel responsible. There were not enough hours in the day to handle all the disasters. I went home to Ed and Timida exhausted.

- Wandered to Goulburn, Bowral. Stole some early lilacs. When Timida came in she did a strange thing. Smelling the lilacs, she reached up to the table in the bedroom and jumped up to sniff each blossom. I asked "Did you love lilacs too in a former life? (as I must have)" It was very interesting since she never got up on tables or counters in our house.

Oct. 6 - Richard Johnson showed up - Lyn's replacement. Lyn had pulled strings from influential friends to get out early.

- A kookaburra came to flap his wings against the window. We've had 8 or 9 such house calls. It dawned on me that perhaps he thinks the lamp cord was a snake. Kookaburras are carnivores. It is a lovely creature with a fluffy crewcut, blue markings, long tail and long beak.

Had Richard, Don Cleveland, Marie H for dinner. Don had been here a month and said it was his best meal in Canberra. Ed was good and even let Don interrupt him.

- Another auction at the warehouse with others participating. I got a chest of drawers I needed for A $160.

- To Ron and Jo Mortensons' African dinner with their old African hands. Couscous for ex-Peace Corps Director they had known before. He was fat and arrogant and had to command the conversation.

- Weighed in at a ridiculous 68 kilos or 149.6 pounds, my heaviest yet! Linda happily took Richard to view houses. I plodded away on reports, collect the traffic. He is not at all eager to take the reins, and is too cheap to rent a car. In eve Ed and I went to see "The Unbearable Lightness of Being" Beautifully done.

- The Ambassador hinted at leaving at year's end, not accepting any appointment by either party. He told Richard he'd pack out by Christmas. I fasted for two days. Karen Allen, Kale's wife, will star in "Glass Menagerie." Baba and Stefano have sold Tipsy Gypsy and are making new plans.

Oct. 22 - I learned I was on the promotion list. Terrific! I told the informant she made the rainy day sunny. Nick and DCM called to congratulate me. Ed and I went to see "Glass Menagerie." Karen Allen was Laura, daughter of Joanne Woodward's Miranda." Fine actors all.

- To Octoberfest with Don Cleveland, Pat Parker. Danced the polka with Don. Heard Richard was a womanizer and his wife was anti-American. Should be an interesting couple.

Nov 5 - Fretted over Robert's hip surgery all day. Sandy later told me that he was on the table 4-1/2 hours and they almost lost him; gave 8 units of blood. It was the 4th time they've gone into that same hip!

- Day for gifts. Greg Polson, ex-landlord, came with beads and fan from Tuvalu, was happy their house was well cared for. The South Korean Embassy gave me a lovely scarf thanking for the loan of 12 transformers.

Nov 12 - to the Marine Ball with Colleen and Roger. Ed had given up on Marine Balls. I danced quite a bit; it was just fun enough but not as much as last year.

- To British High Commission for Trevor Williams farewell. Vernor, the German from our admin lunches and wife Ursula were the most interesting. They love Australia, have been here five years and flew around to see most of it.

Nov 24 - Thanksgiving at Linda Hayes. Lois and her mother, Kate, tried to be courteous to Bill L. Made rice with sage dressing. Rainy on and off. Told to dress casually, so I wore Red Lodge black shirt and pants.

- Spent the day pulling dandelions with Andrew and was weary.

Ed was in the way as I tried to prepare dinner, so he went off in a huff. Later on he was conciliatory but weary me did not speak to him. We went to bed that way, contrary to his mother Woo's instructions: "Never go to bed on an argument!" We woke up friends the next day and went to a second Thanksgiving at the Martins. A nice few hours.

Dec 1 - State Dept doctor Viss from Jakarta was in town, went to discuss Bowens Disease, which rarely metastasizes. My BP was 164/100, highest I've had. Now it is urgent that I lose weight and exercise regularly. (Not to mention get out of here!)

- I made rice and tomatoes, my favorite pamper-me dish I had eaten when I had hepatitis. Ed and I walked in the neighborhood. I felt the benefit immediately.

- Dreamed Ed and I were forbidden to fly out of some country and we ended up in a light plane, barely making it over trees and buildings. Then we were literally flying on our own, soaring and swooping and it was thrilling, coming down fast onto some lovely view. It was great. Dream aside, I settled down into work for the brunch, beavering away on the hottest day of the season. Pat Parker, Gertrude Carpenter, Rosie and Richard, Colleen and Roger. Rosie thinks she is cute and coy being controversial, hates Willie Nelson, cats, Americans. She's also in love with her own voice, therefore having the least to offer. Colleen is good, entertaining a crowd with her stories.

Dec 10 - I awoke in the middle of the night after the strangest dream. Ed and I were planning to poison ourselves and die together. We ate household cleaner and felt the numbness, waiting to die. Timida was there and her body was stiff, she was in on it too. I awoke to feel her warm supple body and I was relieved. Told Ed and he said you can be glad it's only a dream. I love the weekends home with my Big Darling and my Little Darling. We have a lovely house with a charming view of the Brindabellas. Timida shows up at many glass doors. She'll climb up the gum tree in the back of the house and end up on the veranda. This she does when she is showing off a little. How I love the little precious! I tell her so constantly.

Dec 11 - To an IBM brunch, with a nice couple from Arkansas. Later to see "Babette's Feast" a warmhearted story about insulated folk who stay home all their lives vs. the ones who wander off. Wherein does contentment lie for both? Babette's Feast, of course!

Dec. 12 - Dreamed of a snake draped around the fish pond, big, long and brown.

Dec. 14 - Gino the painter, treated Don Barnes, Richard, Linda, Colleen and me to lunch at La Scala in Civic. He was sweet, and it went well. I wasn't feeling great, went home to bed for a couple hours. Ed was impatient and annoyed that I went out to Torville and Dean and the Russian All-Star skaters when I wasn't well. I appreciated them though. Home 11:30 pm.

Dec 16 - Stayed home with cold. Ramage had called me and told me I had been invited to the meeting he had with Richard yesterday. I said "that's interesting, I never heard that I was." I don't trust Richard and I don't really like him.

- Lunch with Pat and Colleen at Tivoli. They gave us 3 bottles of champagne and treated us to lunch for Christmas. We were pretty happy by the 3rd bottle, could have stopped at 2.

Dec 23 - Gift drawing game was fun, with everyone stealing from one another. Christine came, I gave her Red Label. Peter and

Art gave me champagne, Bernie a wooden piece, Gino port.

Dec 24 - Brought homemade egg nog to Colleen's. Daughter and friend, at least half of them were smoking. Ed came with me at midnite 11:15 service Uniting Church in Kingston. Hot, candlelight service. At least some singing to put one more in the mood for Christmas.

Dec 25 - We gave each other six classical compact discs and played them all day. Ann and Bill and the kids, Colleen and Roger came to eat. Turkey, stuffing, Waldorf salad, pumpkin pie. Ann made pecan. I was quite weary by the time the guests arrived. Heavy rain in avo (as the Aussies say).

Dec 26 - Slept 10 hours on Boxing Day. Asked Baba and Stefano over for leftovers. They brought Tahitian chef named Phillipe, who said Marlon Brando had no style, sleeps on the floor like the natives. Said the island is divided between Brando's ex-family and his present one, with a line drawn in the middle.

Dec. 27 - Met Ann and Bill at Bateman's Bay, two hours to their rental place. Had junk at lunch and in eve lovely oysters kilpatrick and natural lamb chops, salad. Tasted divine after earlier junk food. Home 8:45 p.m. Timida in all day.

Dec 29 - Pampered Timida and Ed in morn. Got a perm. To Baba and Stefano for delicious stuffed cabbage dinner, Two other Hungarians there, entertaining. They spoke of Sydney and settling in the Blue Mountains. Timida came to cuddle between my legs. What a wonderful creature she is!

Dec. 30 - Pat and I went to Tivoli for lunch and I told her that Tony's son was the MacArthur rapist. She was shocked. Later Timida didn't come home for dinner. Ed and I went to Woden, looked around a bit, bought some things, home at 8. Still no Timida. Ed went to the back veranda and there she was sitting by the tree limb she had climbed up. I gathered her in my arms and told her how much we loved her. She didn't want to be held, ran upstairs and went under the bed. I pulled her out again; her black coat had a dull sheen, she was almost pale. Let her back under the bed and saw she was breathing, I kept wondering. Ed said let her rest, she'd be okay. Then a thumping and I realized she was in convulsions. Called the vet and met there. He wanted me to help as he shaved around her paw area, I was shaking and of no help. He said it had to have been a black snake, she would have died instantly if a brown snake had bit her. Gave anti-venom serum. She had this pitiful sound, glassy eyes, unconscious, semiconscious. I said "Timida, come back to us because we love you!" He took her home with him and said he'd call if anything happened to her.

Dec. 31 - Got the call at 8:00 a.m. "I thought she'd pull through at 3 a.m. but just after 6 a.m. she gave up." Our little darling died. We were down to the clinic at 9 and Dr. Pilkington talked with us and I asked to see her. "Are you sure you want to?" I nodded. There was Timida in the cage, curled up and dead. I asked if she'd suffered in the end and he said "you can see how relaxed she was." I petted her and she was cold. Her sweet white foot, I petted that. Ed remarked how beautiful she was. I wanted to see her face again, but it was faced downward and rigor mortis had set in. I petted her head again and said: "You were a special kitty cat!" tears streaming down of course. Ed and I had to run away from home, the memories were running rampant. We packed a few things and went to Bundendore's Carrington Hotel. We picked a pleasant room. Ed had brought five newspapers and we purchased books at the bookstore and read a lot to occupy our minds, I cried for at least 12 hours, intermittently at lunch. They must have thought we were divorcing. Spent most of the time in the room. We had takeaway Chinese for our New Year's Eve. They had a five-course meal in the hotel dining room and a band that blasted away until 2 a.m.

Australia 1989 (last 6 months)

Jan 1 - Ed and I made love at the Carrington to begin the New Year. Drove to Batesman's Bay in pouring rain. Got some oysters for good luck and Ed sang to the Greeks at the takeaway. To Ann and Bill's. I cried and couldn't talk about our loss. So sad to return to Timida's house. Felt compulsed, had to vacuum under the bed, our room, trying to get out every hair, every reminder. Washed 3 or 4 loads of laundry like Lady MacBeth run rampant. I cried oh how I cried and asked Timida's forgiveness for not taking her in earlier. Oh what a sad, sad life!Wondered over and over again if Timida had been on the back veranda all the time we had been at the shopping center, how long was she in agony? One kicks oneself over and over again. I liked turning my anguished self over to Ed, to let him care for me, tend to me. Everytime I told someone about Timida at the Embassy, I cried. I kept telling them and after awhile I could do it without weeping. I had no interest in work or Australia. I kept expecting a warm little body to curl up on the bed between my legs. It did not happen. Ed did not want to live in this house anymore, but we had almost six months to go. After a week I then wanted to save Timida's hairs to put into a box.

- Ed had a bad day over Timida, home all day with the memories. Had a wild, fast storm like a hurricane. I told Ed Timida came to say hi. Moped around feeling sorry for myself. I thought about what a rough life Mom had, losing her father, her son, her sister, two husbands seemingly every few years. She had always maintained an optimistic attitude. I hadn't had grief in 24 years! (When I lost her!)

- Christine came over and we talked of cats; she spent $4500 caring, feeding and quarantining hers for nine months when she moved from the States. I gave her catfood and supplies, past Cat Fancy magazines. She offered to lend a cat, has 3 US and 1 aussie. She went ape over the CDs and records she would copy for the ice skating classes she taught.

- To Dr. Ingram, dermo. Froze off more Bowens from my ankle and was chatty, left others waiting. Talked about Aussie anti-US sentiment, how socialism had taken over, everyone felt a right to his share without working for it, how unions blackmail to get the job done at his daughter's dress shop in Sydney. He had to pay $200 per week "confidence" money for the foreman's special tea, etc.

- The big event at work was to unroll the new dining room rug at the Residence to the glee of Mrs. Lane and the Ambassador. I got a lot of undeserved attention. The Ambassador went to his wine cellar to give me a 1983 good chardonney, so I kissed him on the cheek. Richard didn't appreciate the attention, I could tell. The Lanes will stay at least until April, though it won't be definite until Bush has an Ambassador named. They had a big, friendly yellow Labrador who managed to damage their carpet. I had suggested to the Admin Counselor that they pay for the replacement. Don't know the final answer on that one.

On a trip to Sydney, I saw Art Gallery exhibit "Gold of the Pharoahs." Loved it: coffins, funeral masks, lots of jewelry brought into eternity, 300 slaves as well! Ed went to a meeting and I to the pokeys. Had a grand time on $10, kept winning 100 coins, 50s.

After two hours of thorough enjoyment I walked out with $12 profit. Returned home to a sad house, no Timida awaiting us.

- I've come to the realization that Colleen plays one person off against the other. Later a hard storm blew up to release tension. I love them. I feel Timida has roared in with her spirit to pay us a visit.

- Richard and Colleen sneaked off to Sydney to be spoiled in Xerox's Cricket box.

- Had a harrowing three weeks of having a stray black cat come around wanting adoption by us. I forbade myself to touch her in memory of Timida and not allowing myself to become attached. I did feed her out of sympathy and Ed and I finally got her into a box to take her to the shelter. Donated $50; they deserve a medal. Took "Kangaroo" out at video place. D.H. Lawrence said of Australia: "the place seems to have almost a physical indifference to either soul or spirit." Freda thought the landscape sad, "as if man had never loved it." I am in accord with both.

- To visit the multicultural stalls in Canberra; lovely weather and it was nice to see all those foreigners. Ed had paella. I had spring rolls and Czech beer. To the movie "Maurice" E.M. Forster's autobiography. Enjoyed it.

- Felt compelled to write a Letter to Editor about people who abandon their pets.

- The Residence had a lunch of pasta salad, etc. for GSO people with thanks for the new rug. I talked with the Ambassador about retirement, his and mine, visiting Sunset magazine. He talked about riding horseback with his friend Reagan into the sunset.

Jan 26 - Australia Day. Breakfast at Hyatt. Movie: "Who

Framed Roger Rabbit." It was clever, stupid and violent. Fireworks at Red Hill in evening were disappointing.

- Stickell DAO (Defense Attache Officer) told DCM who told Ramage ADM Counselor who told Richard who told me that I had said Dillpickle (my nickname) was forbidden to enter their house until we were finished with it. A wondrous game of telephone, and illustration of how Beverly hates bureaucracy. The naval person's wife had been pestering painters and others getting her house ready for the inhabitants. She had a pronounced sense of noblesse oblige.

February

- Richard Johnson had 3 or 4 opportunities to introduce me to FBO people from Washington and he chose not to do so. Bernie's 10 yr. service ceremony was at the Ambassador's office and Johnson didn't tell me. I was livid. I ranted to Letty and Rod so the FBO guys could hear me. Later I took the FBO fellows to see Embassy-owned houses and shopping so they could buy their Akubra hats and dryzabone coats. Managed to have some fun with them.

- Robert from the Burmese Embassy came to get a grounds tour of U.S. Embassy. I walked him around. He was most impressed by all the space we had. In eve I had my first pottery class. I struggled with the clay.

- I'm offended by the treatment doled out to me by Richard and Ramage and thought about a rebellion.

- I didn't even call in today. Richard called 9:30 a.m. wondering. I said I felt I didn't exist around there, so didn't think anyone would know I was gone. I told him I would make a list of my grievances, didn't know how far I'd take them. I met Carol Poulson (ex-landlord) in Manuka and we drank 1-1/2 bottles of white wine. She told me her Tuvalu stories, how an intruder had punched her in the stomach and caused a miscarriage, got peridonitis, etc. and that is partially why they came back early. If they'd stayed, we'd be at Red Hill and Timida would be alive. Is that stinkin' thinkin' or what? I delivered my list of grievances to Richard and said I'd be glad to discuss them. Made better pots at class in eve. Some urchins had stolen the Mercedes symbol from the hood of my car.

March

- We set up the Cheshire Foundation meeting. Jack was bartender and cook. I gave drinks and cleaned up. Ed made coffee. There were 18 there; it turned out well: 13 Aussies, 1 Canadian, 2 Brits and 2 Americans. Enjoyed it thoroughly, the weather was perfect, view lovely and no insects.

- Ed was feeling down after seeing a nuclear waste program on TV and what humans do to one another. Lunched at the Yacht Club. Richard and I had a pow wow and he went down my list of complaints to "explain." Some I fell for, most NOT. Not worth the hassle for 3-1/2 months. I felt better anyway and will try to dwell on the positive in all of my affairs.

- Read "Magic Presence" and was upbeat much of the day. About this time I learned I was to be Personnel officer in Managua, Nicaragua. Wrote Harry Bergold asking his opinion since he had just been Ambassador there. It would fill the retirement post, with its differential pay.

- At pottery class, did three. My creations are certainly distinctive. No one would mistake their thin walled creations for mine, which are bulky and heavy, like commie peasants.

- I was ranting in general to Charley Jackson one day and Peter kept whispering "pure thoughts!" After finishing Unveiled Mysteries, I had then said I must think "pure thoughts." After my diatribe I then said " I must think pure thoughts: Bless you, my children!" In the eve I walked with my French neighbor, married to a Pole; she still misses France after 35 years.

- I stopped at Poulsons after work for a drink. Other women stopped in, one was in Fiji with the Johnsons and called Rosie a bitch. Carol is kookie, her children drive me crazy. The Tivalu savage unzipped his pants and urinated off the porch.

- To Robert's Burmese farewell lunch: 4 Burmese, 2 Aussies, 1 Israeli, and myself. I was the only woman. Enjoyable. Peking duck and other fancy things. He's sorry to have to return to Burma, worries about his children's schooling. Ed and I later went to a Texas barbecue.

- We took an old second class train to Melbourne. I heard you can get a No Drinking carriage as well as a No Smoking one. Then a flight to Tasmania, how I love the sound of it, how it rolls off your tongue. To Derby where Rod was raised, an old mining town. I looked up a Kath Delaney for Rod and delivered a candy gift he had sent her. She spoke fondly of him. It was a long drive to Swansea Lester Cottage, built 1830. Iron rods inside our room held the foundation together. We roamed the 3-block town, ate at the hotel, crawfish cocktail. Our temporary house is filled with lovely antiques, gorgeous bed lamps. Bed at 8.

- We drove to Freycynet National Park lighthouse for a view of all the bays. Lovely. Tasmania is green and clean. Richmond is a lovely historic town. I found a colorful watercolor for a Tasmanian souvenir, $230 A. To Mt. Prospect for a colonial accommodation, charming. The meal was elegant: tomato/basil soup, chicken divine, best meal in a long while. A British couple from Melbourne were friendly. Had a fantastic egg/bacon in a custard cup for breakfast. Saw the oldest bridge in Australia, had ducks chase us for food. I saw a woman in a shop with a washstand for sale, and we worked on a deal for $255 Aussie shipped to Canberra. Lovely!

- Hobart, a lovely town. To Nelson through Huon Forest and back to Hobart. It was difficult to believe that such a peaceful, gorgeous island as Tasmania had been the scene of such slaughter of the aboriginals 200 years earlier. It was the only spot in Australia or New Zealand that completely wiped out the indigenous population. Today it is economically depressed (did God get even?) with little industry. Much of its population has sought employment on the mainland and left the natural beauty to few inhabitants and occasional tourists. We lunched at an Italian place and she served me a glass of wine even when not licensed. On a mini-tour we saw mules, cows and horses all nestling one another's necks. So Tasmania today is a real love-in. We dined at Mure's on the Victoria Wharf. Ed had great ocean trout; I wasn't as lucky with my mushy prawn salad.

- When we left after another congenial breakfast, I had the feeling we were leaving home. Stopped by Mt. Field National Park to see Russell Falls. Lovely cool weather. Saw Lower, then walked up to Upper Falls but not to the horse shoe falls. Kate and Lois had done the whole trek. Onto Lady Denham, then Queenstown, 362 kms. The most travelled day thus far, roads were winding and slick. To Gorham River chalet with a nice view, small boats on the bay.

- Took the Gordon River cruise and saw the same British couple for the third time. She bemoaned not buying a certain wash stand and I exclaimed: "Guess who bought it!" She laughed and hoped I'd enjoy it. To Stanley and to the town's elegant restaurant Sullivans. Very fine food, three courses, and overloaded with people.

- Mrs. Kennedy had won the Laughton House at auction. The antique dealer Rod knew had closed. She left him two pieces for us to deliver. The nearby pub Longford had delicious cauliflower and pumpkin soup.

- To Launston. At the Boatwright House we had the largest, most charming room of them all. We walked some hills and vales, back to nap. At Shrimps we saw people Ed and I knew from Canberra, Kitty Kemp and Victoria de Long. Ed went to a meeting and I chatted with them about Canberra and Tasmania. They walked me back and began their trip to Tasmania as we ended ours.

- The Aussie Prime Minister admitted to infidelity to his wife in the past and had tears in his eyes as he admitted it on TV, and spoke of the special person was his wife. To the 12 Apostles, no film for camera: London Bridge and other formations. Strolled through Warrambool, nice old town. Crossed into South Australia, much less lush than Victoria. Camels showed up at one spot, suggesting more desert. Went to Kingston, S.A. with a giant lobster as the town's symbol. Decent meal at Homestead kitchen of our hotel. One client played the organ. We had a gorgeous sunset behind two pine trees. I would love to paint it, streaks of red flowing through a wine red horizon.

- Into Adelaide around noon. There were long distances of barren desert land between towns. Ed's cousin's friends Shirley and Harry Hartwell came for a brandy. We chatted an hour and they invited us for Easter. Quite congenial. To Gerranos restaurant; the pasta was wonderful.

- Ed went to a convention, I went to the zoo and photographed a koala in a tree. Wandered into church on Good Friday, but walked out before the service.

- Had a perfectly lovely day. Went to an art gallery and meandered through their things, lots of old world but some fresh works. Saw Japanese ceramics for $5 and was absolutely enchanted with them. Dashed to movie: "Working Girl" with Harrison Ford and Melanie Griffith, and was likewise enchanted with it. They were charming together, very well done. Recalled how I felt I had to do more than be a secretary, just to prove it to myself. Had lunch with Ed at the apartment and he was quite chatty and talkative. Then we drove to Bridgewater to see Shirley and Harry's lovely home. Their cat Benjamin came to sit on my lap and Shirley said it was very unusual. She took me to Handorf German settlement, which I enjoyed. Bought an exotic two-piece dress with Shirley's encouragement. Dined at Jolleys on the river. There are a lot of smokers in Adelaide.

- Searched for flowers and went to Easter dinner at the Hartwells. Harry's two sisters, a British man Frank, and us. Ed was engaging and charming. Had goose (not so tender) and pork (very good), scrumptious dessert. We sat at the table four hours. It was a pleasant afternoon. Benjamin came to say hello outside. Do I have a new power? In the evening we waded through lots of newspapers.

- Took time packing. Saw Kale on Another World, about three years behind the actual series in the States. To the airport and the flight was prompt to Melbourne, switched planes to Canberra.

Army fellow next to me talked about his wonderful skiing and sailing trip to the U.S. Ann, Bill and family met us at the airport with Ed's car. A few words and we parted. I got the Mercedes from Roger. Our house had not been washed downhill with the rains.

- Lots of junk to sort through at work. Raved on about how great our trip was to Tasmania. Lunched with Letty, She's thinking about living in London to get away from her family, which expects her to handle everything for them.

3/29 - Mom would have been 83. I could have done so much for her, and I could certainly have used her love and support during these times.

- To Ramage's office to prepare for the preadvance group for VP Quail's visit. To Pavilion to book 16 rooms plus the control room. Karen, Kale's wife was on location near Melbourne filming a movie with Brian Brown, a noted Aussie actor. (In fact, we had seen the crew from a distance and Ed thought we should introduce ourselves to her. Again, my messy hair called the shots and I refused to do it!) Kale joined them later and had thought he might see us in Canberra. He called to say he was taking Brian Brown's charter plane to Sydney, it was too complicated getting out of Mt. Gambia. Said he'd see us in Washington.

April

- To Rod and Meg Jeffrey's house. She went wild with a 6 course meal: pumpkin soup, quiche, chicken veronique, two desserts and cheese. Served on antique china. All were quite congenial. I particularly admired the affection their daughter gave them. We were shown their antiques and Rod's Tasmanian potters' collection (McHugh and Campbell).

- Airport farewell for Don Ramage, Admin Counselor. I have seen two go, plus my immediate boss Dent. Time for me to do so! I recall that he left the letter from POL person, requesting her money back for transportation they paid upon leaving. He never dealt with it, hid it at the bottom of his file.

- To see Lanes at 4 ish. He gave me a farewell gift of two wines for my "support and friendship."

- Made stuffed sea perch for Baba and Steve. They came and acted in their usual quarreling, disruptive manner. She needed to emphasize the tragic in any situation. Both Ed and I got nervous around them, should cool the opportunity for any gatherings.

Somewhere in there came Mong, Ed's childhood friend, and Edith his new friend. I believe they left after a week.

4/25 - Anzac Day. Had breakfast with Jack Thurgar and Leonard Cheshire of RAF, ex-wing commander, group captain, most highly decorated bomber pilot, awarded Victoria Cross in 1944. He gave a home for handicapped veterans after WWII and established the Cheshire Foundation. That foundation established also the leprosy home in India to which the Australian chapter contributes. Ed was excited, spiffing himself up for the Anzac parade. He was in the front row of the U.S. contingent, looking proud and professional. He had been interviewed by CBS from Tokyo and gave them the company line.

- Dave Lambertson from Saigon days was in the Vice President Dan Quayle party. I showed him to his room; looks about the same from 20 years ago, more grey. I later had a few minutes with him. He said he's usually happy "relatively speaking." Talked about Hal and how he had used me. He said he was the last to know about such things.

- Sent off the Art in Embassy works back to the States, through Grace Brothers. They were quite experienced, confidence in them was restored.

- It's surprising to me that fish in ponds can give you pleasure. They come a runnin' and I play the count game: 6 black, 1 gold in the front pond and at least 17 gold, 6 black, 1 white "shark" below in the lower pond.

- To the Martins' home and Allison's first communion at the Catholic Church. Saw Dr. Nugent there for his daughter. Neighbors gathered at the Martins' and it was all enjoyable.

May

- Dr. Ingram told me that my Bowens disease was on the run, looked good but I'm not to be too confident. He's going to leave Australia and head to the U.S. next year. To Burns Club for lunch with Kate. Lost $10 on pokeys, she won a bit. Met Ed at Matilda's Tavern in eve. Devoured the ribs, so good. Ed bought a Professor Higgins cardigan sweater which had attracted him.

- We had three offers for the day. To see Wendy at the sheep station to hear her woes; to Tidkinvilla with Kate and Lois and face that uneasy feeling that Lois is Kate's protector; or to join Baba and Steve in the afternoon or evening to hear their bickering and discontent. I chose the option: "Maybe I don't have to!" Made meatloaf, stayed home, and had a long nap with my love.

- Kate gave a dinner in my honor, the first for her in two years. Went all out with chicken, veggies, homemade rolls, 2 cakes. The Mortensons, Lois, Colleen and Roger and we gathered for a pleasant eve: foreign service talk, some laughs.

- Neighborhood cats visit. I overbought Aussie souvenirs, koala, kookaburra jewelry, coral. To the Martins for oyster rockefeller and filet mignon, two hours late per usual, but tasted divine.

- To pottery class. Made an almost nice chunky thing.

- Had GSO farewell lunch at the Yacht Club. Bernie's gift: made a lovely wooden bowl out of Australian black bean, I gave a farewell speech about GSO abuse, which they liked. It mentioned all the abuse GSO received, not what we gave! It was a 3 hour lunch. Later a Hail and Farewell at the Residence where I gave DillPickle a cold shoulder. She irked me no end. Then to meet Baba and Steve at their house. Onto Phuket Siamese restaurant, lots of people. I can't bear to think of all the food I've been imposing upon my ever-expanding body!

- Greg Poulson's 41st birthday. Chatted with Carol's mother and ignored all others. The party lasted 3 hours without Ed in attendance.

- Dreamed of a sweet black cat on our bed with us, and that was Timida. I hoped her sweet soul was with us at that moment. Had Beverly's Basic Brunch with Jan Cleveland, Lee Anderson, Bill Martin, Greg & Carol, their houseguest Ann from Sydney. It went well.

- Weeded 2-1/2 hours of volunteer slavery. To Steve and Baba's for peasant bean soup; it was more of a stew. Again the bickering, but had some laughs and a roaring fire. For the first time she mentioned her weight, told us that she had accepted herself as is a long time ago. Her fat son resented his inherited weakness.

- Bought souvenirs, to tannery to get sheep skin for Thomas' stroller, as per my assignment. Had a fire in the eve, with lovely

Mozart and Vivaldi. Ed had ambitious ideas for his paper and Harvard Law Review. I hope he's not disappointed. He does have a tendency to tilt at windmills. I do love him!

June

- Bob and Barbara Arthurs had us for a farewell breakfast with the Mortensons. I had forgotten about it and dashed over late. Gave us some nice wildflower coasters. The forgetfulness had obviously been a result of my scattered brain those last days of my long, long frustrating posting!!

- To Fred Vinson's for lunch at the invitation of his Thai wife Luk. A united nations of Thai, Philippine, Korean and us. Good food. Home to work on air freight.

- Stacked the air freight in the carport for pickup. It was the last day the neighborhood cats could visit. I glimpsed at my last views of the Brindabella mountains. Picked up some pots from the pottery place. Some are even decent. Lunch at Margaret and Don Cowie's. Ed backed out so I took Richard. They have a lovely place on 12 acres of woodland. She had great taste. A huge fireplace divides two rooms. There was another pleasant couple there; we whiled away two hours. They have some lovely Aborigine dream paintings, which were just then becoming the rage.

- Fourteen people for a final farewell lunch at Tivoli's. They were in their glory, for the place was filled with others as well. Fun. Orchids from three Xerox people, an Aussie record from Christine Bird. Later a happy hour farewell at the office. Ed was lively with Bernie, comparing their POW stories in WWII. Bernie had 4 years, Ed just 6 months. Colleen and I drank a bottle of good $21 duty free champagne and got sentimental. She wrote a poem and gave a picture, a collage of her family's photos.

----Mini glossary of Aussie terms: arvo=afternoon evo=evening lavo=lavatory milko=milkman smoko=rest period bickie=biscuit/snack sickie=day off work (real or imagined) bussie=bus driver lizzie=lizzard mozzie=mosquito lollies=candy sheila=woman bloke=man feeling crook=sick to try=give it a go in nature=outback, bush

- I didn't say real goodbyes, touched on a few. Barb Whitesell, social secretary at the Residence, said a real spark would be missing from the Embassy. She said people wanted to come to the airport to see me off. I said we'd be hiding in a separate room. Farewell at the Tivoli after insanity at the bank transferring money. They treated Colleen, Linda and me, gave champagne cocktails. At home Ed and I were both weary and neurotic as we left. Henry took us to the airport, Jack met us and took us to the Ansett Lounge. Overnight in Sydney at the Park hotel. Steve (ex secretary) had been on the plane. I went up the street with Steve and Paul, one with a carport (?) hairstyle and one with spikes. All seemed to think we were an incongruous sight.

- To the Consulate for a check for dollars, to buy a suitcase, get Hawaiian Air tickets. A taxi to the airport and it was heavenly checking into the Business class section. A stop at Aukland, New Zealand. It was smooth sailing except for one minute of strong turbulence that scared me to death. I clung to Ed. Our steward Steve went out of his way to be charming. Gave us hints about Kahuai, and a bottle of champagne with a red carnation and white linen napkins. Never before had I that treatment! So up we came from down under to discover another paradise closer to home, Kauai. We landed gratefully in Honolulu at 6:30 a.m. Friday June 16.

GSO, Housing Officer, Australia 1986

Ed collects for Cheshire Foundation, which benefits leper colony in India.

Colleen and Steve as we protest million dollar fence being built
around our compound in Canberra.

Bev and Secretary Steve - Australia

Suzy and Stan on their visit to Sydney Opera House 1989

Sydney Opera House

Ed and Bev at British High Commissioner gathering 1989

Kookaburra in the old gum tree. Australia 1989.

Colleen van Cornewal, Purchasing Agent, U.S. Embassy and Bev, general slave. 1988.

50th Birthday balloons "50 and over the hill" compliments of secretary Steve, 1987

Precious Timida! 1989

Suzy on Heron Island, Australia, 1988

Mignon Emmanuelle Martouzet at Berkeley, California before
becoming Mrs. John Edwin Ledbetter in 1988. Born in Nantes,
Brittany, France.

John Blacken, Bev, Ed   1986? Wash D.C.

Big Four once more: Bev, Mary, Joyce, Phyllis aboard the riverboat Spirit of Peoria on the Illinois river.

Cathy's ex David, Donny Osmond's look-alike.

Admin Counselor Paul Sadler and guest. Paul was a gourmet chef with great artistic taste. Australia 1986

Fairy Penquins near Melbourne - Mamas loaded up with fish coming to feed their kids in the bushes -1986

Sydney Harbour Bridge - 1988

A visiting Kookaburra on our back deck, Australia 1989

A temple in Thailand, 1988

Colleen and Bev on our Asian trip 1988

Colleen, Bev and Letty, Bangkok - 1988 of Australia tour

Christmas dinner at Colleen and Roger's home, Canberra with boss
Lyn Dent and visiting daughter Suzanne and friend Stan, 1987.

Bev, Colleen, my secretary Linda and B&F officer friend Kate
Danforth - Australia 1988

Camping with Lois and Kate - 1988

After Australia - 1989

June 16 - We were permitted to live one extra day compliments of the international date line. From Honolulu we dragged our luggage to the domestic terminal and boarded a plane to Kahaui, fighting the Japanese tourists. Drove to Hanalei Bay Resort. Had a lovely view of Bali Hai, mountains as backdrop for South Pacific, the movie. Quite restful surroundings. At that point I began to unwind from the three year strain of Australia. We had lunch on the terrace overlooking the beauty of Kahaui. Warm, humid. Surveyed the immediate area of Princeville. Rain. Cooler. Walked a bit, bought a colorful muumuu at Hilo Hatties, shirt for Ed. In the evening we went to a bar for a MaiTai and two appetizers: Pu Pu's they call them. Delicious shrimp and deep fried seafood, congenial waitress, good female singer, flute and brass and piano. A fine ending for the day.

- We drove as far as we could on the North shore, ran into Charo's (Xavier Cugard's wife) restaurant and thought she was a part of it, but she's in Waikiki. Lovely beaches to view. Local restaurant Breamfront provided very good bream, great scallops and salad. Viewed a gorgeous sunset. Australia's winter was seeping out of our system.

- Made love in proper fashion. Then went to a little green church in Hanaleis. It was lively with a show biz atmosphere, a woman entertainer. We meandered to a plantation and Gaylord's restaurant where we lived it up on pasta/shrimp. The outside sitting was nice, with Thai antique horses. We found the beach where they filmed South Pacific. The water was rough, the sun came out eventually. Onto another small beach with lovely water, color of deep blue aqua. Some hint of volcano in the sand, cool tradewinds.

- Upon departure we checked five bags through to San Francisco for a smooth flight. Took a Wikiwiki bus to the International terminal in Honolulu. It was a full flight and we ran into the Testerman family from Canberra who had spent four days in New Zealand. Mary, Gabby and Karen came to visit us during the flight. Mary was uninhibited, climbed onto Ed's lap.

John was waiting to rescue us. Small house in Berkeley. Suzy was there to welcome us, along with Emmanuelle with her cute little belly. Ate al fresco in back yard. Suzy liked her koala necklace and Emmanuelle loved her kangaroo earrings. It was a hot day. Suki, our Brazilian cat, was adorable. He's been through lots of moves with John, has lost weight and John sez he has more energy. Is that a message I should heed?

- Suki slept with us all night on the living room futon and cuddled up against the chill. Also played monster game attacking our feet in the early morn. How I love the little darling. I forgot once and called him Timida! John and Emmanuelle were given almost everything for the baby. Now have a koala, kangaroo and kiwi. I gave Suki a good brushing and his coat looks better. Also put sun lotion onto his pink ears.

- Emmanuelle wanted a picture taken in her bathing suit to show her French sisters, so I took one. She is cute about her pregnancy. Took us to the airport for a rental car. We trickled down the coast; the route through Big Sur was gorgeous on Highway 1. I had never realized how spectacular the rocky shores and crashing waves could be. We saw the original cannery of Steinbeck's novel in Monterrey. It was now a cutesy tourist trap. Pacific Grove's old Victorian houses and the shoreline were beauteous. We ended up driving eight hours to San Simeon and stopped in the fog at an $85 motel with a fireplace.

- To Joyce in Burbank to sleep in separate beds. She and Bob will soon be divorced.

- Saw Cathy and David. They are talking marriage and buying a house. Had a lovely brunch at an outdoor cafe.

- Onto San Clemente to visit Ed's ex-brother in law Jut and Martha in their lovely condo by the sea. They are in the same development as the Nixons.

- Back to Berkley to await the first grandchild. Ed had been pigging out. It was difficult being an expectant grandfather.

- Emmanuelle and John were at the hospital. Her pediatrician father kept calling. "Il n'est pas encore!" I kept saying. Suki walked over to me and crawled into my lap and gave me more loveys than I ever can recall. I was so touched and loved him so much. Still the horrendous wait at the hospital. John finally came out in hospital greens, worn out, with tears in his eyes. "It's a boy!" It was an ordeal but Thomas Zachary Ledbetter, 7 lbs. 4 oz was born 9:46 a.m. on June 30. After 60 hours of grueling labor, they gave tiny Emmanuelle a c-section. John had had 3 hours of sleep in two days. They had all sorts of problems with Kaiser, changes of shifts, understaffed with a record 300 babies born per month.

July

- Left for Denver, Judy and Wayne collected us. The peacocks are flourishing, now 32. Thirteen or fourteen roosted in the large tree above us as we sat outside.

- To a cabin in the mountains at the North Fork of the South Platte river. Peaceful. Judy and Wayne's friends and a bunch of relatives to visit, some of them Aussies. Volleyball, horseshoes, bonfire. On 4th of July they placed sparklers on wood chips to float down the river. I lit one sparkler for childhood memory's sake.

- Their friend Don had been in the navy and travelled both to Trinidad and Brazil, and it was nice to share memories of both places. In 101 degree heat we headed back to Judy and Wayne's place in Englewood.

- Onto Dallas and Ed's niece Judy met the plane. Looking good, now separated from Roby for two years.

- Bob Davis asked me to lunch at City Club high up in his office building. He's now on his 3rd wife, his secretary. He said I wasn't available so.... His 1st gave him 3 sons. He is powerful now, people listen to him. All other prominent tax attorneys live on the east coast. He offered that he was willing to talk with niece Judy gratis, about how the divorce game is played. I really like him. Saw Joe in eve for tequila and grapefruit juice.

- Rented a car and went to see Mary Nelson. She finally looks old at 92. She and her 86 year old brother agreed that 75 years was long enough to live. Later, onto Joyce and Ray's to visit the very wholesome Asay family. Four of us went to a Mexican restaurant. Ed said he felt uneasy around Southern Baptists, even though J & R were okay people. Early bed for him.

- Judy and Jennifer went to church. Ed went swimming and I couldn't resist jumping in in my nightgown. The water was so lovely, did some strenuous leg exercises. Want my own pool for body discipline! To Copelands, a New Orleans style restaurant. Jennifer was rotten picking at her mother, the food was cold. I escaped to Joyce and Ray's to see Sherrene and Sherilyn, all sweet of course. Sherrene is beautiful. Then to visit Joe and Helen. I learned that Joe had been on business in Manila the very time Colleen and I had been there at the Silhaint Hotel!

- The one way Southwest flight to Little Rock was $19 for Ed over 65, and $61 for me! Bill Sr. aka Skilkey, met us. Saw Clara and then on to Emily's.

- To Ed's friend Hippo (don't you like Arkansas nicknames, they stick for life!) to look at cars. Bought a Ford Bronco for $10,400. The title, registration, insurance hassle accompanied us. To coffee at Bill and Clara's. Alice Faye, her prodigy granddaughter, reads very well at 6 yrs. old, with inflection. Dinner at Jim and Patty's place: lasagna, salad and goopy dessert. Travis is a favorite. He's a precocious showoff, but sock full of personality.

- Got a license plate, took the Arkansas driver's test. I got 92 and Ed 84, we passed. A gang of 9 went downtown in the evening to Place to Eat. Accompanied by wild thunder and lightening.

- Farewell to Conway. For breakfast Emily made biscuits and two types of gravy for her little brother. He has been spoiled. Off to Little Rock to see Ed's Harvard friend. I waited a half hour in the car to avoid his cigar smoke. Then we dashed off easterly to Cobden, Illinois to meet Loretta, my college friend. She had added a large studio to her A frame house. When I say "she" I mean she built it all herself, along with a stone fireplace. She said she will paint again. She excels in whatever endeavor she chooses. We savored the lovely twilight. Her timid cat came right to me and she was astounded. Then she took us to a cabin in Giant City park nearby. We ate at the lodge and all were pleased with the meal. Ed and I were worn out and soon retired.

- Loretta brought us over coffee on Bastille Day. I gave her a kiwi key chain and an Aussie wildflower towel. Ed and I walked in the early morn and climbed the water tower, in no hurry to leave. Made love and both needed it. Sauntered toward St. Louis to Robert and Sandy in mid afternoon. Greg is "finding himself" in Cape Girardeau, Robbie attends school and works full time, Robyn is a schoolteacher (computers), Cynthia a sales rep and popular with the boys, and Stephanie, 16-1/2, just starred in "Hello Dolly" at school. Robert was without pain for the first time in many years, and in good humor. We were to dine at Steph's workplace but had a 40 min. wait, so we ended up at greasy Long John's Silver. Robert and Sandy teased one another and were so much more relaxed this round.

- Robert said he had not forgotten what he owed me, now had a better job. I left a check for $500. We farewelled and headed for Peoria. Joyce and Larry awaited, with sandwiches for lunch. She weighed 107, had been sick two weeks, including pneumonia. She was gentle about my weight gain, but said I had circles around my eyes. After a hamburger cookout in the evening, we went to see "Dead Poets Society" with Robin Williams. An amazing film at the amazing cost of just $1.50 per person at their cheapo theatre.

- To driving range to hit balls: Larry, Mary, me. Joyce had planned a murder mystery night. I had a white boa and was to be a beautiful actress, Larry a doctor, Ed a lawyer with ascot. Phyl had a bad day, came without Rich and no outfit on. Mary came in a suit and was an efficient secretary. We began with a handicap, two characters missing. Phyllis didn't cooperate so we put the game aside, to Joyce's chagrin. She had been so excited about planning it. But we four women managed some laughs for old times sake.

- To get Pat. She was heavier, hair long and greyer, looked like a fat hippie. I contained myself on weight nag, since I have my own sins with which to deal. I offered to get her a haircut, but no, she liked it that way. Had a huge tenderloin sandwich at the Lariet Club. Recalled having been there with both John and Bill Larke in past years. I discovered Pat had had a hysterectomy for cancer of the cervix before Christmas last year; she had told no one, poor thing! Dropped her off and went back to eat with Joyce and Larry at Avantis. I had wanted to treat at a nice seafood place, Larry wanted Steak n Shake, so we compromised.

- To Walmart with Pat and $200 worth of groceries and some clothes she wouldn't try on. Salad lunch at Joyce's. Dropped her and the Big 4 went to Vonachens for fajitas and laughs.

- To Chicago. Laura, Donna, Ed and I went to a nice Chinese restaurant in the teeming rain, too much food. Ed got a new pair of shoes from Mr. Czukla from his backyard shed. Laura sacrificed her bed and slept on the couch.

- Lazy morn. Met Bev Enslin and Scott for lunch. He is happily unattached now and is thinking of joining the Merchant Marines once again. Always have some laughs.

- Left and headed for Ashtabula, Ohio. Met the Sao Paulo crew of 5: Leslie, Ted, Danielle, Paulo and Jackie plus Mrs. Dieffenbacher and Leslie's mother Sarah Rowe. Jackie, our goddaughter, is cute, now almost four. Danielle is a vixen, big and solid. Paul has the same face and is sweet, more shy than Dani, but then the whole world is! We checked into the Cedar's motel, showered and went to dinner with the entire group. No liquor served, and I needed a drink! To bed at 10.

- Picked up some Swedish and Finnish bread from Olsen's bakery and went to search of coffee. Sarah was up. Leslie came and we bid farewell to the rest of them. Leslie, Ed and I headed for Washington, D.C., they talking all the way. 6-1/2 hours with stops, lunch at Breezewood. Dropped her off in D.C. and went to Jack and Liz, why? Because they asked. Liz cooked a nice chicken meal, pasta salad, green salad and a very rich chocolate dessert. Jack got a touch testy, but was generally well behaved.

- Liz went to church, Ed to a meeting. I did laundry and washed my hair. Ron Spiers had a fascinating article in the Washington Post re the "trashing of Foreign Service" because of all the political appointees. Bush is worse than Reagan in granting political favors. We four went to Arties restaurant for lunch. Later Leslie, Gail and I went to a place in Fairlington after caiprinhas at Gail's house. Leslie loves being Principal Officer in Recife, Brazil. Gail is now in Senior Foreign Service and will attend the Senior Seminar for nine months. Gail and I dropped Leslie and went back to her place to sip wine. I dragged back to Jack and Liz's place at 10:30 pm. Ed had fretted over my absence.

- Went to the State Dept. for the hassle of photos and new IDs. Back to pack and check into the Hyatt; it was so restful to have our own place.

- Ed went off to Capitol Hill with Hal. I went to the Terrorism

Seminar. At lunchtime I saw Rosalinda from Mexico on the street and then in a shop Celeste Bergold. Have to meet for lunch or dinner. Looked at apartments, we're on the list for a two bedroom. Ate at Cantinita, a Cuban restaurant, for beans and rice.

- Split a jogger's breakfast: 2 poached eggs on spinach and yoghurt on the side, good. Had a so so hairdo from the salon. At State Dept. saw O'Mahoney (Trinidad) at cafeteria and had to say hello. Realtor John Martin arranged for us to see our apartment in Alexandria and it was a pig sty with the ex-husband babysitting the cat. Structurally it seemed in okay shape. A heavy thunderstorm clapped around us, with dramatic lightening. It was flooding going back to hotel, treacherous driving. We'll offer our place for Georgiana, the tenant, to buy. In eve Meg and Dick Searing came to dinner at Hyatt. She's a real lady, quite charming. He never did especially impress me. In a few days Meg would return to France where Kathy and Jim are, he being assigned to Geneva.

- To Dept. for lab work. Weighed in at 155 at five feet tall!! That's disgusting. Ed was 182 with his shoes on. David B joined us as we had a quick breakfast. The desk officer told me the Nicaraguans weren't giving diplomatic visas and haven't since June. I had no intention of ending up in D.C. without an assignment, just waiting and without per diem. We checked out of the Hyatt to Westpark, downgrading. Called Joyce and she and Larry still planned to come visit.

July 28 - Our tenth legal anniversary. Ed was horny, so we imbibed, or is that indulged? I saw Hume Horan and he chatted a bit with Ed as well. Went to State for our visits with the doctors. Mine was wonderful, Beverly Oliphant. She introduced herself with

"I never met a Beverly I didn't like!" She was very congenial, chatty and professional at the same time. I had higher cholesterol 244 but the HDL is high enough to counterbalance it. Ed has 210. My BP was 138/88 and his was lower, so he wins. Met Pat Parker for lunch. She was late, a cloud about her as usual. Ed and I walked to the Japanese steakhouse for dinner. In the afternoon he brought me ten red gorgeous roses for our anniversary. We had a background hassle with the house in Los Osos, CA. The tenants locked themselves inside, wouldn't answer door and were late on the rent.

   - To Lyn (Australia) and Carol Dents for dinner. Cornish game hens on grill. He had opted early out of Australia for a cushy job on the 7th floor, travel with Secy of State. Their children are happy in the U.S. Had a nice house with a deck facing the woods.

   July 31 - The first day of the Personnel Course. We had big fat module stacks to work through each day. At lunch I dashed to Dent's office to type an affidavit for the west coast attorney to evict our tenants. Ran into Hume Horan again, we've got to stop meeting like this! He worked in the Director General's Office. He seemed to want to chat but I was already late in getting back to class.

   August

   - To FSI (Foreign Service Institute) early. The old cafeteria looks like a den of iniquity since it's the only spot smokers can go. Ed ran into Philicia, Ron Kramer, and Nivea Ribera. I'm not ready to handle them all. Went to Washington National to buy an open ticket for Joyce and Larry.

   - Ed and I took the metro to the seedy part of town where Saudi Arabia staged a huge exhibition in honor of fifty years of good friendship with the U.S. Had tents and sand and crafts and film showing models of Mecca, souks and houses, and robes you could fondle. I found it all quite magical, male guide was in his native dress. Then to Grand Hyatt across the street with a table at water's edge. Piano on an island, pianist in tails. A very nice diversion.

- Ed had car loaded and we went to our new digs at 2500 Clarendon Blvd. I had enjoyed working the modules at Personnel course, making things more clear which I had known only vaguely. In eve did basic shopping and to a Mexican takeaway; generous and good.

- Hot and humid day. Had a joint session to hear how we should protect the spooks overseas. Ran into Ron Kramer (Monterrey) at Dept. cafeteria, lunch with him and a friend from his Barbados days. I'd forgotten how witty he could be, he is being transferred to Nuevo Laredo, Mexico. Saw Lee Graham (Lisbon) who asked about lunch. Then Earl (Sao Paulo), Philicia (Trinidad). It's rather maddening. Too much input, as Ed sez. To Woody's sale and found six dresses for $219, some great bargains.

- To local beauty college, Ft. Myers commissary for supplies for us and Gail. When we made her delivery, she offered a sandwich and drink in appreciation. We then dragged our 20 bags upstairs to Apt. 219, wearing ourselves out. Steak and salad, our first meal in, feeling a bit more settled.

- We tidied ourselves up and went to the Willard Hotel for a reunion with John and Philicia, Laurie and Greg (Spanish course). Elegant surroundings. Heard all sorts of dirt on Harry (Panama). Said to have a "royal" complex, too bad a reputation, and didn't get his ambassadorship to Morocco. We had a good time, chatted for hours. Later Barbara Cake came over. She's in charge of operations of some sort for the Defense Dept. She's at the top of the civil service grade.

- Had colonoscopy at Dept. - all clear. Back to class to catch up on my reading.

- Enjoyed the answers and sources in the course, felt assured they'd be easy to track down when needed. The Personnel FAM's are sensible, in sharp contrast to the messy ones for Consular Services. Lunch with Lee at Szechuan. Talked about all his objet d'art from Africa which he needed to sell. Later Ed's niece Karen and Rex came to call, took us to the Washington Harbor in Georgetown, fountains and build up at Potomac river. Lovely. Da Vinci restaurant was our treat. Rex was entertaining once he warmed up. He's an attorney for FDIC and Karen an attorney for the Justice Dept., then working on Defense Contractors' scandal.

- Coolish day. Work done early. Air freight from Australia was delivered today. Ed was glad to have his books. Lean cuisine and salad. Worked on Awards recommendations for Art, Bernie and Peter in Canberra.

- Met Celeste at New Orleans House for lunch. She said Harry (her stepfather) and Karlene deserved one another, admitted that Harry used people.

- Got through to Nicaragua on the secure line. The person I'll replace said the Embassy didn't expect the Nicaraguans to come through with the visa until after the February election! I hope that is not true! In the evening we went up the street to a Salvadorean restaurant. The chicken fajita was good.

- Our traditional Saturday tunafish lunch was revived. To cotton knit outlet, to Gail's for caipirinha, Chinese food on wok. Had a lively time.

- Talked Ed into going to Hirschhorn Museum and then the Museum of African Art, which was the best one. Bought a gourd for $12 in the shop.

- Lunch with Leanore Paine at Holiday Inn; she's now the Spanish coordinator at FSI. They will work me into a class. Got a strange free hair cut at the beauty college, cut by committee! Hair looked like a mixmaster had gone through it. I was later entranced by a serialized movie: "If Tomorrow Comes." I was enthralled 3 hours yesterday, and my eyes were still glued to it.

- I get exercise to and from the metro. To Hunan restaurant for chicken, broccoli and Chinese beer. Ed sent me a love note in the box. Had a wild sexual fling when I got home. It was the night of the lunar eclipse, the first in 7 years. Reminiscent of the time when we were in the Bermuda triangle returning from Panama in May 1975.

- Took metro to SA-5 to talk about FSNs, compensation, possible insurance benefits, position descriptions. Metro to Foggy Bottom. Personnel assignments officer Val Graham is sympathetic to my plight. I heard David Wilson's (Lisbon) voice and there he was, half his face collapsed, nerve removed from squamous cell cancer. Had to transplant skin from the back of the head, chemotherapy and he's still not sure it's all gone. His eye was droopy, so sad to see. When I saw him I exclaimed: "David what have they done to you?" At least he talked about it. Ran into Bob Homme (Panama), then Dennis Hearne (Sao Paulo).

- My hair looks worn out! Where is Petra (Spanish) or Maggie (Hungarian) when you need them? No wonder I wore wigs. Jannice our instructor is such a stickler, keeps us past lunch and also past 4 p.m.. Had a little chat on how we are doing. I said she was doing fine and she said I was. I dashed to the airport. Joyce did it all on her own, including the commuter line from Peoria to Chicago. I don't recall why Larry didn't come, but I was proud of her for coming anyway! We took her to El Caribe in Georgetown; generous portions, good gazpacho, beans and rice. Joyce was impressed. Walked to Washington Harbor. She enjoyed the Friday night action, all the foreign languages spoken.

- Took Joyce to Farmers Market, Vietnam Memorial, Willard Hotel, old Post Office. A nice Middle Easterner at a camera shop assisted her with her camera, and also a group of Mexicans. Back to collect Ed and headed for Alexandria lunch at old Seaport, crab and shrimp salad for Joyce and me. To Lee's boyhood home and Ed had fun comparing historical notes with the guide. Then to Mt. Vernon. Joyce and I went in. Compared to the Lee home it was shabby inside. I was weary but yet we continued. To Saudi Arabian exhibit by Metro, her first subway ride. To the Hyatt afterward, listened to the pianist on his island. What a day! She is indefatigable, Ed did well. She told us that Larry had a melanoma removed from his back in April. He's now become aware of his own mortality.

- My feet were mutilated by yesterday's activity. To Manassa and Ed and Joyce looked into a museum. Dashed back to the zoo to see the Pandas but Ling Ling wasn't available. Saw her husband inside. To Carl and Beverly's (Sao Paulo) for lunch. To Kennedy Center at 5 pm to see "Road to Mecca." It was well done but was not enthralling or spellbinding as they had claimed. Quiet eve at home with BLTs. Joyce wanted to stroll in the dark, but it's not

Washington, Illinois.

- I went to class and took Joyce to the airport at noon. We began FSN compensation module and tape on retirement plans. It dawned on me that friend Nancy Lowrie, divorced from Art (Tunis) was eligible for a good part of his retirement pay. For this bit of info she was to become eternally grateful.

- Tried Iris' 3 day diet. Lunched with Leanore at Tivoli and ate my meager tuna and soggy toast lunch. Ed and I went to commissary later; had beef slices with beets and stringbeans for my evening meal.

- 2nd day saltines and cottage cheese lunch. Met Ed at noon for a hug. Went to Briefing Center and there was Mrs. Jonathan Rickert. We growled over Trinidad. She hadn't appreciated being victimized either. I called my predecessor now in Florida. She didn't care for the Nicaraguans, did not seem to mix much. Did love her computer and swimming pool. I ran into the ex-desk officer and Post management officer, more articulate than their successors. Said Nicaragua had great housing and the crime rate was almost nonexistent. That seemed more hopeful.

-Began Position Classification segment. Long session of two units. A 15 minute break for a hard boiled egg.

- Day was blank so I have no idea of how much I lost on the 3-day diet!

- Suzy came from California to see Papa and Tony went to N.J. to see his Mama. We went to a Mexican outdoor place in Alexandria. In eve to see "Sex, Lies and Videotapes" Rather good, a low budget film. Showed her Washington Harbor, ate at Mona Lisa restaurant. A long day.

- Went by Union Station in morn. It is gorgeous, completely renovated, elegantly done. Went to lunch at Karen and Rex Taylor's, niece of Ed and cousin of Suzy. Big meal, Suzy ate half. Pleasant enough, fresh tomatoes in back, civil war dead beyond the fence. Then to see Charley McCaskill and his wife and two sons. Lots of chatting about their shared postings in Cyprus and Athens. A few hours there, tea and home.

- Guided Suzy to the metro. She went off to exercise club and a museum. I invited Art Trezise (Sao Paulo) to join us for dinner. I'm sure Art was glad to get out. I think he was enamored with Suzy, kept saying her name and he sure wasn't using mine that often. He's quite a talker, an okay eve.

- Next eve we went to the Italian Terraza restaurant in Alexandria with Rosita and Hal, Suzy and Ed. Suzy looked stunning in bright colors and wowed Hal and Rosita. Our treat. Rosita gave Suzy and me silver plated cheese graters from Italy. She and Hal were on their good behavior tonight; all were very congenial.

- Took Bronco II and Ed to the dermo Braun for his skin cancer operation, then dropped Suzy at Union Station to meet Tony in Atlantic City. I drove the Bronco to collect Ed at lunchtime. He had a very large bandage and fifteen stiches on his cheek from the MOHS method. Individual layers of cancer tissue were removed and examined under a microscope one at a time until all cancer tissue had been removed. It is a thorough, yet timely method. Braun had also operated on President Reagan.

September

- Had an interview today and I played a distraught Muslim

woman with a scarf on my head. Got some laughs. We were let out at 12 and Ed picked me up and we headed for Dulles. A long, long 5-1/2 hr. crowded flight on a DC 8 or 9. Ed and I both sat separately in middle seats. I got very edgy and restless. Man next to me treated me to a headset, complimentary chits for a drink. Emmanuelle and Thomas Zachary were our greeters in San Francisco. T. Zack cried all the way back and finally Emmanuelle pulled over and I had to drive so she could quiet him. Then John attacked me as we walked in the door about drinking some valuable wine of his on our last visit. I was so shocked and weary I went to the cottage and cried a long time. He came to apologize. I hadn't opened any special bottles, Suzy might have done so. I was very injured, esp. after all the money we've "loaned" him, I could have said, "yes it was a $4000 bottle of wine, John!" We had dinner there, lovely trout. I catnapped Suki to sleep with us and he settled down at the foot of the bed. I love him!

- Not quite right with John. He delivered coffee and bread to our cottage which John calls a B&B. I had a sinus headache. Shopped at Price Warehouse. In eve Betty babysat and we four went to a Thai restaurant in Berkeley. Suki stayed all night with us again. I was thrilled.

- Ed went off to early morning meeting. Emmanuelle and I went to a cutesy neighborhood in Oakland with expensive antique shops, used clothes for Thomas (T. Zack). Betty came over for barbecue. Good chicken, salad. Betty is #4 grandmother: Estelle, Renee, me, her. Estelle called wondering about her checks.

- Lovely weather. I held Suki for the longest time in my arms. He was so trusting he made me cry. I have to admit I love him more than the baby. He's my baby! Went to Muir Woods to see the giant sequoia trees, quite majestic. Took a tramp in the woods. To a great spot with a view, restaurant on deck by Mt. Tamalpais. Felt reminiscent of Switzerland. Had some good chardonnay and food and I finally felt okay with John. He and Emmanuelle love each other and their baby. Guess that counts. Had one last night with Suki, my darling cat.

- We evacuated with our suitcases and Suki wouldn't say goodbye to me. He looked so sad; I know I was. They dropped us at the airport, off to Chicago and a 40 min. dash to another concourse for the plane to Dulles.

- Had some presentations; things are winding down.

9/8 - Last day of Personnel Course. Brown bag lunch with Jack Leonard, Charge at U.S. Embassy Managua. He tried to exclaim over the lovely country, great housing, food and servants. Lots of unanswered questions. Made some rounds. Saw Gloria from my past at I.O. (International Organizations). Hugged each other. Ed and I went to a Salvadorian restaurant in eve, the waitress from Peru. At the next table the couple was from Monterrey. He was another Javier type with a lovely wife from Bolivia and a darling 3 yr. old livewire daughter, a Latin Shirley Temple.

- Tunafish lunch by Ed; for eve I made chicken divine, rice, salad and green beans., Jack and Liz and Carol and Lyn Dent came. Went rather well. Carol wins as the talker.

- Took Ed to Unity Club in Falls Church. Explored Tysons Corner; it has changed a lot from the olden days. Then Ed and I went to Clyde's at Tyson's, fine food. We split a caesar salad and Reuben sandwich. Had a long afternoon nap and stayed home in the eve. Picked up Spanish book for first time and reviewed the dialogues in book one. Tracked down Paul Sadler in Pennsylvania and he called back.

9/11 - First day of Spanish. Reviewed with a bunch of tapes. Ran into Paul Hoffman (Brazil) in the lab, studying French for Algiers. In the eve picked up Winifred (Trinidad) in Alexandria and took her to Hal's restaurant Turazo. Had clams and spaghetti. Wyn looked good with her natural grey.

- Ed began computer classes, 10 for $60. Leanore didn't have a chance to test me today. D.J. called (Tunis and Saigon) and is moving to Sarasota soon.

- Plowed through three units of Spanish. Made beans and rice for dinner.

- Dedicated myself to Spanish. I've gotten enough inspiration by being able to recall that it was somewhere on a shelf in my brain. To commissary, meandered over to Ft. Myer officer's club, but it was booked up. To Phoenix Greek restaurant near our place, no dolmados, but had some Greek musical accompaniment, which was nice.

- I was able to sleep until almost 8 a.m., felt luxurious. Went to see D.J. Looked good. She said I never change, had a good time catching up. We went to lunch in the rain to Alexandria, a French restaurant. We both got wistful over the wine; she over Paul's death and me over Timida. Paul Sadler came at 5. He liked Paul Miller very well in Monrovia and the Philippines. I made clams and spaghetti, salad. They left 10:30 p.m.

9/17 - Woke up depressed. I made Beverly's Basic Brunch. The weather cleared up. Barry and Judy Copenhaver (Monterrey) came with champagne and that cheered me; then Barbara Morrison with more champagne. She built my birthday cake before my very eyes: four layers with grated chocolate, strawberries and whipped cream. It was divine. Judy's in Bonn and Barry's at GSO course and will go to Lahore. She'll follow, to be a tandem couple. Turned out to be an okay 52nd birthday.

- Reviewed 3 units of Spanish and had a session with Malisa and did well. We enjoyed each other and she was dramatic, asking what she did to deserve this "castigo." Leanore and I had lunch at Holiday Inn. I studied units 26 and 27 today, they are getting more difficult. She wanted to put me into a class tomorrow.

- Surprised to learn that nowadays Spanish students have Weds. afternoons off to handle administrative details. What a thrill, no one stayed to study in the lab. Bought a London fog coat on sale from $215 to $160, an umbrella, book, some Brazilian coffee, and as I walked out, the bells rang. When I got home I discovered the SY anti-shoplifting tag was still on the coat. I was quite annoyed.

- To Hechts with my trauma; they cut off the tag. I think it happened all the time. We met with an Area Studies fellow, four of us are tagged for Nicaragua; a congenial group.

- Hugo the Hurricane, they said, was headed directly toward D.C. after heaping a lot of destruction on Charleston, S.C. Some schools were closed. The USG had a liberal leave policy. We were let go at 1 pm. Ed and I had a hurricane picnic at home. Nice, then a long nap. The hurricane was a no-show, but there was an air of uneasiness in the atmosphere. We went for a walk, no rain. Ed would have taken me out to dinner, but I wasn't in the mood.

- To commissary. Ed saw and spoke with Ambassador Robert

Sayre (Panama). He was with OAS and had raised a few million for Nicaragua. To Gail's and heard her Alaska stories, lunched. Home to nap and sleep off two vodka collins. Ed to meeting, I got into an "attitude" thinking about how we didn't do much of anything together. We agreed to do something the next day.

- Ed went to an early morning meeting. Then we headed to Occoquan, Virginia to a fair; had a line of cars to contend with, okay, with which to contend. All the crafts looked alike, saw some good deals in antiques., My feet were worn out when we finally trudged back uphill to the car. Home again. Called Kale in Massachusetts. He said he rarely saw his wife, who was then in London. Their TV movie would be released in early 1990. He said to come up anytime; a cutie.

- Did some study in Spanish, but one becomes lazy when the class is slow. Had lunch with Barbara Cake at Szechuan place.

- Had Spanish Dept. picnic. I wrote the skit : Annabel Lee, Eduardo Allen Posey. We dedicated it to Annabelissima, our instructor. Sang with the guitarist, had a good time.

- Gail had a feijoada for Ed and me. Lots of people: Celeste and friend Ken, Jack Pavoni, Paul and Patti Hoffman, Kevin Brown, Fred Kaplan, Jack Davis and friends of Gail. There was great food in the feijoada, had two caipirinhas. All and all, a lovely day.

October

- Moved from 219 to 816. Six loads on cart. Much smaller. To David Wilson's place, old house in Adams Morgan area. Ralph Nader was his neighbor. To mideast restaurant.

To Barbara Cake, Alexandria. Moça the Lisbon dog is thinner, and she also had a friendly cat. In Spanish Arabella is becoming more annoying, spoke English too much, talked a lot about herself, not overly concerned with our Spanish practice. Lunched with her and others to an Italian place run by Bolivians, free cheesecake and champagne. Spoke primarily in Spanish.

- Dottie Magee, the ex-Parisian, came over in an elegant Chanel suit and shoes. Made clams and spaghetti. Ed to meeting. We drank a lot of scotch. She ended up loving Paris, will retire to San Diego.

- Drove to Spartanburg, S.C. to see Paul Sadler. A lovely day to travel. Had a picnic lunch alongside the Roanoke river. Stopped at an antique place and bought Rod (Australia) some McCoy pottery. Paul had another marvelous house: Chinese screen, Philippine four poster beds, mahogany tiles. We got a kingsized suite upstairs. Pina colada, stuffed cabbage leaves, apple pie. Sat on screened porch and chatted.

- Trip up to mountains and Saluda. Gorgeous weather. Paul was homesick for the Foreign Service life and activity. Barbecue lunch out and dinner at home. A chicken and rice dish, a weekend of gluttony. Sent us off with a waffle breakfast. Nine hour drive home.

- Did what they call a bridge in Spanish on a fictional terremoto in Peru. Received a phone call, and had to be an Assistant Military Attaché.

- Ed checked out a used computer for over $1000. To Bailey's Crossroads to see "Shirley Valentine". A woman left her dull husband in England and went to Greece and stayed. We both enjoyed it. To a Mexican restaurant for fajitas, a full day.

- Hair done, met Alba of Trinidad fame, returning from Bogota.

Had some laughs, dredged up old times of craziness in T&T. Philicia joined us, Nivea Ribera stopped by. Saw DCM Teare (Australia).

- It was Annabella's last day, had lunch at Hunan Restaurant. We all resented not having more practice in our Spanish class with her. Barbara Cake came to check our computer, there is some kind of glitch. I made chicken from Paul Sadler's recipe.

- Couldn't find Mom's engagement ring from Harry and panicked, was in anguish. Found it twelve hours later in a purse's zipper section where I had hidden it. Cried in relief.

- Gail had lunch and Gustavo, Ed, Steve, she and I went to the pumpkin festival. There were piles of pumpkins in a charming autumn atmosphere. Apple cider, home again to make love.

- We had a new Spanish teacher, Pedro from Bolivia. He was astounded we had been so undisciplined and did not have a regular routine. We stumbled through the day. Maria McGrath (Sao Paulo) came for raging rigatoni. Had moved into our building.

- Our class was better prepared today. At 9 we learned there was a 6.9 earthquake in San Francisco. Cathy called, lines are blocked.

- Got through to Suzy and she and Tony were okay. Fretted over John. The Oakland highway bridge collapsed in a section, crushing cars. Finally John called. He and Emmanuelle were on their way to the World Series game and in the BART underground when it happened. The train stalled under the Bay. When the train eventually made it to the San Francisco side, they spent the night at a strange woman's house. T. Zack was with Betty in Berkeley, three months old. They are predicting 200 deaths. I cried with relief; Ed was suddenly jubilant. Went to see "Fabulous Baker Boys". Celebrated walking in the rain to a neighborhood Indian restaurant.

- Leanore had heard that Ed was missing in San Francisco (not his son), and all the Spanish teachers were concerned. Went with Ed to an INS ceremony for Annabella's U.S. citizenship. Gordon Daniels had taken her and suddenly Ed and I were thrown together with them for wine, the four of us! Que disastre! He had not been kind to Ed in Panama when he acted as Charge. In eve Barb returned to check the computer, fixing the glitch. We took her to the Alpine restaurant, expensive meal but fun.

- Have been meditating each day since the earthquake panic. More rain and colder. The Spanish class went better than expected; I told the earthquake story. Pedro is loosening up. To lunch with Maria at Hunan. To book fair later with Ed. Taxi home and lamb chops for dinner.

- To PX. Jack and Liz in eve for hamburgers. The last of the Notre Dame game was exciting.

- Gorgeous day, Ed was in the mood to go somewhere. Barbara Cake picked us up to go to Glen Echo Inn for $23 champagne brunch. Delicious gluttony. Did get Ed out for a walk later. Encountered cute cats along the way, which made me more homesick for Suki. Ah, life!

- Certainly got drilled more, practice more, get more out of Pedro than we did Anabella.

- Spanish has now been extended to Nov. 30. Lunch with Leanore. While talking with John in the evening, Suki crawled into his lap and I talked to him. John said he was purring loudly. That made me sad, I want him back.

- I'm caught in the middle of Leanore's problems with her co-workers, all sides being friendly towards me. They don't know she confides in me.

- Ed and I sauntered to Harper's Ferry, onto Antitem cemetery, impressive. At the battlefield memorial I let Ed go in and I read a book. To B&B Candlelight Inn for the night, South Mountain Inn for dinner. It was a beautiful day of activity and weather.

- It was a cool night, comfortable sleeping. Morning lovemaking, the rake! Had a nice breakfast with our hosts; they had a lovely collection of antiques. To Hagerstown, Maryland to a lovely park with swans. Dashed to Bavarian House, a huge resort, and wended on home, tired but happy.

- Was going to diet, brought celery and carrots, but Leanore asked me to lunch. She had an anxiety attack Friday night over the war among the professors. Pedro was a good teacher. I recall embarrassing him once when I asked him how to say "hot flashes" in Spanish, since I was then experiencing them. He blushed and said "Ah, Beverly! It is colores." I'll never forget the term!

- Some people were wearing strange things on Halloween. To Barbara Cake's in the evening, carved a pumpkin on her porch. It was fun doling out candy to the little kids. Her friend Ray was there and he was very congenial. She had stirfry roast beef and ice cream and trick or treat candy.

November

- Delivered memos to various sections of the Dept. re waiting, what's next, home leave, etc. Ran into Joe Sullivan (Lisbon). In eve went to Rosalinda and Stu Seldowitz apartment for Mexican cuisine. Ed and Stu did the talking; it annoys me when Ed monopolizes.

- Greek takeout and movie "The Bear." Beautiful story from the bear's point of view. Gorgeous scenery in the Italian alps. We were moved by both the harshness and beauty of existence. To Maria's in eve. Fred Kaplan there (Sao Paulo). Maria's sister told her that Ed was adorable. He can be, I love him!

- The FSI Spanish section had gone downhill from before, selling themselves to other agencies, overloading the classes, overworking the instructors. To Gail's, a drink or two. We are most relaxed and like each other in the quiet times.

- Ed and I sauntered around the Adams Morgan area, enjoyed each other's company. We have managed to have a decent attitude about the uncertainty in our lives just now. Played it a day at a time and I was proud of us.

- To Dottie Magee's house. Had a bloody mary there and onto Old Ebbitt Grill for brunch, her treat. Nice ambiance, poor service. Company nice. Walked to Renwick Gallery to see the Tiffany exhibit, which of course was lovely. Slaves quilts were upstairs. After dropping Dorothy off Ed and I stopped at Textile Museum to see the molas of the Cuna Indians of Panama. We could have assembled such a thing ourselves back in 1973. I believe I'd love that kind of job. Why have I let myself just slide so randomly along the pathway of life?

- Two hours of class and then three hours off. Returned for an hour of class. I clowned a bit, Pedro can't resist me. He really drilled us on imperfect tenses, past subjunctives, etc.

- Took Ed to airport, farewell for now. Suzy was to have an operation. In eve Gail and I went to the Folger Theatre to see

"Twelfth Night". Great seats, they all did an impressive job, quite fun. Ed called, having arrived safely in San Francisco.

- We took Pedro to Hunan for a farewell lunch. He hinted that we could ask for him again.

- Talk now of TDYs. San Salvador was off, would I go to Belize? East Berlin opened its borders today to the shock of the world, 45 years later. Met Gail at her club to play racquet ball for 40 min. Quite a workout! Felt so much better after a shower. Ed called from Suzy's hospital room. She was in quite a bit pain after having a bone in her leg transplanted to her wrist. Carpal tunnel operation. Ed said that T Zack looks like Emmanuelle.

- Veterans Day. Went to see "Crimes and Misdemeanors" by Woody Allen. It did not quite coagulate with me, but the message was "We are defined by the choices we make in life." Talked with Ed and we were both feeling low. He said he wouldn't mind if I retired on Monday and we took Suki and found a home somewhere.

- On diet. I took pill that made me hyper, so straightened the house and dug into papers, sorted through mortgages. To see Jack and Liz.

- Had a long chat on the phone with Ed, missing each other. Barbara and I went to the National Theatre to see Neil Simon's "Rumors." It was really sophomoric; I personally got only a few laughs out of it. Onto Washington Harbor, scallops and linguini, shared a bottle of wine. Diet, what diet?

- Got home leave approved through the first week of January. Heard horror stories about Belize and began to have other thoughts. They feel I have the experience and am best for the job. What they want me to do is straighten out the GSO property mess in two weeks. Impossible!

- Ed's homecoming! On the way to the Dulles airport in a downpour, the car radio told me people should stay home, we were in a tornado watch. Thought about Ed in the air and panicked, missed the turnoff, went out 50 west, was frantic. I finally made it after an hour of hysteria with wild winds and heavy rain! Ed's plane was 1/2 hour late. They had circled over the area until the winds calmed down. So glad to see him alive! Stopped at a greasy spoon, got home and went to bed to hold each other. Another wild storm came through with hurricane strength winds, but I no longer cared, I had my man. A tornado hit in nearby West Virginia and also in New York. Ed's plane had sneaked between two fronts. We made love. Ed went to a meeting, the weather now clear and crisp. I called Ed Ferguson to say we would not go to Belize. He was disappointed. I had reached a stage where I would have gone but Ed would not.

- I was relatively quiet in class and Pedro was shocked. Lunched with Leanore and talked retirement, hers and mine. To neighborhood crab house in eve.

- Pedro out a half day, had Annabella and it was the same old thing. She did an interview with me, but the rest was her show.

- It was the first Thanksgiving Day snow in 20 years in D.C., but 51 degrees in NYC. Had two inches on the ground, lovely. To Karen and Rex's for Thanksgiving dinner. Had turkey breast, cranberry sauce, all the necessities. Stayed over three hours. They tried to convince us to meet them at Disney World mid December. Rex had an unhappy childhood and made no effort to keep in touch with his mother and sisters. Went home with turkey leftovers.

- Got more passport pictures. Still awful. Do not know what we're doing from one minute to the next. Tried a Salvadorean restaurant, took Maria, quite chatty. Spoke Spanish to the help and they were quite congenial.

- Kale called and came over for a long chat. Looked good. He and Karen Allen are right for each other he said, and she is unaffected by stardom. They'll go to Liza Minelli's party next week. They are friends of Tom Hanks and Katherine Turner as well. Ed's a bit jealous of my affection for Kale. I mean, it's not every day we have an actor in the family!

- I was domesticated, and made a roast, just like the olden days on Sunday with our mommies. Am using up food in our freezer. Ed was appreciative.

- In Spanish Maggie had taken over the class from Pedro. It was a surprise to him as well. She was very animated and concentrated on priming me for test-like conversation. Talked about kangaroos, crocodiles, etc.

- My test in Spanish. Maria Carmen was the examiner, did all she could to make me feel comfortable. I felt the conversational part was fine. I got stumped on the briefing and really screwed up. I couldn't think of the word for treaty (tratado) and it was downhill from then on. I received only 2 + 2+. Leanore said I was just a 1 when I came eleven weeks ago, so that was good. Got depressed. Home to prepare for my Happy Hour in party room downstairs. Ed picked up empanadas. Quite a group showed up: Stu and Rosalinda, Bill Kendall (Monterrey); John Blacken (Panama) and new wife from Guinea Bissau; Dave Wilson, Lee Graham, Barbara Morrison (Lisbon); Leanore and Charley Payne, Celeste Bergold

(D.C.); Charley & Jackie McCaskill (Cyprus) for Ed; Maria McGrath, Lee and Steve Dachi, Dennis & Sylvia Hearne, Gail Gulliksen, Paul and Patti Hoffman (Sao Paulo); John and Philicia Collin (Trinidad); Kathy and Ted Reinhart (Spanish class). Survived it okay, but barfed four times in the night. Residue tension from the Spanish exam?

- Career Counselor appointment with Gussie Rodgers. Home to movers. Mong and Edith came over in the middle of it all; went to Wendy's for lunch. They had been eating their way through Buffalo. We were then to commence an additional home leave. Our car was loaded to the gills. I went alone to Lee's with Maria, Ed's replacement. Cold out, Lee lived in sleazy NE, condemned housing next door, but Mayor Barry lived in the same block, so that keeps it safe. His house is overstuffed with his mad purchases. Would have sold me a blue/white vase from Portugal for $30, but I had no room in the car! Loaded our clothes in the Bronco and were at Gail's at 8:45 p.m. She acted a touch huffy but got better when she realized we were suffering. Had beans and rice, part of a beer. I felt then we were taken in out of the storm. The basement was cold, but had a comforting electric blanket.

Dropped off tapes at FSI, hair done by Viennese woman near Gail's place. Went to Lawyers Club for Harvard Law School luncheon. What a seedy looking bunch of characters, lots were elderly. Ed was the best dressed in his vest. Talked beforehand to the guest speaker, who was First Secretary of the Russian Embassy. Asked if I had ever been to their Embassy and he was going to arrange it. He'd been six years years in D.C. I asked if he was Americanized. He admitted to being a Redskin fan. He had been in Canberra as well. Talked about Nicaragua not giving diplomatic visas. He said "You don't look like a spy!" He spoke well, admitted his country made some mistakes, but was willing to learn.

To Gail's in later afternoon. She came home a bit disgruntled. My stomach was in a so-so mood. The three of us went to Carnegie's. Had a brandy alexander, which soothed my stomach. She's a genial host, asked us to stay even longer, even past Saturday to go to her feijoada for the Hoffman's. All indications are that she'll be PAO (Public Affairs Officer) in Lisbon. That would be terrific, we'd have a place to visit!

December

- Dropped Ed at Crystal City. Had a goopy delicious hot dog at Ollie's Trolley. Finally got my final orders. Back to Gail's. We wouldn't decide until we woke up whether or not to stay another day. Guess Louis and Donna were in town. They passed the word to Gail through their maids, which Gail considered an insult and not worthy of response.

- Decided it was better to hit the road, loaded up, Gail took pix and we were gone. Headed for Washington's birthplace in Tidewater territory in Westmoreland county, VA and Lee's birthplace at Stratford Hall. Lovely, but had a phony aged southern belle docent in hoops and petticoats. Ended up lost in Williamsburg at 6 pm, took us nine hours to go 200 miles! We lunched at an ancient inn in Montrose, VA. Slept in Williamsburg.

- Left Princess Anne Court, lunch at Greensboro. Ed recalled a fellow who had been in POW hospital with him, Carl Gibson. He got his number from information and we met him at High Point, NC at the Radisson Hotel. They rehashed old memories from 1945. He looked like a real southern boy, big belly, waist up to his chest, spoke of his "grand boys". They hadn't seen each other in 44 years. Ed had worn much better. Then a mad dash to Spartanburg, SC and Paul. We were lost fifteen minutes or so. Paul said he was ready to send out the St. Bernard. Made pork chops, was a bit in his cups.

- They had a record 20 degrees overnight, the furnace kept going out. Paul went out four times to reset it. The furnace man came at noon. We had a tunafish lunch made by me and homemade bread made by Paul. Went to an outlet place and video store. Home to drinks and home spun chicken pot pie and salad. He'd always been a great cook since we've known him. It was warmer weather wise this eve.

- Paul left for Florida to see his sister, and the house was ours. We tidied up, took showers and celebrated our independence day by making love. We both needed it! Did some general cleanup, wandered Spartanburg. Paid $30 for a facial and it was one hour of pure heaven given by a pleasant girl. Had Paul's chicken pot pie leftovers, made some phone calls.

- Had car tune up, put in platinum sparkplugs for its Christmas present. Walked the neighborhood, 2 dogs accompanying us. Walked up to two horses and they came to greet us. The South is so friendly! Kale was on "Another World", drinking a double bourbon!

- Explored some shopping centers, got a video of Karen Brown in "Backfire." Made clams and spaghetti for dinner.

- A rainy day, mailed off packages to Gail, Pat, and a tee shirt for Meg in Geneva. Did some cards, Ed to meeting. Bought a microwave for Paul, hoping he'd like it. Made raging rigatoni for eve.

- Sleet and ice all over the trees, quite dramatic, but roads were clear. Had hair done and when I left the shop there was a blanket of snow on the ground. Ed and I got into a mini snowball fight, fun.

- Paul returned home. I had made a chicken and rice dinner with broccoli. Paul had driven 11 hours, bringing back his sister with him.

- We left for Ashville, N.C. after breakfast. Met Ed's niece Susan at Biltmore Dairy bar. She's a pleasant 40 yr. old. with lots of hair! Showed us the Grove Park Hotel, with an enormous fireplace, decorated splendidly for Christmas. There was a huge decorated tree and also a poinsettia tree. Went by Thomas Wolfe's birthplace, childhood home. We had to return to Spartanburg since we had driven away with Paul's garage door opener. He wanted us to stay overnight but we went on to Clemson, SC to a Ramada Inn; early bed.

- Onto Dahlonega, Georgia to see Ed's Aunt Irene and Uncle Orby, Susan's parents. Had a lovely town square. Caught up on family, Irene was a character, Orby a former college professor. A four hour visit, then down the road past Atlanta in teeming rain during the rush hour, past Macon and settled on Centerville, an AFB town. The Holiday Inn was nice with Christmas trees in the gazebo. I shocked the Southern Baptists around me by ordering two old fashioneds.

- Determined to pass through Plains, Georgia, Jimmy Carter territory. We made a detour. It was a cold day in Plains with friendly people at the welcome center. Saw his first cousin, a state senator, bought peanuts at Billy Carter's gas station, tried to see their house but it was surrounded by a gate and secret service headquarters. And that was it. There was a note on a store window: "Jimmy Carter will teach Sunday school this Sunday." I saw my first cotton field on the way, in lovely terrain. Onto Florida, stopping at "Old South" barbecue place. Called Iris in Nakomis, FL, and before long we were welcomed into their charming house. Don was in Bellevue, Illinois. She made us a typical Honduran meal of minced meat, beans and rice. I made an old fashioned, did dishes, and we pooped out before 11 pm.

- We had juice from oranges from their trees and Honduran coffee. Ed went to a meeting, she and I to thrift shops. We split a sandwich at a German spot with a rude waitress. The evening meal was shrimp, scallops and rice - very good. We did 15 minutes of her Jane Fonda exercises, quite energetic even for beginners.

- Homegrown o.j. once again. Don was freezing in Illinois snow in the morning and was back in balmy Florida that afternoon. He made delicious martinis. I helped Iris make her Montezuma Pie, which she now called Limpia. Ed got annoyed as we drank too much. I stopped long before they did. The food was wonderful, as usual. My French chardonnay was fine.

- Christmas tree shopping and found a full one for $20 at the first stand. We stopped at a redneck bar for a beer and a lottery ticket. Back for tunafish and tree decorating in the afternoon. Iris was hostile about Ed not helping to decorate. There was a mess of lights and bulbs, but we three got it up and it was lovely. To Holiday Inn, danced a bit with Ed, back 10:30 pm.

- Ed to meeting. Had a big breakfast farewell. Iris gave me a beaded necklace her sister had given her 20 years ago, which I had worn last night. Art Lowrie (Tunis) returned my call and he's divorced from Nancy and living in Tampa with his former secretary Pat; did oral histories of ex-Ambassadors living in Florida. We made it to Orlando in two hours and I conned Ed into going to MGM Studios, festively decorated, but we missed two major events, the movie ride and the live entertainment portion. Weary, early bed.

- Ed woke me early with lovemaking. We were overdue.

- Karen and Rex came late last night. We picked them up at 10 and headed for Magic Kingdom. Rode the Mississippi Steamboat, Thunderbolt Mountain roller coaster (fun, Karen and I were in the front seat and she was more terrified than I was). To Hall of Presidents, kiddie Snow White ride, Space Mountain, a more harrowing roller coaster ride in the dark, several exhibits, 360 degree shots of America, Parade of Progress, and then to Adventureland for a boat trip with a comic pilot, and the Pirate boat trip, which I enjoyed. Some shopping, ice cream. Sandwiches at noon. Rex was in good spirits, cracked corny jokes. In eve Ed was pooped.

- Woke up to teeming rain and the news that the U.S. had attacked Panama. We were mesmerized a couple hours; of course they could not find their target, Noriega. We ventured onward after saying our goodbyes. The turnoff in Northern Florida was horse country and quite charming. The armpit of Florida was pine trees and more pine trees. Ended up at Apalachicola, Florida at the Gibson House. It stood out like a blue-grey mirage on the highway, $55 with government discount. We dragged our valuables to our room, had a drink downstairs; a small community. Teenagers came to carol full of enthusiasm, but with no harmony or voices. We split a seafood meal. It was a pleasant enough place, early bed, 8:30 pm.

- Walked around the neighborhood. The town is about to be restored in cutesy fashion, but is as yet still unaffected. The spanish moss dripped, languished in the trees. A pleasant dash through Alabama and Mississippi, picking up pine boughs from the road, to put them on the dashboard, our stand-in Christmas decor. Stopped at some famous McGuires pub near Pensacola for lunch. Biloxi Miss. has lovely antebellum homes right on the gulf. Ended up in New Orleans around 5 p.m. and found the Saint Helene hotel. They gave us a suite for $58.50, normally $80, right in the French Quarter. Dragged half of our earthly possessions upstairs. It was cold. Went to the Royal Cafe and had wonderful gumbo, beans and rice, and shrimp creole. Everything was quite tasty, enjoyed the roaring fire, no complaints. Talked with a trumpet player around the corner, walked by jazz joints. The French quarter was almost deserted. Our room was warm and toasty.

- Had thoughts of leaving today, but an ice and sleet storm changed our minds. A crust of ice to walk upon, 28 degree record for sunny New Orleans! Ed crunched off to a bookstore. I hunted things for Judy Mize, pralines and coffee and such. We had coffee and beignets at Cafe du Monde, onto the flea market. Ed bought me a scarf and eel skin bag. Saw a freezing cat I worried about, popped into a seedy lunch place for a drink and beans and rice. It was full, everyone talked about the weather. In the eve Ed took me to Antoines; the head waiter was very pretentious. We tried 2 oysters rockefeller, 2 thermida, 2 another. The French onion soup was divine. Ed liked his pompano, my main course of garlic chicken was inedible. We split a pear dessert. We toured 15 rooms, all quite charming. Helped make up for the loss of $92.

- We had a morning tiff when Ed was worried about the roads and really wanted to hole out in the French Quarter for eternity. I wasn't so sympathetic, felt we had to move on. When I got assurance from Channel 6 newsperson that the roads were clear, he acquiesced grudgingly. Lots of cars were stalled or abandoned on the highway. To Baton Rouge, then Natchitoches, LA where "Steel Magnolias" was made. Stopped at a real hometown restaurant called "Landings" and the waitress said the town had been starstruck for six months; a cute place. Onto Dallas. We got to Judy Mize's residence at 7:15 pm. Ed's sister Emily was there to greet us and fed us macaroni and hamburger casserole. Caught up on chatting a bit. Judy had a bad cold. Their tree is out of Neiman Marcus, huge, flocked and beautiful. They change the color theme each year, must get expensive. Ed went to bed early and everyone else was in bed by 11 p.m. on Christmas Eve.

- Had a big breakfast of sausage, bacon, eggs and toast. Judy and Emily cooked. While Ed and Emily caught up, I went to a shopping center to have hair combed, bought skirt and top. Jennifer and I set the table. The feast was turkey, chicken, sweet potatoes in oranges, cornbread dressing, pumpkin pie. There followed ostentatious gift giving. Ed went to bed and said "thank you for not giving me 15 sweaters!" Emily gave us matching red/white striped flannel nightgowns.

- Jennifer pouted because there was no Christmas stocking. Ed and I went to visit Mary. We had the attendant have her pull a long red ribbon until there we were at the other end. She yelled and was happy to see us. We brought her a heart shaped wreath. Stopped at Joyce's awhile, the others were playing tennis. Judy gradually felt better with her cold.

- Coco came to clean. So nice to see her again! Went with Joyce, Ray and Sherrene to lunch. Sherrene is a stunning girl. Had a very pleasant time. Ed and Ray talked war stories. In the early morn we took the Mize family: Judy, Emily, Jennifer and Roby Dan to the airport with lots of luggage, on to ski in Colorado. The house was ours!

- I screwed up the burglar alarm, $60 charge for that! Roby Sr. (now divorced from Judy) roared in to check, since they had called his office. Took us in stride and asked if we had a free night. I made shrimp stroganoff for Joyce and Ray. Lively conversation, they liked the meal. Ray was now in management at UPS and Senior 847 pilot training.

- Saw Mary. In eve Roby took us to his favorite Swiss/Austrian restaurant. Delicious food. Roby felt that Emily was a saint, as was Coco, as was Woo. I told him that Judy was like Woo and her mother, but he couldn't see that.

- Earthquake at Newcastle, Australia, 11 killed at local labor club, It was Ed's 17th anniversary of not drinking. Bought medicine for Mary and delivered it. Told her it was my birthday gift to her for Jan. 1. She was a new year's baby. Ed and I went to see "Blaze" with Paul Newman as Earl Long, ex-Louisiana governor.

- Rainy, dreary day. To Baylor hospital to visit dermo. Said I had impetigo, a staph infection, who knows what caused it? Antibiotic and meds. U.S. forces invaded the Nicaraguan

Ambassador's residence in Panama, a diplomatic no-no. Ortega then kicked out 20 U.S. diplomats from Nicaragua. I don't blame him. Ed and I went to Galleria, a lovely shopping center with an ice skating rink and enormous trees, ala Rockefeller Center. Talked to Judy, Emily and Roby Dan in Colorado. They had loved their skiing.

- Visited Mary with a birthday card. At 5 we took our motorcade of Mercedes and Bronco to DFW to pick up the ski bums with their furs and equipment. Judy, Jennifer and Roby Dan all had New Year's Eve plans. I went to Joe and Helen's with three masks. We drank pina coladas and made it until 11 pm. They are thinking about moving to British Columbia or Oregon-Washington.

End of Career 1990

An explanation of our journey heading southward: We were looking for warmth as the majority of our winter clothes had long ago been sent to our alleged new posting at Managua, Nicaragua. So we were surviving on just a few winter outfits. It was our unhappy fortune that the south just happened to be in a deep freeze!

New Year's Day - Judy and Emily made a traditional New Year's feast in Dallas: garlic grits, ribs, black-eyed peas, jalapeno cornbread -- all divine. To see our friend Mary on her birthday. She said she was sorry she loved us so much, because it hurt to see us go. Jennifer said the house was fun with us around and we shouldn't leave.

- Pancake breakfast send-off, onto San Antonio. We stopped at Abbott, TX, Willie Nelson's birthplace. Dined at Turkey Cafeteria, the most delicious, moist turkey sandwich I ever had. Then to Mong Kelton's house, and to Edith English's place where she had prepared dinner: ham, green bean casserole, and chocolate pecan pie. She provided a queen sized bed for us. Told us Mong's place has become uninhabitable with his collecting (hoarding) papers and assorted paraphernalia. When we were out for dinner, the TV in the bar announced that Noriega had surrendered in Panama. The American military had blasted rock songs at high decibel all hours, driving the papal nuncio to distraction. Noriega had been afraid of the crowd outside but was finally convinced to give himself up to American military authorities.

- Took off for Laredo, Texas and to meet Ron at the Consulate.

Maricela took me to her hairdresser, always a first priority.

- Called DCM Bob (Lisbon) in Mexico City, and he offered to put us up. John Negroponte (Saigon) was the Ambassador. Labored with Ed over memo that they drop me from Managua. We had tortilla soup at the Cadillac Bar, luscious, and headed for Monterrey. Made it to the Consulate at 4:15 p.m., almost a three hour drive. Anna Morales was so pleased to see us; many came up to hug us, names I've forgotten since we left in December 1983. Maru was married with a son, Anna was 29 and unmarried. She and Diana had been speaking of me the other day, how I was the best. The Consul General's secretary had died of cancer. Anna got us reservations at the Hotel Gran Ancira. It was still decorated for the Christmas season, and looked the same as before. We had a drink there and then went over to Sanbourne's. Nice to be back with friends. Made arrangements for Hotel Tortuga in Acapulco. Ran across the river to look up Maria Theresa and Javier. Learned they had moved two years ago up the hill toward the mountain but could not give an address.

We checked out of the hotel and took a taxi to the airport for Mexico City. Upon landing in Acapulco, we discovered that the Hotel Tortuga was not the 4-star it advertised. Had loud musicians, no A/C regulators. Kept us awake until 1 a.m. We were both out of sorts.

- Called Washington collect. Lisa wanted me to go on TDY to Panama after our invasion there. Acapulco is hot. We ate downstairs and arranged for a room on the other side, mas tranquilo. To a seafood place on the beach with a lovely view. We split the ceviche and shrimp curry. There were a lot of beggars, street vendors, lots of noise but Acapulco still maintained a natural beauty. Later to dinner with a romantic setting - horse carts trundled by.

Walked up to the Hotel Condessa for breakfast, lovely views with no camera. Lovemaking back in the room. To the Chinese restaurant up the street. Had a decent daiquiri and we split chicken and barbecued ribs as an appetizer.

Called Lisa in D.C. It took the operator 50 min. to get through. Suddenly she was not so friendly, had read my memo requesting the break on the Managua assignment. It was a pending "policy decision" she told me. She also had the flu. She'd send passports and orders to Conway for my TDY to Panama. No dependents were allowed in Panama as yet. We went to catch a flight to Mexico City and onto Monterrey, exhausting. Hotel Gran Ancira welcomed us back. Onto Nuevo Laredo after picking up our car . Onto San Antonio and we were whisked off to Luby's Cafeteria. Mong has received all sorts of calls for us. I believe he enjoyed the drama, calls from the Department in D.C. etc.

Made calls to D.C. and travel arrangements to Panama. Mong and Edith were off to Barbados tomorrow. Another stop at Willie Nelson's hometown for that turkey sandwich. Ed wrote a fan note for him and left it with the people there. In Dallas Judy was sick and hacking with a cold. Lulu and Mar stopped by for a visit. Later Judy and I watched TV re the investigation of the murder of a DEA agent in Guadalajara. Farewell once more, we left for Conway and were on Emily's doorstep at 5 pm. Ed was so weary and worn out from our travels that he went to bed immediately. Emily made her little brother (four years younger) his favorite meal of cornbread, chicken and dumplings. Bill, Clara, Alice Faye came over. The latter has become tall and looks like Patty Hearst.

Ed was in bed with a cold, compliments of Judy. Patty, Jim, Travis and Katy came for Sunday roast beef dinner. Sug has had twins and Clara has taken over the tending of them. She also teaches and has her mother Mrs. Nation living with them. Martyrdom! Ed needed a lot of attention in his suffering. I sorted our things in boxes. Clara and Bill, Emily, Ed and I went to a Cajun place in Little Rock. Everyone had good fish. Clara rarely got out. Ed's treat $99. Earlier, went to Emily's hairdresser for a perm, which she is wild about. I must have looked like the wreck of the hesperas. Don't ask me where that originated!

Ed went to the emergency room across the street and was diagnosed with the flu. I tended to him, got his medicine, answered his clapping hands. Emily wanted to give him a cow bell, but I advised her that she'd be sorry. But Ed insisted on being in the car as Emily drove me to the airport. Farewell for now. Poor Emily at 70 will have a lot of extra work. Onto Memphis for me. Instead of a 50 min. wait, it turned into 3 hours with weather in Detroit. Into Miami at 12:30 a.m. Barely got someone to help with the luggage, barely got a taxi to a hotel. To sleep at 2 a.m.

Panama Redux

Had four hours sleep and three security checks before the flight to Panama. I was put into a transient apartment with two other women, Gail and Joan. Joan was the grumpy one and smoked. Everytime I asked a question I got "I have no idea!" I called Ed, depressed. He tried to cheer me. We three went to dinner at Bavaria and were joined by two USIS TDY fellows. Had a lot of wine and it was fairly congenial, the corbina was good, and I felt a touch better.

1/18 - I turned myself into the Embassy at 8 a.m., albeit reluctantly. I landed in the middle of the invasion, which didn't end until January 31.

When the American military brought forth their operation "Just Cause" to get rid of Manuel Noriega at midnight December 20, 1989, the protection of the U.S. Embassy fell through the cracks. I recall sessions with Fort Clayton during my tour 1973-75 where officers from Fort Clayton and the Embassy went over the E&E (Emergency and Evacuation) plan. Troops from the U.S. Southern Command at Fort Clayton would come to defend the Embassy on the Panamanian side from any and all aggressors. When "Just Cause" went into effect, so many military personnel came to town to countermand the directions of another command, and the Embassy was forgotten along the way. It is not a story they tell. They were busy bringing forth the Army, Air Force, Marines, Navy seals, and Coast Guard.

The Embassy was attacked by the Panamanian Defense Forces with only the Marine Guards who had been stationed to protect the Embassy, there to defend it. A mere handful. On the night of the invasion about a dozen people had been working in the Embassy and were forced to find refuge in the Embassy vault where the encryption machines were stationed. For two days they ate C-rations provided by the Marine Guards while panicked calls for help brought the tardy arrival of assistance from the military in the Canal Zone. When I arrived there was still a patched hole in the windowed wall of the Ambassador's conference room. At least 3000 Panamanian civilians were killed, with over 20,000 losing their homes. The U.S. military admitted 23 casualties, with 205 Panamanian military dead.

Bo (Admin) and John (GSO) joined me and talked about a lot of work. I hadn't seen it yet. To the commissary and PX with Taylor, also Consular TDY. The same Taylor of the old Panama days 1973-75. The Personnel nationals were nice and efficient. In the eve we ordered pizza in. Had a stilted conversation with Joan. Early to bed.

I got the impression I had been too pushy yesterday in talking with Admin. So I sat back in my office and waited for Bo to come to me. He never did. I read FAMs and generally took it easy. Sent out a cable for someone's lost household effects. Lil Mary Gaber came in from Managua, tiny and 64, all enthusiastic. I took her to lunch at Marbella next door and had my corbina con salsa verde, as fine as I remember it! Mary had a wide-eyed approach, full of questions. They wouldn't assign her here or anywhere because she was obligated to retire at 65. TDYs can be expensive for the Department of State.

To a grocery store for wine, walking six hot and humid blocks. Got two bottles of wine and a small rum, hot and dripping, me, not the rum! Mary told me that Joan said we shouldn't go out alone. I told Joan when the security people told me, I might listen. They hadn't even given a security briefing. In the evening Taylor, Mary and I went to El Panamar restaurant. The outside was exactly the same as 1975. Had ceviche and lobster. I hadn't had lobster in 15 years. I recall having been there before but not with Ed. Had a nice cool breeze and it was very pleasant. They did most of the chatting. Military around the Embassy said there was no problem walking, just to be careful. Grafitti sez: "Yankee Stay Here," "Bye Bye la Pina." (Noriega's nickname because his skin blotches looked like a pineapple.) Heidi took us to the pool for Mary to swim. She was in a spacious 3 bedroom aprt. with a great view. To bed at 8 p.m., read til 9. I was lonely for Ed, lonely for some sort of destiny for us. I got wistful thinking what it had been like in Panama 15 years ago. There were at least three who proclaimed their love for me. (Ed, John and ?) How soon I forget!

Mary was assigned to work for the advance team for VP Quayle's upcoming visit. I got the control room setup, made many lists of what had to be done. The DCM came by with Bo and wanted me to get the background on Awards and type of awards for those with harrowing tales of their activities during the invasion. My main project was to write up hero awards for those who had harrowing tales of the invasion, both within the Embassy compound and outside on the streets. There was an influx of security officers, our own Marine Guards and various Embassy personnel with stories about their participation, even accidental involvement in "Just Cause." John Blacken popped in for 3 or 4 days; I went up to say hello. He was at the Marriott. VP Quayle was coming Saturday, the Undersecretary of State Weds. or Thurs. A busy week for some. Took a taxi to via Espana and checked out the area of El Panama Hotel (closed), Continental (dead), Sardi restaurant (closed) and Exejutivo where I had spaghetti and listened to journalists complain. Took taxi back. Called Ed and he was anxious to come join me.

Glad not to be really involved in the visit - got to ignore the countdown meetings I hated so much in Australia. I felt l had lost weight here, did not have regular meals. I heard El Panama Hotel was being rebuilt with drug money. The "cocaine" they found at Noriega's headquarters turned out to be tamale meal (maize) in banana leaves. Funny!

A retired Pan Canal Commission Chief financial officer was killed at his home by masked robbers some claim were from "dignity battalions." That inspired Ed to worry about me and plan to come, legal or not. I still had to wait for permission, Bo said, since the Ambassador also wanted his wife to join him. I sort of made work, accounts of acts of heroism trickled in. To Marbella for my corbina and felt better. So bored here.

A 9 a.m. meeting with the Undersecretary of State. Saw the Ambassador for the first time, came in with a cigar, rough and tough. He announced that the Undersecretary should announce that dependents were now permitted into Panama. That inspired several calls from Ed, he couldn't find his passport, had to get a clearance at travel agency, etc. Esther arranged a free lunch at the Marriott with the handsome Asst. Manager Daniel Sarria. He was charming, had buffet with Esther, Marta and me. He had been kidnapped, along with a CBS newsman, and held six hours. Their orders were to kill Americans but he protected them, a real hero. He had moved 45 Americans around into different suites during a 24 hour period. I started on thank you letters for the Quayle visit. Learned that I could move into an empty apartment. To the Marine House happy hour after Marta and I did about 85 thank you notes from Quayle to the Embassy staff. Taylor Blanton was there and generously bought drinks. Had about three. Laura, Consular officer, dropped me off.

Embassy car and driver helped cart suitcases, minor groceries and clothes to 15A Torre Almar, Punta Paitilla. It was a spacious apartment with nice water views. I packed a suitcase and went to the Marriott. Got the keys for fourteen rooms. The VP plane was late. Ed was on the Eastern flight, happy to see me, I love him! We had an overnight at the Marriott. I went to the control room. Suddenly Bo wanted to talk, after ten days. I introduced him to Ed. Ed and I ate downstairs, ceviche and corbina and ravioli. He went to bed early and I was in the control room with Esther and Alicia until 11:30 pm. Quayle got in okay.

Ed and I breakfasted downstairs. There was a fax panic for Quayle before his interview. After three meals I was bored with Panama's No. 1 hotel. At 3 p.m. Ed and I went to our new place. He liked it. Phone not working. Door slammed shut and I had to climb through a hole in the maid's bathroom, practically breaking my leg and neck to get to the other end of the apartment. Walked with Ed to McDonalds for chicken and hamburger take out. Felt vulnerable on the streets, expecting thugs and AK-47s to find us.

Ed was in a lovemaking mode. Tried to get a taxi to take me to the Embassy but the driver refused because Quayle's motorcade had blocked the traffic. So I took another taxi to the Marriott and had a motor pool car take me to the Embassy. Ed walked. I lunched with him at Marbella on my corbina con salsa verde, which I dearly loved. We split a big salad. George, the Ambassador's aide, would write an AFSA award nomination for the DCM. He was a bit of a hot shot. Ed and I walked to a new grocer in the evening, $4 for dijon mustard, etc. Had a Danish spam sandwich and peas for dinner.

Took taxi to Embassy. Worked on awards. Had a hectic morn

sorting out accounts by RSOs (regional security officers) of dangers they had endured. Had a 28 minute phone conversation with an RSO who was here on TDY and had a heart attack. They are all trying to name their own awards, so modest of them. Pat Brania, the Ambassador's secretary, came in from Costa Rica. I had met her in San Salvador. She was nice, a night and day difference from grump frump. She'll make quite a difference in the front office. Ed had found the pool and has done his exercise. Spaghetti, meatsauce dinner.

Esther was out sick, would have an ulcer operation next week. That prompted her to see if I'd stick around another month. I agreed, Bo agreed, Ed agreed. Heidi came down to my office, all neurotic regarding the Foreign Service here, having to buy a car, move to smaller apartment, her father dying in Las Vegas. I gave her a few options and told her to think it over and let me know if I could help. I think she just wanted to rant. Ed and I walked to Gran Morrison and found a nice souvenir section with mola bags. I bought one for Emily's birthday.

Ed found an old contact from 1975, Rolando. The Panamanian girls think of me as one of them. Bo was disorganized and lost things. I worked on awards. There are lots of Awards for Valor, Security guards, FSN's and Marine Guards. In the eve to Laura Schmidt's gorgeous apartment. We were loaned an ice chest and snorkels for San Blas by Pat Perrin. Taylor and Brian were there. I told her that hers was the first friendly voice to come out of Panama in over two weeks (among the Americans, that is).

It was a very tiny plane that took Brian, Taylor, Mary, Ed and me to San Blas islands. We were the first Americans to visit after the invasion. People from the Oceanographic group in the San Blas area had been kidnapped and held hostage by Noriega forces during the invasion. I made up and we signed an agreement that we would not hold the Embassy responsible if something were to happen to us. The Cuna Indians had become more modern since 1975. They now had a hotel, but less desirable than the bed on the sand in the thatched hut. Still no plumbing. Went to other islands for molas. Quite a difference from 15 years ago. Their children ran rampant. Before they had been in the background hiding while their mothers sold their wares. Since we were the first foreign tourists since the war, they desperately needed to sell their molas to build their economy. The lobster lunch was lovely. Taylor, Mary and I went to two larger islands, too many desperate people, too many molas for sale. Sang with Mary in our hammocks,

We are eating too well. I've bought too many molas, felt responsible to help the token mola economy. Collected shells. The motor stalled on our dugout boat when returning. One paddle and no life preservers. Made it back almost an hour later. The water was various shades of gorgeous, pristine. Another lobster lunch, a large plane came to pick us up a half hour late. We all were weary and glad to be back at home in Panama City.

Had the awards ceremony. Bo wanted in on the act, almost 40 people. Esther stopped in and we went to lunch at Marbella. In eve we had dinner with Ed's old friend Milton Henrique at the Union Club. He was the same man 15 yrs. ago who told Ed that he had won me in the lottery! He bragged about his senator son, doctor son, business son, and his daughter in Austin married to an electronics engineer. Wanted me to tell the Ambassador that the business people needed loans. His company was looted and lost half a million U.S. dollars. Off he went in his jaguar.

Esther was operated on February 7. Ed worried me, with nothing to occupy his time. Did a lot of walking, swimming, but no exercise for his mind. In eve we took Pat Brania to El Panamar; it was quite breezy. Delicious corbina, Ed had great asparagus soup and beef stroganoff; Pat had langostinas, giant shrimp. $69 with tip.

Ed made a tunafish lunch. He's working on a round robin letter so that occupied him a bit. I worked through write ups by special agents. They really blew their own horns. We wandered a bit near via Espana and found Irene and Bernadine's old apartments. I had still not a clue where ours was, somewhere left of Einstein's head. Pork chops and green beans and early bed.

Amorous Ed woke me at 4:30 am. Caught up on necessary requirements. Ambassador Hinton was off to pick up his wife, car, son, father, with a slew of bodyguards meeting him at the border of Costa Rica to escort them back to Panama City. Ed and I met at Casa de Mariscos and had a great meal: ceviche just perfect, his red snapper wondrous, and my veal fine. To Centro Medico of Paitilla to see Esther. Had a regular suite, lovely. Her mother, son, sister, husband all there.

We were both in the mood to rediscover the bases, so drove over to Amador, going along the causeway. It had run down; Panama had taken over some of the bases. Balboa looked familiar; to Ft. Clayton and back to Albrook for groceries, and Corozal for the PX. Home to hamburgers and other things.

Took Ed and Mary Gaber to El Valle, a favorite Sunday drive in the olden days. Stopped at Punte Chame. It was a long ride out and suddenly: a gorgeous beach. To El Valle on pot-holed road. The market was in full bloom, lots of people. We lunched at the El Valle hotel on corbina. Bought a $6 wooden bowl I loved. Had a super highway part of the way but it was a long journey with a lot of traffic. I recalled back fifteen years, stopping to watch a 3 toed sloth in a tree. Ed's predecessor used to bring his pet sloth to parties. I wonder how long he lasted at that fast pace. It had a heart rate of about 46 beats per minute.

Worked on the awards, had hair done at noon. The cable was on the way to extend me to mid-March. To retire or not, that is the question. Mr. Jones continued to be good about lending me a car. Ed and I set out in search of a library and Ft. Clayton had one. To Albrook officers club. I had ceviche and an old fashioned. Blew $3 on slot machines, didn't even know they had them!

The Panamanians wanted me to stay, they said I lifted their morale. I teased with them; Bo is usually heading for a meeting. There is always something popping up to interrupt my work. Like wanting to hire someone on a PSC (Personal Service Contract). Polt in POL sez I should stay as well. Lunched at home with Ed, soup and sandwich. Received a Christmas card a month or so late from Joelle Mortensen in Canberra with a couple pictures. If Quayle had been the most exciting thing that happened to them in 1989, that's every reason for leaving the Foreign Service! I went to the hospital to see Esther, who's much better - had part of her stomach taken out. The doctors said there was a beginning of a tumor and they are happy they operated. Nice to sleep with a cool tropical breeze.

Bo was in good humor early on, talked about his days in Brazil, the sexy women there. I tried to concentrate on Awards, and had other distractions. Ed came in with a big bunch of flowers for the Admin/PER women and a smaller one for me. So lovely and romantic. The Panamanians make something of Valentine's Day. It's a touchy, feely, friendship day. Marta gave little boxes of M&Ms. Ed and I lunched at Casa de Mariscos, ate well, corbina. Alberto, the manager, knew the missionaries in the book I was reading. In 1925 the Cunas rebelled against the Panamanian rule and became independent. A nice man, Alberto.

It was a day for meetings, two long ones. Carlos from Colon visited Ed and they visited treatment spots. Had an Awards meeting with Bo and DCM. Hashed over the types of awards, who should be in group one, etc. I didn't hesitate to put in my two cents worth. So we'll rush to get out the valor and heroism awards, plus the general one for the Embassy as a whole. Made waffles and sausage and egg dinner for Ed and Carlos. He was 77 and still hanging on, with skin cancer and hardening of the arteries. Carlos returned to Colon/Cristobal. Received four boxes from Nicaragua, one set of training materials, two from Australia, including my last pot from the kiln. My two favorites were broken. One came from Colorado with Christmas garlands and Ed's winter jacket. Bill Barr CAO (Cultural Affairs Officer) asked us to a party at his spacious apartment in La Cresta. Lots of TV, news types there, a token few from the Embassy. A duo of oboe and guitar played - very nice and civilized.

To Albrook Club for brunch. Then to Howard AFB where he registered for free flights out of here.

Washington birthday holiday. To library for more books. Mopped most of the apartment floors, cleaned sinks. Drove out in search of Iris's and then John Blacken's place. I think we at least found the street. I didn't recall where we used to live, but looking back, I could have found the address in Admin. Ed went for a haircut. He accidentally recognized the old Bella Vista children's home. There was a nice woman missionary there from Chicago.

The hairdresser was worried about Panama once the military leaves. Remarked how much Panama owed the Americans. Wait a minute, WE were the invaders, right? To Milton's house in the evening, about 16 people there. Met his sons and others. Good ceviche, tacos. An Ecuadorian invited us to dinner the next day. Ed said he had plans.

Marta felt she was efficient and I was the trainee, which could be annoying. Remember, Beverly, you are leaving soon! This Sunday they'll show the Challenger movie with Karen Allen and Kale.

Turned in some of my awards for the DCM to sign. Ed and I dined at Casa de Mariscos with Mary and Taylor. We three all treated Taylor for making all the arrangements for San Blas.

On February 24 I told Ed I would retire. It was beginning to sound final. Up early, taxied to Punta Paitilla airport for our plane to David. Drove to Volcan and then around a long bend to Bambito. Had a big hotel, nice, very slow service at lunch, trout. Read, back to room for nap. There was a roaring wind earlier, beating at the hotel windows, thought they'd break. I went for a sauna (Finnish, you know!) up the hill. Another drive to Volcan and found a great shop of cotton-stuffed birds from El Salvador. Up the hills and down the vales. Lovely scenery, of course I didn't have my camera with me! Dinner in the dining room was romantic with nice courteous service.

Early morning love. The wind has calmed down. Had to go all the way to David to go up again to Boquete and the Hotel Panamonte. They were friendly. The Swedish woman Mrs. Elliott, had died at 82 in 1979, the year we were married. Her daughter ran the place and also grew coffee. She had six children and three grandchildren. The place is just as we left it 17 years ago. Rustic. We spent all afternoon in the bar/restaurant area reading. Listened to a wonderful singer on TV, Marvina? from Spain. She sang songs from Jesus Christ Superstar, Les Misérables, Cats, and Evita; had a beautiful voice. The only venture into Boquete was a walk to the river bridge. Our room was $33 plus tax.

To the airport at 6:30 a.m. Stopped on the way to look at the stars. Saw both the Big Dipper and the Southern Cross in the sky at the same time! It was windy and a bit bumpy on the flight of 8 passengers. Taxi home and an Embassy car took me to work. It is official that Chamora won the election in Nicaragua. I called D.C. regarding my retirement alternative before they got any idea to send me there, one faraway day.

3/1 - Sent the retirement cable to the State Department. Once I did it, it felt that it was the right thing to do!

I had said I'd have Taylor over before he left. Pork chops dried out in the oven as he was late. He was annoyed that I wouldn't go to Nicaragua and join the fun. Mary kept saying, "You'll love your house in Nicaragua, Overton loved it." I was proving that it just wasn't in my destiny.

To Rodman PX area. To Howard where Ed registered for MAC flights. So many young GI's are at the mercy of sexy Panamanian girls who lay the trap for them. To Pat Brania's in eve. All there smoked and Ed got dramatic over opening a window. He could have done it calmly but he enjoyed being crotchety. Maybe like the Ambassador, from what I hear. In spite of him, I enjoyed most of the company.

Taylor asked to see Ancon Hill so we took him on a mini-tour. He took pictures and was his usual Taylor self. Ed and I ended up at Argentine Las Malvines for lunch. Shared soup and my meal and had our best flan here - Argentinian. Ended up walking through the fair on Balboa - an effort to get the nice people of Panama back together. It was an easy saunter and I enjoyed it. A grenade was thrown at a bar called "My Place" last night, frequented by U.S. military. Many were injured, one died.

Ed felt amorous so attacked. I must be old - I needed the sleep. I loved to have the cool tropical breezes wafting over our bed and onto our bodies with such a delicate touch, so refreshing. Now that is sensuous! The Undersecretary for Administration came over the weekend on a seven-nation tour. He said people like me, assigned to Nicaragua but going everywhere else, are the "unsung heroes of the Foreign Service." I raised my eyebrows and he said "It's true!" I was invited to lunch with the boys but chose Esther and her sisters, Alicia and Marta. We had rice and shrimp casserole and wine at her house. She said she'd be back in the office Mar. 19.

- When I saw Ambassador Hinton today, I said "I knew you couldn't be all bad, being born in Montana - my mother was from Red Lodge." He said well everyone has some saving grace. I felt the people in the front office felt I was brazen, or it could have been my own thought. Retiring does give one a special freedom. Real PER work interferes with my awards. I lunched at Marbella, had my usual. Asked for the recipe before I left the country. Carlos was there with Ed. Bacon and waffles for the three of us in eve. Carlos complained that his social security check was late each month. Seventeen years ago he wasn't receiving any at all until Ed saved him by getting the process going. I bid farewell to him and went to work.

3/9 - Poopsie's 66th birthday. I got him a card and that was all. He said all he wanted was my love, so I took him at face value. USIS person complained about their boss, saying he was demoralizing all of them, is crass, rude and intimidating. I called Carl Howard in Washington, who is deputy secretary for ARA. He was shocked. Ed and I lunched at Casa de Mariscos. The awards committee was hectic. Bo said he was leery of me at first but now would love to have me stay longer. When I came he was hesitant because I wasn't an experienced PER person, but I'd done a good job and he didn't know what he would have done without me.

- Another frustrating day, we had a little blowout. Ed had too much time on his hands and needed my companionship. My side, I need to do some Embassy reorganizing. I felt tied down spending time with him when I should have been working. He felt I was trying to push him away, felt rejected.

- Pat called to invite me to cake and champagne for the Ambassador's birthday. I think he was 68; his wife and child were there. She and Pat both had face lifts while assigned to Costa Rica. Looked good.

- I managed to get some things done, but I was always besieged by employees for personnel advice. I was getting better at it. Dottie, the DCM secretary and the DCM had a blowout and weren't speaking to one another. I mailed our mortgages, Virginia and California. There was a happy hour farewell for Art Brunetti at 5, ceviche, etc. I asked Art for a drink since it was his last night and none of the boys had asked him out. So he had a spaghetti farewell, and went home to San Francisco.

- Had lunch once more with Ed at Marbella and got the recipe for my favorite corbina con salsa verde! They were very nice about it!

- I knew there was to be a hail and farewell for incoming and outgoing DCMs. Also knew that George the Aide didn't like me and I wasn't on the list. I talked with Pat Brania and told her I was insulted and she, the Ambassador's secretary, put me on the list. Had hairdo and manicure, wore my Brazilian red/black silk dress, brought to Panama for such a possibility. The Residence looked lovely, the table splendid in its offerings, a side table with palm fronds, very tropical. It was the best buffet table at any Residence I'd seen. The food was fine, I was kissed by VP Guillermo Billy Ford, who said "God bless you." I had told him I wanted to shake his hand, and he said "I want to kiss you." I did shake hands as I was introduced to 1st VP Caderon Arias. I met the Chief of the Supreme Court, a mild, nice little man. Ed met a ballet dancer who was Margo Fontaine's protégé.

On March 16 Ed learned there was a MAC flight to Charleston that he could get on. I took him there, farewell for now. I went to work at 8:30 am. I suddenly got a sinus headache that turned into a sick stomach. I vomited nothing in the ladies room. At 11:30

a.m. I went home to be sick again, felt awful. I slept fitfully until 1:30 p.m., went back to work at 2. Had a 3:30 p.m. Awards committee meeting and was cantankerous during it as they attempted to rewrite that which DCM Bushnell had already signed. In the eve Esther had a happy hour which turned out to be a dinner as well, a farewell for me and an anniversary party for them, she and Carlos. I had some weak drinks and a bit of the paella and rice. Went very wearily home at 8:30 p.m.

- A mad day, sunned a little, went in search of souvenirs. To the mola place near the El Panama hotel. The woman was wild, ranted about her robberies, all out looting. She had the dresses pinned together to make them more difficult to steal (or to try on). I bought some cosmetic bags, two dresses, one huaca (silver dipped in gold) for $43, my souvenir to myself. Onto Colleciones, a lovely shop with Mexican imports. Bought paper mache fruit which would have been half price in Mexico, and a lovely leaded mirror. I had a $300 day of purchases. Had hair combed out. Went to Marta's and was surprised to see a nicely decorated house. Marta was the queen, Mel cooked. Earlier I had dropped off a map for Tom, to lure him to Marta's to meet lovely Mayra. She had been there and finally left when Tom didn't show. Marta's Mel got drunk and was an ass. The next day Mel called to apologize for his behavior. Tom reported that he and his driver had gotten hopelessly lost.

Ed called from Conway. He had gone through some rough weather over Atlanta with thunderstorms, but was safe . I went to the Embassy, wrote some letters, picked up Mary to go bowling at Albrook, my first in centuries. I wasn't so hot, 120 high for 4 games. I returned Ed's library books at Ft. Clayton. Pat Brania called, went to her apartment for a drink, hors d'oeuvres, and chat. She's 48 and looks 35 after eye tucks in Costa Rica. Put me in the mood to do it. Dr. Marten's the name. I liked Pat.

- Esther returned to work looking tired, stayed stubbornly to 4 pm. Bo wasted 1-1/2 hours in his Admin staff meeting, with a lot of bull. I wasn't amused. I asked where my awards drafts were, said I had 8-1/2 days left and would like to have my goals accomplished. I was so disgusted with him that I went home to eat lunch at him. John's birthday card to Ed came late. At least one remembered.

- Barr came in to check the regulations on marrying a foreigner, a Brazilian. Esther stayed home with a fever and sore throat. I bought Judy a mola purse in the Canal Zone, succumbed to a wonderful chili dog at the PX. I finally found the one I'd been looking for. Marta announced that Mel liked me. (I'm honored.) I've discovered not too many people had respect for Bo.

- Avoiding Bo, I've washed my hands of him and his promises to provide award recommendations. Ed won at the races yesterday. I finally got an awards package together for Washington. The weather was changing gradually with warmer nights, less ideal tropical breezes.

"Worry is a substitute for action" sez the morning inspirational message. That fit the bill for Ed sometimes and Bo a lot. He fretted over reports rather than charging in to do them. My new theory was to ignore him. I dashed out to the base at lunch to buy more tee shirts and mola bag. Found a salad in the snack bar particularly divine. Since I hadn't been eating much greens, I found that I craved them.

- I continued to be frustrated by Bo's non action on his award requests. Lunched with Esther and Alicia. I went home for a change of clothes and to Dorothy Hecht's apartment. Very pleasant, had drink and she and I went to the nice restaurant at the Marriott and onto the casino (on my list). She had all sorts of luck, took a long time to lose her $5, I spent $10, not much luck, but it was a pleasant diversion.

- No call from Ed. I went alone to my fate to Contadora, for old time's sake. Progress has slapped it in the face, was much less rustic, had a new hotel. I walked to the shore and asked the sea what it had been up to these past 16+ years. My room was okay, no TV. I felt generally blue for a past that is now lost. It was Mexican buffet night with authentic mariachis from Veracruz, lively dancers, very enjoyable. Saw Judite's sister with her Japanese husband and sat with them awhile. I felt conspicuous as the lone person there.

- I read, had breakfast. Walked over to Marina beach, found a private area behind some rocks and got some sun, read about two hours. Back to room to shower, 1 p.m. lunch, corbina good at the buffet. I was quite ready to leave at 3:25, lined up for the plane, recalled our "hijacking" incident some seventeen years ago. Home again. Ed called at 6. Bad boy lost $275 on horse races at Oaklawn in Hot Springs today, receiving a lot of bad advice.

- Promises from Bo were to no avail, so I was trying to tidy up my own act. An unenduringly long Admin meeting as per usual. The new DCM asked if I thought the post needed a Personnel officer. I replied with a strong yes. I had been surprised by the number of people who sought me out with their concerns.

If I had been assigned here it wouldn't have been so bad, would have had a nice apartment. I'm glad to be free of Bo's indecisive action and George's blundering. But I certainly liked the Panamanians and they would have made it bearable. Ed called: he was lonely and sad. He said "Why do you always do this to me?" Who left whom? But it helped to appreciate each other.

- What a day! It was time for everyone's troubles. USIS girl came to tell me how maligned she was by Barr, so I advised her. Linda sought advice over an award nomination she had written. At 11:30 a.m. I went to pedicure, manicure and hairdo. I felt spoiled for $20. Dashed home to cook a hamburger. Back to work until 7 p.m. to make up for lost time. To Pat Brania's apartment for "gawumpkees", good. Dorothy will be DCM secretary in Managua. We three had a pleasant time. Good goopy dessert called Tres Leches.

- Wrote nomination for award for Martade Souter. The driver took me downtown to buy cuna material for a skirt. Got him to go by Pan Canal building to take a photo of the two flags. The Panamanian flag would not unfurl, and he said "esta trieste!" We laughed. Back to more work. Seven FSNs took me to lunch at Marbella. It was very tender of them. I received three gifts, earrings from Esther, and hadn't opened the others yet. Had some laughs. Back to work madly to prepare the awards for the meeting. It was a no-nonsense one and we approved 7 of them in less than an hour. Marta was thrilled at what I wrote for her regarding her award. We three (Mary, Jan and I) had a decent meal at Casco Viejo. Ed called at 9:30 pm.

3/30 - The Embassy car collected me at 6 am. Another TDY fellow was in the car to the airport. The flight was full to Miami, smooth, and had a decent breakfast. An hour before the Memphis flight, more time to kill there. A long day of perspiration. Ed met me in Little Rock. Sweet Emily, home from the beauty shop, had chicken and dumplings ready. We then went directly to bed, following Ed's mission to make up for lost time. To the races the next day with Bill, Clara, Emily. Ate the track's luscious corned beef sandwiches, margueritas, chocolate yoghurt. At least that way we knew where the money was going! Otherwise, betting was a $54 loss for the day. Instead of curing me, I want to go back tomorrow to make it up! Have Ed and I contracted the Ledbetter horseracing disease?

Miscellany

Englewood, Colorado in Wayne and Judy's model A Ford

Stateside what year? Kathy with lovable little Meg. Meg was born in
1975.

St. Louis area. Half brother Robert at 6'5 with wife Sandi and Bev.

Wisconsin reunion 1981. Ed's mother Hildur (Woo) and her two
octogenarian brothers Edwin and Art, plus Ed, John and Suzanne.

Ed's daughter Cathy at a wedding.

Front Row: Ramona, Cheryl, and half-brother Wally Stetson.
Back row: Rob, Hal, Shirley (Eliah), Gary.
In Montana, rarely seen!

Aunt Irene (Daddy's sister) and her 5 daughters Lumina, Pat, Marie, Louise, Irene - Christmas 1984 - Aylmer East, Quebec, Canada. Her only son Paul died many years before of a brain tumor. Her husband Remy was also deceased.

Dear friends Joyce and Ray Asay, Dallas 1989. Ex-school teacher and ex-Braniff pilot. Had five children (one set of twins), all lovely and outstanding.

Bosom buddies Joyce and Bev in Dallas.

Dr. Roby Mize, Jennifer and Judy, Dallas.

Mary Nelson. I thought of her as a crusty Ethel Merman. Quite witty, wrote poetry, worked at Dallas Country Club where I met her in 1970 when I pranced back and forth from school in Iowa, work in Peoria or doing a Dallas tour. She made it to age 99.

Ed and Bev , Peoria between postings.

Kathy and Bev, buddies for life!

One of Big Four Phyllis and husband Rich Boland.

Emily and Paul Knebels whom we met back in Panama. From Wilmington, Del., had printing business. Spent a few week-ends at their place at Ocean City, New Jersey.

College friend Loretta Vincent. A self-made woman. Every task self-assigned, was done with utmost perfection. An artist, house builder, stained glass maker, wood chopper. Built her home in the woods, gradually acquiring 21 acres to surround herself by nature unmolested.

47th birthday on trip to Lisbon 1977. Flowers were so big we used
the bidet for a vase!

Ed's cousin Ralph Reynolds, his brother Bill Ledbetter, sister Emily
Montgomery, and Ed. At that point all were octogenerians. Several
became nonogenerians. A tight loving family of Arkies.

Robert and Sandra Drewitz in front.: Robert, Robyn, Cynthia, Gregory, Stephanie. St. Peters, Missouri

Ed, Bev, Hal Marley, Washington,D.C. area 1989

Rosita and Hal Marley, Wash.D.C. area 1989

Suzanne Ledbetter and husband Tony Graef

Clara and Bill, Emily and Ed.

Son James and Patty Montgomery. Ed, Emily, and daughter Judy Mize.

Wrap Up

After my reunion with Ed in Conway, we did usual visitations to Dallas and Peoria. In Dallas we shopped for a house and chose one, making an offer on it and kept moving. We stopped in Cincinnati to visit Jim O'Donnell and his flock of Canadian geese, and landed on April 23 in D.C. Visited the Department for medicals and entered the procedure for retirement. I was advised that I should have filed a grievance for being on hold ten months for the Personnel Job in Nicaragua. It was a major job to sort out Annual Leave and Home Leave after Australia, Panama, and all points in between. I received 10% differential and 25% danger pay for almost three months in Panama.

The retirement seminar began April 30. It was a nice surprise to discover familiar faces such as the Povenmires, Ferrers, Hume Horans, Ardith Miller. A week later began the Job Search Program. Saw Ed Peck from Tunis days and Roger Kirk from Vietnam. Peck, Horan and Kirk had all become Ambassadors after our first acquaintanceships. We were introduced to the Myers-Briggs test. Ed was an INFP and I was ENFP (the only one in the class). Extrovert, Intuitive, Feeler, Perceptive were classifications. Ed shared my last three classifications but was more of an introvert. John Blacken showed up later and was returning to Lagos, Nigeria, having a great offer from some company there. He had retired as Ambassador to Guinea-Bissau.

It was great to renew old acquaintances, met the Spanish

language instructors again. Pedro had lost 18 lbs, and said his wife gained them. Saw friend Gail Gulliksen from Brazil days and she offered an occasional bed, as well as dear Barbara Morrison, and even spent our last few weeks at her place. We housesat as she and her mother went to Brazil in search of an adoptable child for Barbara. (She later adopted two boys from Bolivia.)   Saw the Collins from Trinidad in their lovely new home in Maryland. When they complained of the high mortgage payments, we countered with "how about three?" (California, Virginia and now Texas). They felt better.

In between sessions we were preparing our condo in Alexandria for sale. About a month later we agreed on a $90,000 sale price. A Spanish colonel bought it for his daughter who had been assigned to World Bank.

Meanwhile we were introduced to a buffet line of job seeking items: how to seek another job, critiques of resumes, cover letters, job lead sources, financial planning advice, interviews by prospective bosses. The worst for me was the video interview. I did okay on the questions, but was shocked to see what I looked like to the world. I had gained so much weight the past frustrating years. I had thought I was Leslie Caron but I was really Golda Meir! (At 52!)

June 1 was the last day of the Seminar. We left D.C. area June 8, 1990. Stopped in High Point, N.C. to see Ed's WWII friend Carl Gibson, bought Bill Jr.'s BMW he couldn't afford in Conway, and landed in Dallas to our empty house on June 13. Within two weeks we received three different deliveries of household effects, having been stored in various places. My official date of retirement was August 3, 1990.

I was so excited to begin my memoire on Foreign Service, but as reread my diaries and struggled through my three long years in Australia, my daily offerings were bleak and dragged me down. The exception was when Ed and I were off discovering on our own the variety of landscape and inspirational wonders of Australia that had absolutely nothing to do with my daily labor. So the writing was hardly stimulating much of the time. There were many days of blank pages in my diaries, illustrating the frenzy of daily life I had no time or interest in recording. Theretofore I had always filled each day of my life into those diaries. When the tour was finally over, and the Department of State would not allow me to relax and saunter on my way back to the States, but rushed me through the Personnel course for an assignment that would not be forthcoming, it was a slow leak in the vehicle's tires that had brought me so many divergent, interesting situations in the Foreign Service. If it were not a slow leak, it was simply a running out of gas. The almost three months of TDY in Panama, going back to the spot where I first encountered and began a 43 year wondrous relationship with Ed, proved interesting if not always fulfilling. What is interesting is this: after my retirement I felt lost, and looked fondly on Foreign Service and what it had offered me. But when I plodded through the daily records after all those years, I'm left with a feeling that it dragged me down and wrung me out. I almost regret looking back and seeing the glass darkly when in my mind's eye I was grateful for the 21+ years of adventure. So for whom am I writing this memoire? For myself, certainly, and perhaps to entertain some of whom I met along the way. You can be the judge!

The Author and the Book

Conceived in Montana, Beverly was the first baby born in a lumberjack hospital in Laona, Wisconsin, moved to Illinois at three months, already born under a wandering star. She had an epiphany at age 13 to stimulate her further need and lust for travel. She joined the Foreign Service at age 27 and never looked back. Well, that is, until now! Herein are remembrances of postings in Tunisia, Vietnam, Washington, Panama, Portugal, Trinidad and Tobago, Mexico, Brazil and Australia, along with stateside detours in her career to Chicago and Iowa City. Gathering credits for a Bachelor of Arts was haphazard as itchy feet prompted her to yet another adventure. She finally attained that degree 20 years after it could have been on her list of accomplishments. After Australia she was in a hiatus awaiting a diplomatic visa for Nicaragua because of US interference in the Iran/Contra affair. After almost ten months of waiting, a TDY to Panama after our invasion there, she reluctantly retired in August 1990. She has lived over 25 years in the Land of Enchantment.